Ground Zero On 9/11 with
THE WALL STREET JOURNAL

September Twelfth

An American
Comeback Story

Dean Rotbart

TJFR Press
Denver, Colorado

TERRORISTS DESTROY WORLD TRADE CENTER, HIT PENTAGON IN RAID WITH HIJACKED JETS

Nation Stands In Disbelief And Horror

Streets of Manhattan Resemble War Zone Amid Clouds of Ash

A Wall Street Journal News Roundup

They were like scenes from a catastrophe movie. Or a Tom Clancy novel. Or a CNN broadcast from a distant foreign nation.

But they were real yesterday. And they were very much in the U.S.

James Cutler, a 31-year-old insurance broker, was in the Asser restaurant on the ground floor of the World Trade Center when he heard "boom, boom, boom," he recalls. In seconds, the kitchen doors blew open, smoke and ash poured into the restaurant and the ceiling collapsed. Mr. Cutler didn't know what had happened yet, but he found himself standing among two feet of debris. "It was like a war zone," he says.

Please Turn to Page A16, Column 1

What's News—

Business and Finance

ALL MAJOR U.S. FINANCIAL markets closed yesterday and remain closed today in the wake of the terrorist attack on the World Trade Center. The near-panic reaction in the global market that remained open suggested that substantial damage was done to the psyche of a world financial system already on edge from prospects of an international recession. In Tokyo, the Nikkei stock index fell below 10000 early Wednesday for the first time since 1984.

(Article on Page B1)

The **World Trade Center** housed many Wall Street and banking firms, law offices, technology companies, trading firms and other businesses. Many escaped before the destruction of the buildings yesterday, but the toll of dead and injured is unclear.

(Article on Page A11)

The **attacks threaten to push a fragile global economy into widespread recession**, smashing consumer confidence and disrupting basic commercial functions such as air travel.

(Article on Page A11)

The **dollar tumbled** in global markets following the attacks. In late London trading, the euro stood at $1.44 U.S. cents, up from 44.66 U.S. cents, up from 44.46 U.S. cents before the attacks.

World-Wide

BUSH PROMISED action against terrorist attacks in the Eastern U.S.
The death toll from the hijacked-jet attacks that destroyed the World Trade Center's towers in New York and damaged the Pentagon outside Washington was impossible to gauge immediately. But the president said "thousands of lives were suddenly ended." A fourth hijacked plane crashed near Pittsburgh.

HEALTH TEAMS launched efforts to treat thousands of injured victims.

Please Turn to Page A16, Column 1

Death Toll, Source of Devastating Attacks Remain Unclear; U.S. Vows Retaliation as Attention Focuses on bin Laden

By David S. Cloud And Neil King
Staff Reporters of The Wall Street Journal

Hour of Horror Forever Alters American Lives

Attacks Will Force People To Make Adjustments In Ways Large and Small

---

U.S. Airport Security Screening Long Seen as Dangerously Lax

New Measures Are Likely To Add Inconvenience And Costs for Passengers

---

Attacks Raise Fears of a Recession

By Greg Ip and John D. McKinnon
Staff Reporters of The Wall Street Journal

Courtesy of The Wall Street Journal

• Dedication •

To every journalist who has risen to the occasion regardless of difficulty or personal risk.

The real glory is being knocked to your knees and then coming back.

- Vince Lombardi

• Contents •

Introduction   13

Section One: 200 Liberty Street

Chapter One — "Mir Zenen Shich, Mir Zenen Letzter Eidus"   19

Chapter Two — "I'm Sorry. I'm Going to Interrupt You Right Now."   37

Chapter Three — Baptism By Fire   49

Section Two: Scattered

Chapter One — "This is Clearly our Pearl Harbor"   63

Chapter Two — "I Think We Are Going to Name Her Zoë"   77

Chapter Three — The Kingmaker   91

Chapter Four — "I Don't Want My Life to Be Dust"   97

Chapter Five — "Take Me to Washington, Whatever It Costs"   107

Chapter Six — The Flying Wallendas   115

Chapter Seven — "-30-"   137

Chapter Eight — Project 2002   153

Chapter Nine — "If Not Today, When?"   165

Chapter Ten — "Where Have You Been?" She Meowed   175

Chapter Eleven — September 11 Didn't Happen in a Day   185

Chapter Twelve — Magical Thinking   191

Section Three: September Twelfth

Chapter One — Messenger of Sympathy and Love   203

Chapter Two — The Morning After   209

Section Four: Five Lives

Chapter One — The Origin: Who Doesn't Know That It Was a Horrific Turn in History?   217

Chapter Two — Helene Cooper: The Worst Moment Came on Monday, October 1   223

Chapter Three — Ianthe Jeanne Dugan: Are You Really with The Wall Street Journal?   229

Chapter Four — Bryan Gruley: Comfort the Afflicted, Afflict the Comfortable   237

Chapter Five — Phil Kuntz: Did You Hear About Jimmy Barbella?   243

Chapter Six — Joshua Prager: And He Thanked Me for Calling   251

Chapter Seven — The Book of Habakkuk   261

Chapter Eight — Awaiting John Blanton's Verdict   265

Back of the Book:

Author's Note   269

Afterword: "Don't Give Up the Ship" by Dr. David F. Winkler   277

Source Notes / Bibliography   285

Acknowledgments   287

About the Author   295

Website and Social Media   297

Coming in 2023 — Steiger: A Journalist in the Public Interest   299

Also from TJFR Press   300

Meet the Journalists   304

Index   306

Library of Congress / Copyright / ISBN   311

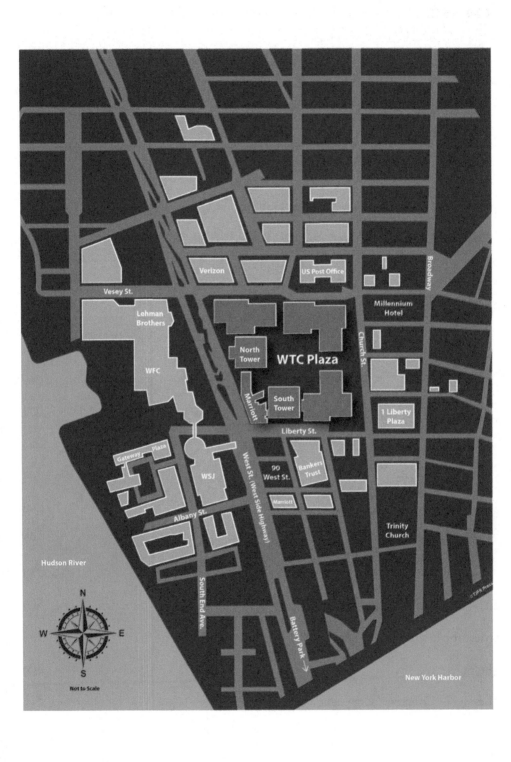

• Introduction •

On Tuesday, September 11, 2001, *The Wall Street Journal* sustained a near-fatal blow. As the world looked on in horror, the twin towers of the World Trade Center – spewing smoke and flames – quickly cratered. The *Journal*'s main global newsroom, located just across the street, was severely damaged by the fallout.

Most of the paper's New York staff had not yet arrived for work. Those who had were quickly evacuated to the streets of Lower Manhattan, putting their lives in the hands of fate. One editor would later succumb to his injuries, while dozens of others would suffer physical or mental illnesses.

Like shards of shattered glass, the headquarters' team of reporters and editors were strewn throughout New York City's five boroughs, New Jersey, and Connecticut.

Phone service was intermittent at best. A few staffers carried BlackBerrys capable of texting and sending emails. Most did not. Incommunicado for hours, it seemed evident that the paper's managing editor, Paul E. Steiger, was dead or seriously injured.

Who was in charge? What were staff members supposed to do? Without offices or computers and unable to locate one another, how could they possibly get a paper out the next day? Was that even a reasonable goal, given the immeasurable human disaster that was unfolding?

Without warning or training, the traumatized staff — business and financial journalists — was thrust into the role of war correspondents.

This book recounts the extraordinary efforts of the *Journal*'s workforce to report, write, edit, print, and deliver the newspaper the morning after. Jettisoning their ordinary responsibilities, employees stepped up — often without being asked — to fill whatever voids in newsgathering and production arose.

Theirs is the tale of journalism at its finest, an achievement recognized months later with the 2002 Pulitzer Prize for Breaking News Reporting, the first Pulitzer in that category in the paper's 112-year history.

More notably, the response that day of *Wall Street Journal* reporters, editors, news assistants, graphic designers, software engineers, compositors, and delivery truck drivers is the consummate comeback story. Theirs is the true tale of a group of lay individuals who would not be bowed by fear or danger in the face of a brazen attack on our nation.

On Wednesday, September 12, in bold, capital letters stretching across all six columns of the *Journal's* front page, the headline read:

TERRORISTS DESTROY WORLD TRADE CENTER, HIT PENTAGON IN RAID WITH HIJACKED JETS

With remarkably few exceptions, readers across America received their morning *Journal* as usual, at their desks, on their front porches, and from their favorite newsstands. To a nation in shock and turmoil, that ink-and-paper daily brought reassurance that the world *would* go on.

The backdrop for this book is September 11, 2001, and how one news organization responded to the exigencies of that day under the most trying of circumstances. But the models of courage, determination, sense of agency, and resurrection are timeless and universal.

Dean Rotbart
Denver, Colorado
August 2021

Section One:
200 Liberty Street

• Chapter One •

"Mir Zenen Shich, Mir Zenen Letzter Eidus"

(We are the shoes, we are the last witnesses)

Moyshe Shulshteyn
Yiddish Poet (1911-1981)

The image haunts him to this day.

The shoes. Primarily women's dress shoes. By the hundreds. Strewn for blocks along the West Street bike path leading from the World Trade Center to South Ferry at the tip of Manhattan Island.

The son of a Holocaust émigré, Jon Hilsenrath had heard the stories from a young age and seen the exhibits at sterile museums and memorials piled with the shoes of gas chamber victims.

But this was not the Majdanek concentration camp in September 1942; it was Lower Manhattan on September 11, 2001, and the images of the shoes were seared into Hilsenrath's memory every bit as much as the horror he witnessed of a woman's decapitated head, and a severed arm, with its index finger still pointing, as if to identify the 9/11 culprits.

Trying to escape the flaming debris and cyclone of smoke, women refugees from the World Trade Center and surrounding buildings literally ran out of their shoes.

Hilsenrath, himself, did an inordinate amount of running that morning. He began the day as a financial and economics reporter for *The Wall Street Journal*, but shortly after 8:46 a.m., when the first plane hit the North Tower of the World Trade Center, he became a war correspondent.

He had arrived early that day at *The Wall Street Journal*'s headquarters, which occupied multiple floors in the World Financial Center, a two-minute walk over the West Street pedestrian bridges that fed directly into the World Trade Center. He planned to attend the annual conference of the National Association of Business Economists (NABE), which conveniently was hosting its day-long sessions at the Marriott hotel located in the World Trade Center complex.

The Gothic-style arches on the lower floors of the Twin Towers, rising to narrowly spaced windows surrounded by aluminum-alloy cladding, were so familiar that many reporters and editors at the paper seldom took note of them, even those with or near windows facing the World Trade Center.

Before heading to the meeting, Hilsenrath wanted to attend to some unfinished business that awaited at his 10th-floor newsroom cubicle.

Suddenly a colleague began screaming.

Startled, Hilsenrath dashed to the newsroom windows that faced the Trade Center and gaped at the flames and debris spewing from the North Tower's upper floors.

It was 8:47 a.m., and in the next 15 minutes, the script of his life was about to be rewritten.

———————————

Few *Journal* reporters or editors had yet arrived at the office that morning. With regular afternoon deadlines that extended to 7:00 p.m. or later on weekday evenings, it was common for *Journal* staffers to use the early portion of the day to meet with sources, commute in, or enjoy a little extra sleep.

Hilsenrath beelined down the stairs one flight to the 9th floor, where the paper's senior editors had offices. Few had arrived there either, but he spotted two of the news department's top executives huddled in conversation, Paul E. Steiger, managing editor, and John C. Bussey, foreign editor.

At this point, no one had a clue what had transpired, but they all sensed it was big.

Hilsenrath wanted in.

I'm ready to go. What do you want me to do?

Steiger, as usual, was unruffled. It appeared to Hilsenrath that his commander-in-chief was still trying to get his head around developments and what they'd mean for the paper. *The Wall Street Journal* had a long and acclaimed history of covering industrial accidents, plane crashes, terrorism, even wars, but whatever this was, it was different. This time, the event was taking place, quite literally, just outside their door. Steiger's response was brief.

Grab a notebook and go find out what happened. And don't get yourself hurt.

Leaving everything at his desk except for a spiral-topped memo pad and a blue pen, Hilsenrath rushed out.

I'll walk over to the Trade Center and try to grab people there. Eyewitnesses.

There was a surreal quality to his movements. Hilsenrath found himself on the overpass that he had crossed from the World Financial Center to the World Trade Center hundreds of times, but now the scene was different. Usually, the bridge was filled with people laughing, chatting casually, or carrying coffee. Now it was empty.

Instead of cars passing under him on West Street, the roadway below was littered with what appeared to be mounds of mechanical debris.

A small plane must have crashed into the building. Or, perhaps, a boiler exploded?

As he proceeded, surveying the scene below, Hilsenrath grew convinced that what he was eyeing was the wreckage of an airplane.

I want to see what's going on down there.

He descended to the street level and started scribbling notes of what he saw. That was his first instinct. Take notes.

Now, the dream-like oddness of his experience turned into a bona fide nightmare.

It wasn't just smoldering heaps of mechanical parts strewn along West Street, it was chunks of human flesh and body parts, too.

Nearby, amidst the chaos of people running and the cacophony of sirens, shouts, and screams, he spotted the decapitated head of a woman with long dark hair, wearing a bandana. Her severed torso was nowhere to be seen.

Like other *Journal* staffers that day, his reporter's notebook became his emotional shield, scrawling notes with a shaky hand and concentrating on getting the story rather than on the horrors that he was witnessing.

There was an arm that was severed around the elbow. There was something haunting about the hand of the arm. It was a finger. The index finger pointing out. The other fingers were curled. But the index finger was pointing out like it was pointing somewhere. It was just an arm on the street.

The debris and carnage that Hilsenrath observed on West Street were dramatic testaments to the force of the bomb-like explosion that the hijacked passenger plane created on hitting the North Tower, blowing out airliner and building wreckage, as well as human remains, in all directions.

Hilsenrath stationed himself on the street just in front of the Marriott World Trade Center, the hotel known as 3 WTC. He was busy recording the sights and sounds in his memo pad when a New York City police officer shouted his way.

You've got to clear out of here. You can't be here.

His adrenaline racing, Hilsenrath weighed his next move.

I should resist. Stand my ground and do what a good journalist would do.

On the other hand, this is a crisis, and do I really want to fight with a cop over whether or not I should be here?

Slowly, very slowly, Hilsenrath shuffled southward, continuing to scan the scene and jot notes as he walked.

And then, an instant later, he was running as fast as his legs would carry him.

What Hilsenrath heard in the sky above was ear-shattering. Sinister. On the attack.

It seemed to him that United Airlines Flight #175 was flying directly overhead, details on the blue belly of the plane clearly visible — its landing gear still retracted.

Anyone who has ever gone plane-spotting on the perimeter of a major airport — watching incoming planes on their final approach — knows the roar and vibrations that turbofan engines generate.

Those are a mere whisper and tap compared to the boom and wind gush generated by a Boeing 767 flying full throttle over the canyons of Lower Manhattan at an altitude of less than 1,500 feet.

This is no small commuter plane. We are under attack.

Because Hilsenrath was running south, he didn't see the actual explosion when the jet struck behind him between the 78th and 84th floors of 2 WTC at 9:02 a.m. Only 16 minutes earlier, he had been composed, at his desk, still planning to attend the NABE conference.

Hilsenrath paused to gather his thoughts at Rector Place, about a half-mile south of the Trade Center.

Ok, I'm out of the line of fire. I can stop here and figure out my next move.

Hilsenrath was familiar with the area known as Battery Park City, not only because it was close to the *Journal*'s headquarters but also because his parents, Joseph and Elaine Hilsenrath, who lived in Manhasset, New York, also owned an apartment in the area, which he frequently visited.

Like the hundreds of befuddled people around him, Hilsenrath gazed up at the towering inferno in eerie silence.

An unending burst of paper spewed from the upper floors of the South Tower, floating and swirling high above.

The scene had elements of New York's famed ticker-tape parades, which showered astronautsc, presidents, military heroes, and sports champions with confetti as their procession moved along Broadway from The Battery to City Hall.

But other things were flying out of the South Tower as well. Horrifying things. Things that didn't float but accelerated in a rhythmic cadence of desperation, one after another every few seconds.

Holy shit. Those are people jumping out of the building.

The image of his wife Cristina flashed before him, followed by those of his three-year-old son, Alex, and one-year-old daughter, Hope.

Hilsenrath and his family had been back in the United States less than a year, having spent his first three years with *The Wall Street Journal* reporting from Hong Kong. Upon his return stateside, Hilsenrath was assigned to the paper's economics group, tracking the ups and downs of employment, inflation, growth, and also new ideas in economic thought from ivory tower universities.

He met Cristina Tiberio when he was 23-years-old, in June 1990. He was on assignment for United Press International, chronicling the cocaine possession trial of Washington, D.C. Mayor Marion Barry. Tiberio, a 22-year-old brown-eyed brunette with a broad, warm smile and dimples, was an intern at CNN, also assigned to the trial.

The couple dated for five years before marrying in September 1995. Cristina was no stranger to the dangers that reporters face or the painful tragedies they must recount.

Shortly before their marriage, she landed an on-air job as a reporter for News 12 Long Island. One of her first assignments was covering the massive "Sunrise Fire," which in August 1995 scorched more than 5,000 acres of pine barrens in eastern Long Island, disrupting service on the Long Island Rail Road, cutting off access to the Hamptons, and sending roiling smoke so high into the sky that it was visible in Manhattan, 70 miles away.

Her cameraman that day was Glen Pettit, a fearless, 25-year-old cherub-faced videographer who talked fast like pretty much everything he did. Much to her consternation, he navigated their live truck — capable of transmitting real-time video by satellite or microwave — around closed roadways into an unscathed forest pocket surrounded by flames and trees so blisteringly hot that some exploded into a cloud of dark smoke.

Glen, I'm not sure this is a great idea.

Pettit pushed her comfort level, but they got the live shot, and the location he chose made for great visuals.

Cristina Tiberio and Glen Pettit, circa July 1996
(Courtesy of Cristina Hilsenrath)

Less than a year later, Cristina was among the first journalists on the scene after Trans World Airlines Flight #800, a Paris-bound departure from John F. Kennedy International Airport, exploded in mid-air, crashing about eight miles off the coast of East Moriches on Long Island.

Cristina spent weeks covering the aftermath of the airline disaster, including time and again interviewing the families of some of the 230 people who perished.

One conversation, in particular, haunted her. It was with Richard B. "Dick" Hammer, a Navy veteran and media advertising executive whose wife and daughter both died aboard TWA #800. Her interview with Hammer was so powerful that News 12 Long Island broadcast it unedited. The video makes it clear that Cristina, choking back tears, was struggling to keep it together.

Working in Asia, Cristina witnessed and reported a different type of horror.

I covered the handover to China in 1997. I was reporting live at the border of Hong Kong as the Chinese military troops were driving scores of their soldiers into Hong Kong, standing on the back of pickup trucks. Another unsettling story to cover— when you live in a place and you watch scores of Chinese military troops crossing into your "home."

As disturbing as covering massive fires, plane crashes, and military shows of force can be, none of them struck Cristina with the emotional punch of the events of September 11.

She was at home when the World Trade Center came under attack. This time, it would be her husband, Jon, surrounded by flames, fear, death, and immense sadness, leaving her to contemplate the dreadful prospect of never seeing him again.

On the streets of Lower Manhattan, Hilsenrath realized his wife might have heard about the first explosion. He phoned to tell her that he was unharmed and to let her know that he was outside covering events.

After the second plane struck, he was sure she would be watching the breaking news on television and most likely terrified by what she was seeing.

Before either tower collapsed, mobile phone communication was still possible, so Hilsenrath phoned Cristina a second time. The conversation was uneasy.

Jon, those buildings are going to fall down. You have to get out of there. You have a family at home, and you have to get home.

Hilsenrath knew it was a crude analogy; even so, he couldn't help but think that for him, this was the "Super Bowl" of journalistic events.

The country is under attack, and I'm a journalist. I can't leave. I've got to be here. I've got to be reporting this thing. I'm all right. I'm fine. I'm keeping a distance from the building, and I'm going to be okay.

Cristina repeatedly warned that the World Trade Center towers would collapse, and she begged him to come home. More than intuition, she reasoned that huge planes hitting such tall buildings would render them structurally unsound.

But like the hundreds of emergency responders who rushed into the Twin Towers that morning, never expecting them to collapse, he couldn't imagine it.

Hilsenrath assumed that his wife was reacting with her emotions, not her head. He ignored her pleas.

Hilsenrath headed back in the direction of the World Trade Center and *The Wall Street Journal*'s offices, even as a crush of people ran southward fleeing the burning buildings.

He was looking to interview eyewitnesses who had been inside the World Trade Center when the planes hit, and he planned to return to the *Journal* building where he assumed — incorrectly, as he would later discover — that Steiger and other senior editors would be running a military-like central command, handing out marching orders.

I want to be part of the action.

On South End Avenue, Hilsenrath skirted the river of dress shoes — discarded by women who abandoned all vanity for safety and speed. He was walking on the east side of South End Avenue — just across from Picasso Pizzeria — a frequent haunt of *Journal* reporters. A giant, hideous roar froze him in his tracks.

My God, there's another plane coming. I've got to get the hell out of here.

Although *The Wall Street Journal* was only a couple blocks further north, Hilsenrath believed a third plane was headed for the still-standing World Trade Center towers. His first reaction was survival.

When I heard the rumbling, the thought of the newsroom didn't enter my mind. It was just, "Get the hell out of here."

From the corner of Albany Street and South End Avenue, the Hudson River was visible to the west. What he couldn't see was the actual source of the sound. It was the South Tower collapsing.

Shit, I got to go to the water.

As he ran, one in a stream of people headed west, reminiscent of the running of the bulls in Pamplona, Hilsenrath was trying to calculate his best chance to survive.

Something bad is about to happen. If I have to, I'll jump in the river.

The South Tower of the World Trade Center began to pancake at 9:56 a.m. Ten seconds later, it was gone.

Like a tornado, a white cloud, dozens of stories tall, barreled toward Hilsenrath.

For the first time that morning, he was afraid. Terrified. He had watched the World Trade Center jumpers make their death leaps, and he understood that it was their inability to breathe that left them no choice.

Now the smoke monster was gunning for him.

This thing is going to overtake me. I could choke in it.

Suddenly, everything went white.

It wasn't heaven, but it was oddly surreal inside the cloud, and inexplicably, everyone grew quiet and seemed peaceful as white snow-like flakes of ash and dust enveloped them. Hilsenrath covered his mouth with his shirt.

Stay calm. All right, I'm not going to choke and die. Get your composure back.

Hilsenrath would remember the strange, albeit brief, serenity inspired by the quiet calm of everyone around him.

Like the others, he was experiencing an almost out-of-body sensation and, undoubtedly, an emotional catharsis.

I can breathe. I'm not going to die.

And then, immediately, his journalistic instinct returned.

What's the next step?

The predicament facing Hilsenrath and the others who ended up on the esplanade just above the Hudson River was the same: Where to go next?

North and east were out of the question. The police had cordoned off much of the area, and the roads and sidewalks were filling with debris. Additionally, the North Tower might yet collapse.

West was the Hudson River. While earlier Hilsenrath had considered jumping into it, now that he realized he could breathe despite the ash clouds, it didn't seem like a good option.

Even if he and others had tried to swim to Hoboken or Jersey City, it would have been ill-advised. In a swimming pool, the distance to New Jersey would be no problem for a reasonably capable swimmer. However, the river's strong currents might carry those who dared to traverse it southward toward the Atlantic Ocean. Moreover, the river was becoming congested with all manner of boats, some trying to escape Manhattan, others arriving to help evacuate stranded commuters.

South was what was then known as Battery Park, now called The Battery. It marked the final landmass on Manhattan Island before reaching New York Harbor, home to Ellis Island, Liberty Island, and Governors Island.

Like a coin-push arcade game, it was obvious that only so many people could jam into Battery Park — and thousands of frightened people were seeking escape there — before the crowd threatened to spill over the edge.

The best solution, and the one Hilsenrath chose, was to horseshoe around Battery Park on foot and head up the east side of Manhattan toward South Street Seaport, a historic district and tourist mecca where Fulton Street intersects with the East River.

As he walked, Hilsenrath repeatedly tried phoning Cristina. He had no cell service.

Shit. She's going to think I'm dead.

Which is exactly what she did think when she hadn't heard from her husband and couldn't reach him by phone.

She was shaking. Hysterical.

Cristina grabbed Alex and Hope and drove to her in-laws, who lived a few miles down the road.

Maybe God sent us back to New York to be close to family because I am going to lose my husband. I just want him home. I just want him home. Our kids are so young.

———————————

Before he met Cristina and had a family, Hilsenrath had visions of becoming a war correspondent.

After completing his undergraduate studies at Duke University in Durham, North Carolina, he traveled on his own around Eastern Europe and the Soviet Union. In November 1989, he was on hand to join those tearing down the Berlin Wall. He witnessed the fall of communism while traveling in Romania, Poland, Hungary, and Czechoslovakia. And he hitchhiked around Turkey.

The idea of covering the genocidal wars in Yugoslavia appealed to Hilsenrath. On or near the battlefields, he reasoned, was where the action is and where great journalism is incubated.

By the time the *Journal* repatriated him to its New York bureau in December 2000 to cover academic economics and forecasting, Hilsenrath's ardor for becoming a combat zone scribe had mostly been extinguished. Economics had proven interesting and impactful.

By September 11, Hilsenrath, 34, had settled into his role as a suburban dad and husband. Or so he thought.

I have to figure out what's my job here. Is my job to get home to my family or stay here and report this out?

What many New Yorkers discovered on September 11 was that mobile phone services did, for the most part, operate, but the volume of traffic was so overwhelming that the providers were unable to connect countless calls.

That may explain why Hilsenrath and his brother Danny, 16-months-older, were able to connect, even though Hilsenrath had not been able to reach Cristina and her calls to him were not completed. Danny, who worked as an electronic stock trader at Jefferies Financial Group in its Midtown offices, had been monitoring CNBC and its continuing coverage of the disaster.

Please call Cristina and tell her I'm okay and I'm making my way out of this.

Hilsenrath also asked Danny to call their parents on Long Island. [Hilsenrath is the youngest of four siblings. At the time, his eldest brother, Craig, lived in Connecticut, and his sister, Shelley, was in Israel.]

Until he spoke to Danny, Hilsenrath had no context for the drama he had witnessed and was experiencing. Danny told him the Pentagon had been hit by a plane and that as many as ten other airliners were said to be targeting other important buildings, including the U.S. Capitol.

[Erroneous accounts proliferated on 9/11, fueled, in part, by inaccurate news reports of an explosion at the U.S. Supreme Court building (1010 WINS Radio) and a car bomb detonation at the State Department (The Associated Press). Actual evacuations ordered at the Sears Tower in Chicago and The Mall of America in Bloomington, Minnesota, added to the confusion.]

I'm in the middle of a war zone. We're at war. I don't know who it is, but they are coming to kill and brutalize people.

Hilsenrath didn't want his brother to come downtown. But Danny insisted he would meet up with Hilsenrath in the vicinity of the Brooklyn Bridge to bring him some cash. His younger brother had not a penny on him, having rushed down to West Street that morning without his wallet or suit jacket, never suspecting that he wouldn't be able to return to his newsroom desk to file his story and pick up his personal belongings.

While many of those in Lower Manhattan surged uptown to get away from the choking smoke and horrid stench of the burning debris that enshrouded the area, Danny hoofed it three miles down Madison Avenue to rendezvous with his brother.

As Jon Hilsenrath approached the Brooklyn Bridge, heading uptown, he was shocked to see the exodus of thousands of people on foot streaming toward and onto the iconic span. The image reminded him of a verse from the poem, "The Waste Land," by T.S. Eliot, his favorite literary figure:

> *Unreal City,*
> *Under the brown fog of a winter dawn,*
> *A crowd flowed over London Bridge, so many,*
> *I had not thought death had undone so many.*
> *Sighs, short and infrequent, were exhaled,*
> *And each man fixed his eyes before his feet.*

Awaiting Danny, Hilsenrath determined he would attempt to identify and interview other survivors of the Trade Center attacks. He searched the crowd for anyone who, like him, was coated in white dust.

Amid the bedlam, Hilsenrath spotted his colleague, Patrick Barta, maneuvering through the horde. Barta, a reporter a few years younger than Hilsenrath, sat right next to him in the *Journal's* economics-beat cluster. Under the circumstances, it was an amazing coincidence.

Hilsenrath could tell by the way Barta was eyeballing him that he must have looked shell-shocked. Which he was.

Barta had tried unsuccessfully to reach the *Journal's* newsroom that morning, encountering one street obstruction after another.

I got to a barricade and told them I was a reporter. I was told, "you can't go in there because there might be another bomb."

Without access to the live television or radio coverage, many first responders assumed the World Trade Center had been bombed, as it had been once before in 1993.

As the two towers collapsed and fighter jets roared overhead, Barta retreated up the West Side Highway. One woman fainted, and he stopped to help her up.

Navigating his way to his East Village apartment on 6th Street, near Tompkins Square Park, Barta collected companions much like Dorothy had along the yellow brick road in the fictional Land of Oz. He was first joined by *Journal* reporters Neal Templin and Jeff Opdyke, then Hilsenrath and his brother Danny.

The five of them wedged into Barta's cramped second-floor apartment, a typical red-brick walk-up, with a nondescript entryway shoehorned between a tavern and retail shops. Upstairs, there was hardly enough space for Barta alone to work comfortably. The bachelor used his refrigerator as a bookcase and slept on a mattress on the floor.

Shortly after reaching Barta's place, Danny headed out to wend his way to his New Jersey home. Hilsenrath, Templin, and Opdyke sat on crates, stools, or the wooden floor.

Hilsenrath was anxious to transmit his observations and interview notes to the *Journal*. At Barta's apartment, the four staffers — now with spotty dial-up internet access — retrieved the dozens and dozens of emails that editors and reporters had been exchanging while the four of them were still on the street. Only then did they understand that the paper's World Financial Center headquarters had been evacuated and effectively obliterated when the Trade Towers fell.

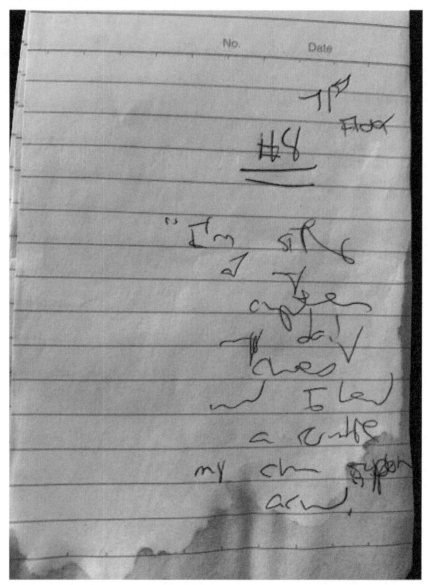

A leaf from Hilsenrath's 9/11 memo pad, where he scribbled notes from his street interview with Vincent Fiori. It reads, "I'm sitting at my computer my daily chores and I heard a rumble my chair spun around." The stains on the page were made post-9/11.

(Courtesy of Jon Hilsenrath)

September Twelfth

From: Lewis, Jesse

Sent: Tuesday, September 11, 2001 12:25 PM

To: Brauchli, Marcus

Subject:

marcus

this from gordon faircloth

Charlie Adams. Verizon in trade center. Standing by WFC when first plane hit the tower. In for 9 a.m. conference call.

Say second plane. look like united coming in from the south and just over the tops of the buildings. and then slammed into trade tower 2.

Reporter went into river.
When the second tower came down, they were evacuating people along the river. still hundreds of people there. Huge clouds of debris and dust mushroomed from building and came down canyon into streete. Some jumped onto fireboard, others in river. Raining down ash. Became almost pitch dark.

Evacuating massive numbers of people to harbor side.

A number of serious injuries. Alot of fire fighters and police officers.

Adam, firefighter, 18th floor of marriott hotel when tower collapsed. Blown down entire floor to 17th floor. Got down to 4th floor. Had to slide down I Beam to wreckage. A number of people were

Datek, assisting with helping EMS people, opened up their building. Like a hospital

Triage center right on the walkway by river. a firefighter with open hed trauma. A lot of people hurt when building collapsed.

Some *Journal* staffers were working from home. Some had managed to make their way across the Hudson River to a Dow Jones administrative office and printing facility 50 miles away in South Brunswick, New Jersey. Much of the day's global coverage was being orchestrated out of the D.C. bureau. And some key staff members, including Steiger, were missing and feared dead.

12:51 pm, from Patrick Barta, NY:

same here for us; i'm in my east village apt. with Neal Templin, Jeff Opdyke and Jon Hilsenrath. 212-XXX*-2989. or my cell, if it comes back on 646-XXX*-4413. opdyke's cell, which is working some of the time, is 973-XXX*-9681. we're available to make calls or return to the scene. (*Redacted.)

Hilsenrath took out his notebook and dictated his day's account by phone to someone in the *Journal*'s Dallas bureau.

"Mir Zenen Shich, Mir Zenen Letzter Eidus"

Neppy Archundia, 31, was sitting in the Marriott in the WTC when he heard the first crash. "I was in a class and I heard the building vibrate and then I saw a lot of debris falling and everybody said let's get out of here," he said. "When the second one hit, everyone ran for their lives."

Vincent Fiori was on the 71st floor of the first building that was hit. "I'm sitting at my computer and I heard a rumble and my chair spun around," he said.

He said people in general left in an orderly manner, but occasionally he saw people coming down the stairs with their clothing on fire. "There was no panic," he said.

Mr. Fiori was covered in soot and stood in the street in a daze. He walked off shortly after the explosion to find his son, who is a policeman.

Mark Heyman was in the Marriott at a seminar on the third floor. "I heard an explosion and felt the whole building shake. We just got up and ran," he said. "At first they didn't want to let us out of the building because they were afraid we'd get hit by debris."

As the afternoon edged toward nightfall, Hilsenrath figured he had done all he could. Fatigue was settling in.

I've had an honest day's work.

It was approaching 7:30 p.m. when the Long Island Rail Road restored its full schedule east and westbound.

With the money Danny brought him, Hilsenrath bought a ticket and caught a train home.

What an odyssey it had been. The expression "to hell and back" seemed applicable. He'd began, as usual, shortly after sunrise, catching the train at the Main Street station on the North Shore of Long Island, whizzing south past his childhood turf in Manhasset, and, along the route, able to catch a glimpse of Little Neck Bay out the train's right-side windows, and closer to Manhattan, the Unisphere and observations towers in Flushing Meadows, flashing by out of the left-side windows.

Hilsenrath had once yearned to cover the genocidal wars in Yugoslavia. Today, he had experienced a Sarajevo-like war zone in the most unexpected of places, his *Wall Street Journal* stamping grounds.

Now, undeniably worse for the wear, he was en route back to his suburban paradise.

Cristina was a jumble of emotions: anger, relief, happiness, and immense gratitude. For much of the day, she'd been shaking and hysterical, struggling not to let her children detect her panic.

Although he was covered from head-to-toe in dust and reeked of smoke, she held her husband and hugged him for the longest time.

All she had prayed for since that morning was to have him back with her and the kids. And now he had been, mercifully, returned to her. But only briefly.

I can't be here. I have to go to church.

The journalist in Hilsenrath wasn't ready to call it quits, even after all that he and Cristina had been through.

Having grown up in Manhasset, Hilsenrath, who, himself, is Jewish, knew that Saint Mary's Roman Catholic Church would be holding a midnight mass for townsfolk who lost their lives that day. He wanted to be on hand to talk to survivors and the families of the deceased.

Like other bedroom communities dotting New Jersey, Connecticut, and Long Island, Manhasset suffered an unimaginable loss on September 11. Roughly 50 of the hamlet's 18,400 residents perished.

Another casualty, the Hilsenraths discovered, was a young New York City policeman, Badge #3815, who followed firefighters rushing into the World Trade Center complex, even as Hilsenrath, his *Journal* colleagues, and thousands of others fled the area.

Glen Pettit, Cristina's former news colleague, had traded in his press pass for a police officer's shield. The eager and fearless videographer, who had driven their live truck into harm's way in order to get the best possible shots of the Sunrise Fire, was still pushing to find the best vantage on 9/11.

Pettit came from a Long Island family of firefighters and police officers, and after leaving News 12, found his dream job as a police videographer. He was 30-years-old when he perished. The last photograph of Pettit, captured as he hustled into the WTC complex with his video camera on his shoulder, was recorded by a News 12 Long Island videographer-friend who wanted to accompany Officer Pettit. Pettit wouldn't allow it.

It's too dangerous.

Hilsenrath and Cristina attended Pettit's memorial service. It was heartbreaking.

Weeks after September 11, Cristina recalls that her husband would still shudder every time he heard a plane fly overhead, which given their home's location on the approach to both LaGuardia and Kennedy airports, was quite often.

One night Hilsenrath dreamed that his Long Island town came under attack.

It wasn't just after dark that the trauma of 9/11 haunted him.

On one occasion, he took the family on an outing to the country to watch one of his nieces horseback riding. He was in the stables with Alex and Hope when he spotted chaps hanging from hooks.

Before his eyes, the leather leggings morphed into body parts, specifically severed arms and legs. Another time, driving through Port Washington, he spotted gardeners mowing the lawn. They placed the cuttings in large burlap sacks. But Hilsenrath's brain registered something else.

Body flesh. It's body flesh.

Parts of Hilsenrath's reporting that day made it onto the paper's lead front-page article on September 12. And he continued to contribute to the paper's reportage for weeks after, gradually resuming his regular beat, examining the economy and how the events of September 11 were impacting it.

As tragic and jarring as the day was, September 11 reminded Hilsenrath of why he chose journalism as a profession and the need to approach his job with humility.

This was a seismic event in my life.

The whole world changed that day.

This is why in some ways, I'm addicted to being a journalist. We're constantly surfing on the edge of history. Things can turn overnight. We have the privilege of watching it and explaining it.

Here is eyewitness from Bussey (via Jonathan Friedland, LA):

Bussey was on the otherside of WFC when first explosition occured "sounded like a jet engine breaking the sound barrier" pieces of buildings flew out several blocks, ems started to arrive when second plane hit the building. ems was trying to find ways to deal with extraordinary fire in northernmost tower. the top dozen or so loors were engulfed in smoke, people began leaping from windows toward the west, one at a time, hitting the ground, shrubery, plexiglass awnings, essentially atomizing. at that point, there were individual explosition in the south building, floor by floor as if charges had been set, going down in rapid succession one after another the skeletal structure of teh building stripped right off.

I dove under a desk and crawled on a floor deeper into the office; WFC filled up with smoke and cement desk and went entirely black because of it. felt his way desk by desk with shirt over mouth. it looked as if everyone had been evacuated, went down a stairwell, impossible to open the door for three or four minutes until dust cleared, exited on southend street. it was coated with three four inches of cement dust and debris. i was like pompeii. the ems people were in disarray, attempting to get organized, the fire trucks and ems units had pulled up close to the northern tower, went it went down, it probably crushed the command centers. there were ambulances on southend street, one of the ems and fire workers broke through window of a deli and we began ferrying water bottles out to ems units and people staggering around on the streets. phones were out, cell phones were down. got a surgical mask, started walking towards liberty street to see whether they'd been evacuated, got closer to street when an intense rumbling filled the air, firefighters began running to get around the corner behind an apartment building on southend street, a wave of debris came washing up the street into the apartment building, pushed ourselves up a corregated tin driveway entrance and we could feel it driving down on our shoulder. the firefighter in front of me took control of the six of us, breathe through your nose, fo three or four minutes there was a question of how long the debris was going to clear. finally, the ems guy got through on radio to a firefighter, we put our hands on each others shoulders and walked for ten to fifteen yard to get through the apartment building.

started walking south to where boats could come in, a few dozen people between WFC and battery park, a makeshift ferrying system of private motor boats and park service police, ferried across directly to new jersey

he 's making his way to either fort lee or s.b.

• Chapter Two •

"I'm Sorry. I'm Going to Interrupt You Right Now."

I heard a pressing metallic roar, like the Chicago El rumbling overhead. And then the fireman next to me shouted: 'It's coming down! Run!' Run where? I had no idea, so I did the best thing at the moment: I ran after the fireman.

John Bussey
Eye of the Storm: One Journey Through Desperation and Chaos
September 12, 2001 - The Wall Street Journal

When Peter G. Skinner ordered John C. Bussey, *The Wall Street Journal's* foreign editor, to evacuate Dow Jones & Company's 200 Liberty Street headquarters along with everyone else who remained in the building on the morning of September 11, Bussey adamantly refused.

It was a matter of principle. Bussey, 44, had stationed himself in a 9th-floor corner office looking diagonally across the street at the two smoking World Trade Center towers. Every few minutes, he went live on the air, by phone, to update CNBC's anchors and viewers on what he was witnessing.

Skinner and Bussey were like two gladiators, both stern in demeanor and uncompromising.

Skinner, the buttoned-down executive vice president and general counsel of Dow Jones, which publishes *The Wall Street Journal*, insisted that Bussey leave, scolding the journalist that by delaying, he was endangering not only their lives but also the security detail that had accompanied the executive.

You've got to get out.

Bussey didn't know Skinner very well, having met him only once or twice in a group setting. The journalist thought the executive was out of line, especially given that Skinner wasn't in the newsroom chain of command.

Bussey weighed the risks, and they were unpersuasive. He calculated that he was safer inside of the *Journal's* offices than he would be on the street.

I'm safe. I understand you're doing your job, but I'm a journalist, and I've got to do mine, too. I'll take on the responsibility for myself.

Bussey's stubbornness could have cost him his job and nearly cost him his life. It also led to one of the most compelling stories to appear in the paper's September 12 edition, and to this day is considered by some to be one of the best single-bylined articles ever published by the *Journal.*

Still photo of John Bussey from "Wall Street Journal: Events of 9/11" video, circa early 2002
(Courtesy of Freedom Forum)

Minutes after Skinner stormed off, Bussey found himself alone, in total darkness, disoriented, and gasping for air. It had never crossed his mind that the towers might topple and that the paper's headquarters, which occupied seven floors of what was known as One World Financial Center, would be heavily damaged by the fallout.

Just get under the fucking desk.

As the South Tower came down, the office he was in filled with ash, concrete dust, smoke, and detritus. On his hands and knees, he crawled beneath one of the standard-issue, commercial metal desks located deeper in the newsroom, away from the windows. The decision to shelter there made about as much sense as the duck-and-cover drills that Bussey, born in the late 1950s, and children throughout America practiced in elementary school to "protect" themselves in the event of an atomic attack.

Reason slowly returned.

This is ridiculous.

He stood, yanking off his shirt and cupping it over his mouth and nose.

Like a blind mouse in a maze, Bussey began feeling his way along desk carrels and walls, searching for an exit, or at least more breathable air. He felt trapped.

This is what it must be like on the upper floors of the Towers.

There was no way for him to orient himself. Sightless, Bussey continued to stagger around the 9th-floor labyrinth, more than once, he later realized, unknowingly passing the exit to a safer passageway.

Then, by sheer luck, he found his way to a larger space with more air, and soon after, an emergency stairwell. He could breathe again. But only momentarily.

Mark, I'm on the side of the building that's on the south side. I am looking up at the buildings from just across the street. It is an extraordinary scene. The top several floors, as you can see, are aflame, and smoke is coming up. The second explosion just happened. I did not see what Maria [Bartiromo] saw because I'm probably on the backside of the building. However, the hole came through the backside. There are gaping holes in the World Trade Center.

It was 9:07 a.m., not quite four minutes after United Airlines Flight #175 smashed into the South Tower, and Bussey was on the air live, briefing CNBC anchor Mark Haines about the unfolding drama.

Only 20 minutes earlier, CNBC had broken away from its daily regimen of earnings reports and stock forecasts to begin wall-to-wall coverage of the terrorist attacks.

Haines, one of the hosts of the business news network's morning show, "Squawk Box," was in the middle of an anodyne interview with Bill Nygren, a manager of the $4.12 billion Oakmark Select Fund, when the anchor cut his guest off mid-sentence:

I'm sorry. I'm going to interrupt you right now. We have what appears to be a very serious [pause]... Is that the World Trade Tower? [Haines continues speaking as a live video of heavy smoke spewing from the North Tower plays.] This is one of the towers of the World Trade Center in Manhattan, which is clearly heavily involved in a smoke situation. And one would assume there is fire.

Bussey had already been on CNBC a couple of hours earlier, when the world was still normal, talking about global news developments and the state of foreign financial markets.

That was his routine.

As the paper's foreign editor, one of the top jobs in the newsroom, Bussey had been enlisted by the *Journal* to wrest himself out of bed in the predawn hours on weekdays and make his way from his Upper West Side apartment to One World Financial Center, where, via a remote-controlled camera, he reported on overseas news.

As usual, on 9/11, he had arrived at *The Wall Street Journal's* headquarters shortly before sunrise for his initial live report at 6:30 a.m. Other than a security guard positioned at the mezzanine-level elevators, Bussey rarely encountered anyone from the paper.

There was, however, always a trickle of employees from other companies milling around the lobby. Among the other tenants that the 40-story building housed were Deloitte and Touche, Fidelity Investments, and Northwestern Mutual.

Typically, after filing his short CNBC report, Bussey would return to his office and try to get some work done or simply doze. As he sometimes did, on the morning of September 11, Bussey decided to head outside to a gym located just around the corner to squeeze in a half-hour of exercise before the business day began in earnest.

That was when he heard the first impact and saw the first drizzle of debris floating overhead.

Bussey had no idea what caused the explosive blast, but as a stream of people — already evacuating One World Financial Center — made their way out its revolving entryway doors, Bussey dashed into the building and rode a still-operating elevator to the 9th floor. In his haste, he pulled a leg muscle and would limp for the remainder of the day.

Even as Bussey was rushing in, the few *Wall Street Journal* colleagues of his that had already arrived for work were exiting, following the emergency voice notification instructions that were blaring overhead to vacate the building using the stairwells.

Among those withdrawing was Lawrence "Larry" Rout, the paper's special sections editor. His office, situated in the northeast corner of the 9th floor, afforded a perfect view of both Trade Center towers.

That evening, Rout and Bussey would assemble in South Brunswick, New Jersey, in a

The office of Lawrence Rout, the *Journal*'s special sections editor, in the aftermath of the World Trade Center attacks. It was from here that John Bussey reported live for CNBC.
(Photo courtesy of Dow Jones & Company)

makeshift newsroom, to publish Bussey's eyewitness, near-death account of the day's events. But at the moment, Rout's now-empty office is where Bussey positioned himself.

There is shit falling everywhere.

Bussey observed cars ablaze along West Street, even blocks from the World Trade Center.

This is a good place to start reporting. I'll be safe here.

Bussey phoned the CNBC control room, located in Fort Lee, New Jersey.

I'm right here. You guys need something?

They absolutely did.

CNBC's Maria Bartiromo, who had rocketed to prominence for her Sophia Loren-good looks and live daily reporting from the floor of the New York Stock Exchange, was in Lower Manhattan and witnessed the second plane hit the South Tower.

But it was Bussey who provided CNBC the first live on-air eyewitness reporting as he gaped out the windows of Larry Rout's office.

Although his career was primarily as a print journalist, Bussey's phone dispatches were lucid and unemotional.

Bussey warned viewers to stay away from the area, noting that huge chunks of metal were still falling from the Towers and smashing nearby fire trucks. He described the fires as ferocious and gaining in intensity.

Although nothing in Haines's career had come close to matching the events that the anchor was broadcasting, the 55-year-old newsman conveyed two particularly pertinent characteristics of the World Trade Center fires.

One was that the only way for firefighters to battle the blazes would be from the inside, what Haines described as an "extremely perilous undertaking." And second, that those occupants of the South Tower were in great peril because the second plane struck at a lower point than had the first plane that hit the North Tower, and the flames would travel up — exposing a larger number of people to the life-threatening fire and smoke.

John. And again, I just want to get back to very quickly to my point of the fact that the firemen have to fight these fires from inside the building. I mean, these are incredibly brave men and women who are going to go into that building right now and try and do that.

At 9:47 a.m. Bussey was back on the air with Haines, still sounding composed, despite the words emanating from his lips.

Mark, this is the most horrific scene I've ever seen. Bodies have begun falling from the building.

There is such intense smoke. I've seen a half a dozen from where I'm standing, which is in the World Financial Center. People either are falling, or they are leaping to escape this smoke. It is as horrific as you would imagine.

The people are dropping. One is falling this very instant. Arms are splayed, and they're crashing to the ground on top of the glass canopy, the plastic Plexiglas canopy outside of the building and onto the street. There are fire trucks all around. The firefighters are either inside the building or standing back from it because of the debris.

And now, this just began about four minutes ago, people having to jump, apparently to escape the flames. I thought at first it was debris. But now, looking at one after another, probably I've seen eight or nine of these individuals have to leap to escape the flames and this intense smoke, falling what must be something on the order of seventy-five, eighty-five floors to the street below.

.... Mark, it is a gruesome scene. It's just blood or red. I can't confirm that it is absolutely bodies. But I can see this sure looks that way. And then red splotches on the street in front of

the building.

Minutes later, Haines, his voice markedly more shaken than Bussey's had been, uttered:

One of the two towers is gone.... The building is gone.... The South Tower, it disappeared. It collapsed.

———————

Nine flights down, and limping, Bussey reached the bottom of the emergency stairwell that emptied onto South End Avenue. The cement dust and debris storm swirling outside was so intense that he paused for three or four minutes before venturing out.

When Bussey arrived at work that morning ahead of a picture-perfect Manhattan late-summer day, both the World Trade Center towers and the World Financial Center, with its 10-story Winter Garden glass-vaulted pavilion, were spotless, ready to welcome the hoards of workers, shoppers, and tourists who would be arriving soon.

Now it was a hellscape that he gazed upon. The sun was shining brightly, but everything and everyone was colorless, coated in gray ash.

Civilians were running in all directions. Cell phones were useless. Firefighters and emergency medical services personnel were in disarray, attempting, with little success, to get organized, their command centers having been destroyed or simply overwhelmed. Ambulances were lined up along South End Avenue, which ran behind the World Financial Center on its west side. Their crews expected a flood of injuries, but it would be a day mostly of fatalities.

Bussey, wheezing, staggered back in the direction of the World Financial Center's entrance in a futile attempt to ascertain whether his colleagues had made it out. His throat stung.

A voice crackled over the two-way radio of an EMS worker.

Steve, Steve, where are you?

A fireman rammed through the door of a nearby restaurant, and Bussey and about a half dozen others took momentary shelter inside. In the café's cooler, they found bottled water, which they grabbed for themselves and proceeded to hand out to those headed their way after fleeing the World Trade Center.

Stories abound on 9/11 of civilians, like Bussey, helping strangers plow through the dross and danger.

Bussey asked one of the ambulance crew members for a surgical face mask and was given several, which he distributed to EMS workers. Without the mask, the air was unbreathable.

When Bussey joined *The Wall Street Journal* in December 1983, he never intended to stay long. A year perhaps.

He'd been working in Hong Kong for the *South China Morning Post* as a Henry Luce Foundation Scholar and needed a job — any job — back in the States. Paul Gigot, currently editor of the paper's editorial page, wrote a letter of recommendation on Bussey's behalf. The endorsement found its way to Richard Martin, who was the paper's Chicago bureau chief. Gigot had been hired by Martin in 1980 before being dispatched to Hong Kong to serve as the *Journal's* Asia correspondent.

Martin saw potential in Bussey, and Bussey accepted his job offer.

Bussey fit the stereotype of a Wall Street journalist: Clean-cut, hazel eyes, with a bald crown and short-cropped sandy hair at his temples and in the back. He favored button-down shirts, dark suits, and conservative ties. He was of average height and build, and bespectacled. When he frowned, his eyebrows formed a bridge across his forehead.

Like anyone who worked in Chicago's Loop, Bussey was accustomed to the roar and squeal of the elevated trains, the "El," that continually passed overhead along State, Wabash, Lake, Dearborn, and other downtown arteries.

On 9/11, the thundering, metallic rumble that Bussey heard skyward as he walked along the street between the World Financial Center and the Hudson River to the west, still trying to get his bearings, reminded him of the "El." Only he wasn't in Chicago, and this din he knew instinctively had lethal intent.

Shouts erupted. A firefighter next to him called out:

It's coming down! Run!

No one knew where to run, but everyone in sight scrambled.

Bussey chased after the fireman as chunks of concrete and metal rained down. Joined by other firefighters and a couple of bystanders, they ran around a corner behind an apartment building on South End Avenue, pressing themselves as flat as possible against a corrugated tin driveway door.

Bussey was pelted with rubble. He tried to press even closer to the entryway but was already as flattened as he could get.

The sky went completely dark. The air was as dense as tar. Collectively, Bussey, the firefighters, and those with them went down in a crouch, struggling to breathe. Minutes passed.

Mike! Mike! Where are you?

One fireman was trying to raise a colleague over his two-way radio. Only static responded.

Bussey could barely see. To brace himself, he reached out and placed his hand on the back of the fireman who was trying to contact Mike. Bussey felt the fireman trembling.

How long will these ash clouds last?

Bussey thought about asking the fireman the question running through his mind and then realized the absurdity.

How would he know? How often does a 110-story building collapse to the ground?

The fireman's radio popped and hissed. Mike was finally responding, and shortly after, he arrived wearing a respirator and carrying a flashlight.

Other than Mike, no one could see clearly. So Bussey and the others, like children playing the centipede game, formed a line, one behind the other, each with a hand on the person's shoulder in front of them. And they walked out of the darkness into the clear air of the building's lobby, which unbeknownst to them, had been only half-a-dozen or so yards away.

Bussey wanted to thank Mike for leading the group out of the ash cloud. But the first responder had already moved on to help an injured EMS worker.

An armada of public and private boats was ferrying survivors from the marinas and boat harbors that dotted Lower Manhattan's west side across the Hudson River to the New Jersey waterfront. Bussey found his way onto a private boat, which deposited him not far from the Exchange Place PATH train station in Jersey City.

I've got to make a phone call.

Bussey looked like an ashen ghost with large flesh-colored circles around his eyes, which he had flushed with bottled water. The "walking dead" were ubiquitous along the New Jersey piers.

He spotted a uniformed Metropolitan Transportation Authority worker.

I hate to do this, but can I borrow a quarter?

The MTA employee reached into his pocket and pulled out a handful of change.

I'm so glad to be able to say that we have The Wall Street Journal's John Bussey on the phone.

We have been concerned about your well-being, John. Tell us what's going on and what you've been through, pal.

It was just past 11:20 a.m., a little shy of an hour since the North Tower collapsed, and using the Jersey City pay phone, Bussey had reached CNBC anchor Bill Griffeth.

Standing outdoors, with Lower Manhattan completely engulfed in a cloud of smoke visible across the river, Bussey picked up the story from where he had left off just before the first tower cratered. His calm voice belied the terror of his day.

Bussey told Griffeth how the floors of the South Tower pressed together like an accordion, imploding [from the pressure] as if destructive charges had been set on each floor. He talked about feeling his way, without vision, out of the newsroom and down the emergency stairwell. He recounted the Pompeii-like scene that greeted him in the plaza. And he related how firefighter Mike led him and the others to safety.

The extemporaneous tale that Bussey told Griffeth closely tracked to the first-person account that he subsequently phoned into Jonathan Friedland, the Los Angeles bureau chief who Bussey was able to reach to take his dictation. The two unscripted reports would form the framework of the deftly written front-page article Bussey constructed that evening for the September 12 edition of the paper.

On the water's edge in New Jersey, he had no idea who among his *Journal* colleagues had survived. He couldn't possibly fathom the way that the *Journal*'s New York newsroom — demolished before 10:30 that morning — had spontaneously begun to re-form in private apartments and homes, a nearby schoolhouse, and a Dow Jones administrative and technology office located 50 miles to the southwest.

But Bussey was determined to do his part, whatever was needed.

We're going to go back now to The Wall Street Journal's John Bussey. And, John, I know, first of all, I want to say I'm very glad you're safe because I was very worried about you. It was great to hear your voice on the phone.

• Chapter Three •

Baptism By Fire

Bob Bartley, one of the nation's most influential conservative voices, served as *The Wall Street Journal's* peerless editorial page editor for 29 years before passing the leadership mantle to Paul Gigot.

Gigot, a Pulitzer Prize-winning Washington-based opinion columnist with the *Journal*, was scheduled to assume his new post in New York on Monday, September 17, 2001. In search of a place to live and aiming to grab lunch with some of his colleagues, Gigot caught the 6:00 a.m. shuttle from Reagan National Airport to LaGuardia on September 11. Thanks to exceptionally sparse vehicular traffic, he arrived by about 7:35 a.m. at what was to be his new office on the 9th floor of the *Journal's* headquarters in Lower Manhattan.

He would spend 50 minutes there and never again occupy the space.

Mary Anastasia O'Grady, who edited the paper's *Americas* column, was the only other editorial page staffer around at that early hour. By the water cooler, the two greeted one another and remarked about the splendid weather that morning.

Rushing to meet his apartment broker for a 9:00 a.m. showing, Gigot hailed a taxi just outside the paper's World Financial Center headquarters and headed north to Greenwich Village. As his taxi slogged its way up Church Street, east of the World Trade Center towers, Gigot heard a massive explosion.

Ok, well, this is New York City. Right? Weird things happen.

Back at the office, O'Grady — whose desk looked directly across at the World Trade Center — felt the entire building shake. Having lived through the 1994 Northridge earthquake, she was super-sensitive to the shaking building.

I raced down to Paul's [new] office wondering if he had returned, but he was gone. I was alone. Sprinting back to my office and shaking, I grabbed my jacket and purse and took off for the elevators.

Gigot's cab driver, perhaps having spotted the smoking North Tower in his rearview mirror, pulled to the curb, shouting.

Oh, my God, oh my God, oh.

Abandoned to the sidewalk, Gigot joined dozens of others gazing up at the smoke and flames bursting out of the North Tower. He was puzzled by what he was witnessing.

What happened? It's such a clear day; it couldn't have been a plane. Must have been an explosion.

A student of history and a former White House Fellow during President Ronald Reagan's second term, Gigot recalled reading about a foggy day 56 years earlier when a B-25 Mitchell bomber on a routine mission slammed into the Empire State Building near the 79th floor.

Fourteen people were killed, including the two pilots, as aviation fuel ignited four floors and hurling plane parts snapped an elevator cable, sending one terrified passenger into a free fall. Fortunately for her, the plunge was halted by the emergency auto brake.

Unlike the World Trade Center towers, the structural integrity of the 102-story Midtown Art Deco skyscraper was not affected, and the Empire State Building reopened two days later.

By chance, in the crowd staring open-mouthed at the burning towers, Gigot spotted the apartment broker he was scheduled to meet at 9:00 a.m. The two men agreed to go ahead with the showing. When they got to the building, they ascended to the roof, where it was clear that both towers were aflame. With no access to television or radio, Gigot couldn't quite process what he was seeing.

Something is really weird.

Gigot wavered, trying to decide whether to return to the *Journal's* offices. He didn't know that the evacuation of 200 Liberty was already well underway.

I have to get in touch with Bartley.

Gigot had a mobile phone with him, but like almost everyone else in Lower Manhattan that morning, he had difficulty trying to get a call through.

Eventually, he reached Bartley, who was already making plans for the editorial page's next-day coverage and coordinating personnel from his home in Brooklyn Heights.

Robert Leroy Bartley, who turned 64 years old a month after 9/11, most certainly would have continued heading the *Journal's* editorial pages for years were he not preparing to undergo chemotherapy after receiving a grave cancer diagnosis earlier in 2001. A Midwesterner and inveterate optimist, he, like Gigot, began his career with the *Journal* as a news reporter in its Chicago bureau.

Bartley, who became an editorialist in 1965 and was appointed editor of the editorial pages in 1972, was known for his devotion to free markets, individual liberty, supply-side economics, legal immigration, school choice, welfare reform, and bashing most things related to President Bill Clinton and his administration.

To conservatives, the *Wall Street Journal's* editorial section under Bartley was the bible, and he their Moses. While many Democrats disdained Bartley and his opinion-writer disciples, the loyal opposition could not deny the editor's vast influence in D.C. and on Main Street.

"For his distinguished editorial writing, the test of excellence being clearness of style, moral purpose, sound reasoning and power to influence public opinion...," Bartley was awarded a Pulitzer Prize in 1980.

Daniel Henninger, who Bartley hired as a writer in 1977 and was deputy editor of the editorial page of the *Journal* on 9/11, knew the more private Bob Bartley; the soft-spoken, Obi-Wan Kenobi-style editor whose quiet leadership sent a loud message to his team: He wouldn't do their thinking for them. He expected them to think.

Eulogizing his boss and friend, who succumbed to his cancer in December 2003, Henninger wrote that while daily newspapering is relentless and can beat a person down, Bartley drew physical energy from the news.

Over the years I watched Bob go through periods of great personal strain, and every time he'd find new energy inside the ink pots of the news, something worth fighting for — or with. Those weekly columns Bob wrote the past six months were often done amid trips, medical treatment and pain that would have worn down any normal person. For Bob, the columns were like a portable generator — pull cord, plug in, come alive.

Unbeknownst to most people, Bartley was also a tech geek, which would prove to be an essential element of the *Journal's* ability to publish a two-page editorial section on September 11.

Bartley was fastidious when it came to maintaining the total detachment of editorial page staffers from news personnel. Like his predecessors and successors, he reported directly to the *Journal*'s publisher, not to its news-side managing editor.

Although the editorial page team was located on the 9th floor at 200 Liberty, just down the way from the offices of Paul Steiger, managing editor, and Mike Miller, Page One editor, the Bartley crew were stationed behind a set of secured doors. The locks were mostly a symbolic feature that reinforced the independence of the two workforces.

Bartley took his section's autonomy so far as to maintain separate software, hardware, and even tech and page-design personnel. He personally fashioned and perfected the production and pagination systems used to create the daily editorial and *Leisure & Arts* sections. In the spacious basement den of his brownstone, he ran a high-speed internet line and kept multiple computers, all of which came in handy when several of his editorial page colleagues showed up at his home on 9/11, anxious to help out.

Bartley did not sound angry or panicked over the terrorist attacks when Gigot finally reached him by phone. As much as Bartley must have been seething on the inside, it simply wasn't in his nature to let his emotions show. He instructed Gigot to head for South Brunswick and handed him most of the responsibility for selecting and editing the editorial page content for the September 12 paper.

Bartley elected to write the lead, unsigned editorial — *"A Terrorist Pearl Harbor"* — for the next day's edition.

The world is a different place after the massive terrorist attacks on the United States yesterday, much as it was after the bombing of Pearl Harbor nearly 60 years ago; a new kind of war has been declared on the world's democracies. Just as Munich led to World War II, so attempts to buy peace in the Middle East are surely behind this attack.

—

For the dead we can only grieve, and repairing the physical damage will take many years. But even within sight of the World Trade Center, life went on, albeit fitfully, yesterday. The airlines will fly again, albeit not quite as before, and new buildings will be built. Modern industrial society, for all the talk of its vulnerabilities, has a certain resilience. Returning to our normal way of life as quickly and as completely as possible is one part of the answer to the monsters who plan and perpetrate such ghastly events.

—

The upshot of this is likely to be a serious turn on a number of fronts. Intelligence, for example; how could the CIA and FBI have no advance indication of so large an event? Homeland defense, for another; can anyone now continue to doubt that someday people like those who conducted yesterday's events will have missiles that can threaten U.S. cities at 30 minutes warnings?

What most needs to be recognized, though, is that the terrorism has a political purpose. It is intended to intimidate America into standing aside humiliated while the Arab despots and fanatics destroy Israel and thereby prove that freedom and democracy are not after all the wave of the future. We can honor yesterday's dead by rallying our diplomatic, moral, financial and as necessary military resources to insure that that purpose is convincingly defeated.

Dan Henninger arrived at 200 Liberty by train and ferry from his home in Ridgewood, New Jersey, a little earlier than usual. His mission: buy a new cummerbund at a nearby retailer to wear that weekend at his son's wedding on the West Coast.

There was time to walk from the South Tower of the World Financial Center, where the *Journal* was headquartered, past the Winter Garden Atrium to a coffee shop situated down a marbled hallway in the complex's North Tower. The cinnamon-raisin croissants were worth the detour.

Henninger never got his sweet indulgence.

I just saw the wing of an airliner below the top of the Trade Center. My God, it hit it.

The plane seemed to Henninger to have vaporized. Floating down from the tower were little, shining particles which other witnesses have likened to the fine powder propelled aloft when skiers and snowboarders schuss through fresh snow.

Henninger's first-person account ran in the editorial section on Page A-18 on September 12. It would be one of ten articles that the *Journal* submitted for the 2002 Pulitzer Prize for Breaking News Reporting.

Henninger expressed the sentiments of virtually every *Wall Street Journal* reporter and editor who, involuntarily, became a battlefield correspondent that day.

I think that in the next few days I am going to wish that I had not seen any of this. There is no benefit in being able to watch two 108-story office buildings fall to the ground after two airliners have been forced to fly into them. It all seems very compelling now, and when you are in this business and you are on the scene, it is your job to provide an account. So this is just such an account, because there is something about us that demands that we provide this detail for the record.

To avoid the massive wall of smoke barreling toward them, some Dow Jones and *Journal* staffers who had evacuated ran toward the southern tip of Manhattan, while Henninger and others joined the thousands of frightened escapees headed north up the West Side Highway.

I decided that if the other tower had collapsed, then this one would too, and I was going to watch it fall.

I was going to bear witness. Let's be a little more precise about this statement. I loved the World Trade Center towers. I have worked in their shadow for almost 25 years. I came to see them the way I saw the Statue of Liberty. At night, in the fall, as I noted earlier, when they and all the rest of Manhattan's buildings were alight against a dark sky, the World Trade Center's towers were just joyous. They shouted out on behalf of everyone in this city, where everyone seems to take pride in working long, hard hours. No matter what, those long, hard silver towers were always there. Way up there.

Of course it fell. It was the most awful, humbling, disgusting sight. All of a sudden, it was just a 100-floor shaft of smoke. As it fell, as it was hitting the ground, the smoke and crap flew upward, I guess along the sides still standing, and the smoke arced away from the building in a series of neat, repulsively identical plumes. I looked at the center of the building and all I could see were a few scraggly black twisted girders pointing upward. Then they fell and it was all gone.

Henninger was not the only editorial page staffer who chronicled the scene on September 11.

O'Grady, who, after searching for Gigot early that morning in the office, made her way to the lobby of 200 Liberty, only to be assured by a security guard that there was no reason to panic. Almost simultaneously, John Bussey, the paper's foreign editor who had been downstairs heading for the gym, corralled O'Grady.

Walk with me.

So she did, joining Bussey back in an elevator and back to her 9th-floor office, where she phoned her parents to let them know she was OK.

They had not heard the news. My second call went to a brother in New Hampshire who works for a small local newspaper. My voice quivered and my heart was racing, but I told him that I was fine. Not two minutes into that conversation, a second, much louder boom shook my offices. I cursed loudly, shouted "I'm getting outta here," threw down the phone and ran for the exit. Only two elevators were working. "C'mon elevator." I said a prayer, then another.

Only much later would O'Grady learn that her prayers had been answered. The window of her office, along with those of all the other 9th-floor offices facing the World Trade Center, was blown in, leaving only shards of glass clinging to the window frames. Her workspace had been crushed by falling debris. Foul-smelling ash and debris cloaked everything: desks, chairs, computers, phones, and potted plants.

Jason L. Riley, a senior editorial page writer, was at Broadway and Liberty on his way from his Park Slope home into the office when the South Tower seemed to him to fall in slow motion.

I kept looking over my shoulder, and it was clear I could not outrun the cloud, so I started looking for cover. I saw a van and slid underneath, hoping it would shield me from the debris.

It didn't. I was having difficulty breathing. Every time I inhaled, more smoke and debris. My eyes were burning and it was completely dark.

Then I started to worry that the van would move, and I would get crushed.

Riley's 447-word email chronicle made it into the September 12 edition of the paper, filling a space intended for a graphic that proved unavailable.

———————

The challenge Gigot faced trying to make his way to the *Journal*'s administrative offices and South Brunswick printing plant was formidable.

By the time he connected with Bartley, the trains, tunnels, and bridges out of Manhattan had been shut down. Thinking that he might escape the city by heading north toward Westchester County, Gigot walked from Greenwich Village to Grand Central station.

Around noon, service north resumed, and he rode the Metro-North Railroad to Yonkers, New York, where he exited, thinking he would rent a car there and wend his way to New Jersey and then south to the paper's makeshift newsroom not far from Princeton.

Yonkers is home to a number of enchanting parks and gardens, a harness racing track, and the Philipse Manor Hall State Historic Site, which in November 1776 served as the gathering place of more than 200 colonial New Yorkers who declared in writing their loyalty to King George III.

But on 9/11, Gigot had no luck finding a rental car agency in the city on the eastern bank of the Hudson River. So he hailed a taxi and headed to Westchester Airport, 20 miles further north.

I know I can always get a car at the airport.

Except, due to concerns about possible additional terrorist attacks, access to the airport was shut off.

Still in the taxi, fortune turned in Gigot's favor when he called the Hertz rental office in White Plains and nabbed the last car on the lot. Gigot navigated to the Tappan Zee Bridge, now known as the Governor Mario M. Cuomo Bridge, 26 miles north of Manhattan, then drove the 70 miles down the Garden State Parkway to South Brunswick.

When he finally arrived, about 2:10 p.m., *Journal* staff were still assembling from their homes and the 200 Liberty displacement. From that point on, Gigot took charge of the editorial section, joined in South Brunswick by editorial writer William McGurn and Ken De Witt, a 30-year *Journal* veteran who oversaw the daily production of the editorial, op-ed, and *Leisure & Arts* pages.

Conversing with Bartley by phone, Gigot also assigned himself responsibility for writing the day's secondary editorial, *Civility Amid Chaos*.

Terrorists may have thought they were striking at the heart of selfish Western capitalism in Manhattan's financial district yesterday. But what they unleashed instead was a show of democratic civility and resilience.

Gigot may well have been describing his newsroom; intense, facing onrushing deadlines, displaced, and traumatized, but civil and undoubtedly resilient.

This is what makes yesterday's anecdotes from New York and Washington more than just individual acts of compassion or heroism. They are all of that. But above all these acts of civility are validations of our own democratic civilization, what we sometimes call Western civilization. This is what the terrorists hope to steal from us, and yesterday Americans showed that the terrorists had failed.

Philip J. Connors was a 28-year-old copy editor working for Bob Bartley on *The Wall Street Journal's Leisure & Arts* page. Coverage of breaking news would be found nowhere in his job description.

The job was so leisurely that I didn't even show up at the office until 10:00 or 10:30 most mornings.

Yet early on September 11, Connors acted like an amalgam of a war correspondent and a Navy SEAL.

His extraordinary adventure was captured in a 2,950-word annal that was included in an extensive compilation of staff reminiscences that Dow Jones provided to the National September 11 Memorial & Museum on the first anniversary of the attacks.

Connors's account displayed the type of journalistic pluck that gives rise to legends.

One characteristic of *The Wall Street Journal's* editorial page that predated Bartley and his mentor and predecessor, Vermont Connecticut Royster, is that the paper's opinion writers consider themselves reporters — not ivory-tower essayists — who enjoy the luxury of offering a point of view. Many times, the editorial section's staff, relying on their own sources, apply the same reportorial techniques of their news-side colleagues to break scoops and trump their rivals.

That Royster-Bartley-Gigot "force" was strong with Connors on September 11.

On his commute to work, Connors was aboard an elevated train in Queens when all the passengers took notice of the distant World Trade Center towers, which looked like giant industrial smokestacks.

I have to get to work. It's going to be chaos, and they'll need all hands on deck.

Connors took the Astoria "N" train to 59th Street in Manhattan and then transferred to the downtown express. At 28th Street, his train halted and remained motionless for 45 minutes. All the passengers were tossed off at the Union Square station at Fourth Avenue and 14th Street.

The sidewalks teemed with people. Nearly everyone moved north, away from the awful cloud of smoke that was now visible down the canyon streets to the south. I worked my way against the flow of pedestrians. Desperate people held their arms aloft for taxis that never came. I scooted out into the bus lane to avoid the oncoming throng.

Connors hoofed it the mile-plus to Canal Street before he was stopped at a police barricade. On any other day, his explanation that he worked for *The Wall Street Journal* and needed to get to his office to cover the breaking story would likely have been sufficient to be allowed to pass. But the New York City cop he encountered was having none of it.

I don't care who you are or where you work. I don't care if you're the President of the United States. No one gets beyond this spot, and if you insist on trying, I'll have your ass arrested.

Rebuffed, Connors headed west one block before running into another blockade. After sneaking past the second one, he encountered yet a third roadblock and a stern police officer who commanded him to turn back.

He didn't.

I'm not going to get any closer without resorting to extreme measures.

On Franklin Street, just above a shuttered subway station strung with police tape, Connors darted past the yellow bands and down the stairs. He was alone in the station, where an empty train sat halfway adjacent to the platform and halfway in the tunnel headed south.

I flattened myself against the wall next to it and entered the mouth of the tunnel, stepping gingerly along a narrow platform a few feet above the tracks. In my left hand I held my briefcase. With my right I gripped a yellow iron railing. Just beyond the nose of the train the tunnel became pitch black. The only sound was a steady drip of water from somewhere ahead.

Moving through the dark, taking baby steps along the center of the track bed so as to avoid the electrified third rail, Connors progressed until after a while, he found himself beneath the halo of a street-level grill. He heard the sound of police walkie-talkies overhead and picked up a strap-on dust mask that he spotted on a ledge beneath the shaft.

At the Chambers Street station, still alone, he climbed up to the passenger platform. His hands were black with dirt from the railing he had used as his guide.

I walked the length of the station to the mouth of the tunnel at its southern end. I cocked my ear toward the darkness ahead and heard a torrent of water as if from a waterfall. Clearly it would be madness to go further; perhaps it was some kind of madness to have come this far. For the first time I felt fear: fear of something menacing emerging from the void, fear of an explosion, a wall of water, a cloud of poison gas. I was alone in the bowels of the city, and if somehow I became injured or sick, I could quite plausibly die here alone, writhing in agony, where no one would ever think to search for me.

Connors surfaced, strapping on the dust mask he found in the subway tunnel. He remained determined to reach his colleagues in the paper's newsroom, unaware that no one was left there.

Avoiding the police and firefighters, who this close to the World Trade Center's cadaver were too preoccupied to take notice of a nomadic civilian, Connors reached the freight entrance at the rear of 200 Liberty and ascended the fire stairs to the 9th floor.

The lights and computers were still on, but no one else was present. He walked over to Paul Steiger's office. No one. He walked to where the Page One staff sat. Still no one. His own section, where the editorial writers and *Leisure & Arts* crew were based, was layered in ash an inch or thicker.

With no intact windows on the east side of the building, the wind — reeking of burnt rubber, metal, and fuel — blew freely into the newsroom and forced Connors to retreat inward toward the west side of the *Journal*'s offices.

I went to my cubicle and blew the ash from my telephone and computer keyboard. I picked up the receiver to check the messages signaled by the blinking red light: frantic calls from friends and family, making sure I was safe and urging me to call them as soon as I could. I took a section of the Times from my briefcase and spread it over the ash on my chair so I could sit down. I logged onto my computer and found colleagues sending email updates almost every minute.

Connors tried calling Bartley at his Brooklyn Heights home to see if he or anyone else needed him to retrieve items from their desks. One of Bartley's crew, who was screening his calls, was flabbergasted that two-plus hours after 200 Liberty was evacuated, Connors had somehow managed to return to the office.

All of Connors's intrepid efforts to be of service proved for naught. Bartley's deputy, no doubt stupefied by what Connors had done, could think of nothing anyone needed, although undoubtedly in the days to come that proved to be a missed opportunity for many of Connors's peers, especially those — including Gigot — who had left their laptops behind. A department-wide email that he sent from his desk to his scattered colleagues, asking them what he might retrieve for them, mostly got return emails urging him to hightail it out of there.

As Connors was headed back to the stairwell exit, he heard the insistent ring of a phone echoing through the newsroom. He darted back to his cubicle to discover it was his phone receiving an incoming call.

"Phil?" a shaky voice said. I recognized it as my mother's. "We've been so worried about you," she said. "We've been watching the news all morning."

After calmly reassuring his mother that he was fine, the adrenaline-fueled fog that Connors had inhabited since exiting the train at 59th Street began to clear.

For the first time I was able to stand slightly outside of myself and judge the danger of the situation. The building may have sustained structural damage and could begin to list or buckle. Further attacks might still be on the way. Gas might pool amid the wreckage and detonate like a bomb. Something unforeseen and unimaginable could happen and trap me in the building for hours or days.

Connors's trek down the emergency stairs seemed to him to take even longer than the trip up. With a digital camera he appropriated from the paper's production department, he snapped photos of the street scene until his film disk ran out of space. And soon, his day's exploits were over.

When my film ran out I returned to the edge of the debris and simply stared. The magnitude of the destruction was unfathomable, although it lay directly in front of me. Only smaller things that put it in some kind of proportion made any sense: water spouting aimlessly from a pump on the side of a ruined fire truck, cars half-buried in the rubble, their tires nowhere in evidence --either melted or blown to bits -- and their paint sheared off as if it had been the skin on a butchered animal. My lungs started to constrict and burn, even with the dust mask on, and in the sunlight I could see tiny particles of glass undulating like anemones on the breeze. The last thing I heard before I turned away for good was one firefighter yelling to another: "Jimmy, have you seen my brother? Any word on my brother?"

Later, on a bus headed uptown, a man who'd been on the 78th floor of the South Tower told me how, as he and thousands of his colleagues made their long way down to safety by stairs, they'd encountered hundreds of firefighters rushing bravely upward to fight the fire that had ultimately swallowed them.

Only then did it sink in that thousands had likely died; only then did I finally allow myself to cry.

Section Two:
Scattered

• Chapter One •

"This is Clearly our Pearl Harbor"

From: *Murray, Alan*
Sent: *Tuesday, September 11, 2001 10:46 AM*

To: NEWS - WDC Bureau; Blumenthal, Karen; Putka, Gary; Friedland, Jonathan

Subject:

Please file ALL copy involving terror attacks by e-mail to:
Alan Murray; Gerry Seib; Bryan Gruley; Marylu Carnevale; Carla Robbins

Also, please file initial files by 3:00 p.m., then updates.

Alan

Tuesday's "Wire Breakfast" was an institution in the D.C. bureau of *The Wall Street Journal.*

Ostensibly, the gathering of the entire staff was called to plan out the *"Washington Wire"* report, which ran on Fridays, occupying the entire fifth column of the paper's front page. The *"Washington Wire"* is one of the oldest standing features in American journalism, offering readers morsels of behind-the-scenes news, gossip, and forecasts.

But the breakfast confab, in truth, was more of an excuse for everyone to come together once a week to promote camaraderie and cohesion.

The breakfasts were held in the bureau's "living room," a spacious area of its newsroom — carpeted and appointed with comfy sofas and mahogany furniture that could have passed for a power broker's library, absent the books. The D.C. bureau was, and still is, situated on the 8th floor of the Blake Building, located at 1025 Connecticut Ave NW, three blocks from the White House.

It was common to invite a guest to join the journalists' breakfast and offer some informed analysis. On the morning of September 11, 2001, that spot fell to James B. "Jim" Steinberg, a former Deputy National Security Advisor in the second Clinton administration, who, coincidentally, was scheduled to make a few remarks and take questions about terrorism.

Only two weeks prior, Steinberg had moved back to D.C. from Manhattan to take up a post heading foreign policy studies at the Brookings Institution. Carla Anne Robbins, the bureau's national security reporter, was the one who extended the invitation to Steinberg to speak.

In the final years of the Clinton administration, especially following the August 1998 bombings of the American embassies in Nairobi, Kenya, and Dar es Salaam, Tanzania, President Bill Clinton and his senior advisors were hyperfocused on the threat that terrorists and hostile nations posed.

Whether physically present in the White House Situation Room or speaking from a secure line in the middle of the night from his home, Steinberg was fully engaged in monitoring global terrorist groups and crafting the U.S. response to their threats and actions.

While the journalists were still grabbing coffee and bagels ahead of the 9:15 a.m. start, a late arrival announced that a plane had hit one of the Twin Towers in New York. The assumption was that the crash was a terrible air accident.

Nonetheless, Alan Murray, 45, in his eighth year as bureau chief, called off the session and trooped to his spacious corner office along with Steinberg, deputy bureau chief Gerald F. "Jerry" Seib, and several others to monitor what CNN had to say about the unfolding drama in Manhattan.

Seeing the top of the North Tower in flames, Steinberg wasn't convinced that what they were viewing was an accident. When the second plane hit, everyone in the room understood it was terrorism, and Steinberg immediately knew who to blame.

This is Osama bin Laden.

There was no doubt in his mind.

The phones in the D.C. bureau began to light up. Soon, they resembled the switchboard at a pop radio station offering free concert tickets to the 86th caller.

Paul Steiger, the managing editor, reached Murray just moments before Steiger and others who had been in their offices across the street from the World Trade Center were forced to evacuate.

We're going to have to abandon the building. There's a group that's going to try and get to South Brunswick to put together a newsroom, but we don't know how long that's going to take. And you're basically going to have to take responsibility for getting the content for the paper together. You're going to have to do it.

Murray took charge unflinchingly. A crowd of editors and reporters soon encircled him, standing. In a calm but resolute voice, he spelled out the challenge facing them.

Look, this is clearly our Pearl Harbor. We know what it was like for our parents who lived through this. The world has just changed dramatically.

As if to punctuate his words, as Murray concluded his brief remarks, the deafening roar of an overhead fighter jet reverberated throughout the bureau.

Alan Murray and the D.C. bureau were well suited for the role Steiger pressed upon them.

Outside of New York, D.C. boasted the largest contingent of bureau reporters, editors, and support staff — numbering approximately 75. The Capital bureau was organized into sections, or "pods" as they were called, each responsible for distinct areas of coverage. The pods were led by player-coaches, senior staffers who did their own reporting but also supervised the work of others.

For reasons that are somewhat vague, the D.C. bureau also had its own long-established news desk, staffed by three or four full-time copyeditors.

One unofficial explanation for why the D.C. bureau didn't filter its stories through the New York copy desk, like other bureaus, centered on the long-standing, intense resentment the two bureaus felt for one another, each defending a separate power base.

The worlds of politics and finance were quite different, and so were the journalists who covered them. While everyone's business cards read "The Wall Street Journal," those based in Washington and those working from Manhattan often viewed their counterparts warily.

In a manner similar to Bob Bartley, the editorial page baron whose stature allowed him to bypass the *Journal's* primary New York news desk using his own copyeditors, Murray and his immediate predecessors — Albert R. Hunt, Norman C. Miller, and Alan L. Otten — exercised their clout to maintain greater control over their platoons' stories.

If there was an official explanation for the copy desk bifurcation, it was that inside-the-beltway news required different handlers than those staffers who edit business and financial markets stories.

Murray never doubted that he and his staff would rise to the challenge, although he worried if that would be enough. Communication with those in South Brunswick and other displaced colleagues was erratic. Whether the peripatetic New York journalists would be able to overcome the obstacles they faced, and whether the layout, printing, and delivery personnel could surmount their impediments, remained an open question.

The D.C. bureau was now the global command center for *The Wall Street Journal* and Alan Murray, its commander.

When the *Journal* periodically ran disaster drills, such as they were, the planners never envisioned transferring the seat of operations to D.C. Rather, they figured that in an emergency, the top New York-based editors would run the show from South Brunswick, New Jersey, or the Dow Jones printing plant in Chicopee, Massachusetts.

But Murray, whose name was often mentioned when the resident gossips got around to speculating on who, one day, might succeed the 59-year-old Steiger, demonstrated unmistakably that he was qualified for the job.

Murray's focus was twofold: coordinating coverage with those in South Brunswick and the news bureaus outside of New York, and overseeing the contingent of D.C. editors and reporters who would be responsible for producing the brunt of that day's major articles.

Clearly, even if the New York newsroom hadn't been knocked out of commission, Murray's team would have had a central role to play, obtaining reactions from the White House, Department of Defense, Department of State, Federal Aviation Administration, Department of the Treasury, and so on.

For the first hour-plus that morning, as those in the D.C. bureau reached out to their sources by phone and monitored the newswires and cable news networks, this appeared to be a New York story that would be compiled in D.C.

Then Ted Bridis, driving into the office on Interstate 395 from his home in Virginia, called into the bureau from his mobile phone.

Bridis, who covered technology policy and related topics, had a clear view of American Airlines Flight #77 plowing into the western side of the Pentagon and the fireball that resulted. Before any of the newswires or television networks disseminated word of the strike, the Journal's D.C. bureau was alerted.

Suddenly, the story expanded from one focused on the World Trade Center to one that included a second theater, this one in Murray's backyard. And not 30 minutes later, a third crash site in a field in rural Pennsylvania emerged.

Steinberg, who had remained in the D.C. bureau to assist reporters and editors with the benefit of his experience, thought the atmosphere in the newsroom resembled that of the Situation Room.

In both cases, the first question is, 'What is going on here? What does it mean?'

Unlike the National Security Council, which can draw on enormous technological and personnel resources to help answer those two questions, the *Journal's* reporters and editors were pressed to make sense of the rapidly evolving crisis on their own.

The phone circuits were overwhelmed and many of the paper's best D.C. sources were wrapped up responding to the attacks, and thus unavailable for interviews. Surprisingly, however, one of the most challenging tasks confronting the reporters and editors was making sense of the firehose of information that *was* pouring in. What information was correct and what was erroneous?

Steinberg witnessed the atmosphere in the newsroom change when the third and fourth planes crashed.

There was this sense of potential personal danger. The dynamic changed because there was this physical sense of fear. Was there more? Because the Pentagon was close, but the White House was even closer.

While Carla Anne Robbins was trying to get a handle on developments, she was buffeted by concerns for her friends and colleagues who worked for the *Journal* in New York. Moreover, there was a steady stream of rumors, some of which were transmitted by the wire services, that other D.C. targets had been hit. Although the rumors ultimately proved false, Robbins and her colleagues had to chase them anyway.

I remember somebody coming in and saying, a bomb just went off at the State Department. It was one thing right after another. And basically, [we were] trying our best to put together [the story] the best ways we possibly could. And when the paper had lost its New York office, it was a pretty scary day.

Making and fielding phone calls, Murray gazed out the floor-to-ceiling windows in his office overlooking the intersection of Connecticut Avenue and L Street and saw sorties of military planes fly past. The streets below were deserted.

Periodically, Murray popped his head out to check on the progress being made. Everyone was working intensely.

No one in the D.C. bureau dared leave the Blake Building to do on-the-scene reporting, fearing, with justification, that they might not be able to return.

At one point — some staffers remember it occurring around 10:00 a.m., while others think it was in the afternoon — the head of building security appeared at the doorway of Murray's office with a pronouncement.

We're closing the building and you have to leave.

Murray is neither particularly tall nor does he cut an imposing figure, but his response was loud and unequivocal.

There's no way we're leaving this building.

(There is also disagreement among witnesses over whether Murray punctuated his response with an obscenity.)

Robbins, who had worked in D.C. since 1993, was seated nearby. She could not recall ever seeing Murray as adamant.

Alan was just resplendent at that moment. He gets a medal from me for that. It was a defense of journalism as its highest point.

The stunned security manager appeared to be weighing his response before he turned, silently, and walked away.

At 10:46 a.m., Murray dispatched a short email to everyone in the D.C. bureau, as well as Karen Blumenthal, Dallas bureau chief, Boston chief Gary Putka, and Los Angeles chief Jonathan Friedland. Their first deadline to file copy would be 3:00 p.m. Eastern.

Although Murray's email didn't state so specifically, the early deadline was necessary in order to feed some content to the editors of *The Wall Street Journal Europe*, who were six hours ahead and would be hard-pressed to get 9/11 coverage into the next day's paper.

Murray began doling out bureau assignments.

He asked David S. Cloud and Neil King Jr., whom he had delegated to cover terrorism several years earlier, to mine their sources for theories about who was behind the attacks.

Cloud was meeting with sources at the Treasury Department when the first plane hit. He broke off his interviews to hoof it the few blocks back to the D.C. bureau and begin calling his sources. Seated only steps away from Murray's office, Cloud overhead his boss on the phone speaking with an unknown caller.

Cloud is doing the best he can.

The deadline pressure was palpable.

Cloud and King wrote the banner front-page story in the September 12 edition: *"Death Toll, Source of Devastating Attacks Remain Unclear; U.S. Vows Retaliation as Attention Focuses on bin Laden."*

Seib, the deputy bureau chief, edited as Cloud and King typed along. A veteran foreign and D.C. reporter, himself, Seib had a deft touch, knowing how to frame the facts into a clear and succinct narrative. Seib rewrote the first several paragraphs of the final draft.

By successfully attacking the most prominent symbols of American power -- Wall Street and the Pentagon -- terrorists have wiped out any remaining illusions that America is safe from mass organized violence.

That realization alone will alter the way the U.S. approaches its role in the world, as well as the way Americans travel and do business at home and abroad.

The death toll from the hijacked jets' attacks that destroyed the World Trade Center in lower Manhattan, and damaged the Pentagon, was impossible to gauge immediately. But it could eclipse the loss of life the country suffered in the Japanese attack on Pearl Harbor, when more than 2,300 perished.

It wasn't immediately clear who was responsible for the attack, though official attention focused on Middle East terrorist Osama bin Laden and his organization. One U.S. official said intelligence agencies already had gathered "strong information" linking Mr. bin Laden to the attacks. If the bin Laden organization isn't directly responsible, U.S. officials suspect, it could have sprung from a network of Islamic terror groups he supports and finances.

The gravity of the challenge to the country was summarized by Sen. John McCain, a Vietnam War veteran, who said: "These were not just crimes against the United States, they are acts of war."

To forecast the possible fiscal fallout of the 9/11 attacks, Murray turned to Greg Ip, who covered economics, and John D. McKinnon, who kept an eye on Treasury and budget issues. Their story, *Attacks Raise Fears of a Recession*, would echo the unique business spin that their long-ago predecessors used to report the December 7, 1941, Pearl Harbor assaults, running a six-column, three-line, next-day, front-page headline.

> *U.S. Industry's Sole Objective: Arms Production Speedup;*
> *Congress Prepares To Act; Tax Bill Will Be Rushed;*
> *N.Y. Stock Exchange To Open As Usual Today, Says Schram*

Much had changed since 1941, and Ip and McKinnon found themselves in largely uncharted territory, as they reported.

Economists groped in vain for historical precedents to help evaluate the potential impact of such a shocking, tragic event on the economy. "I don't know where to look for analogies," said Alan Blinder, economics professor at Princeton University. "Confidence-shaking events usually have transitory negative effects on consumer spending. But we've never seen anything like this that I can think of."

Murray enlisted June Kronholz, who was covering the Department of Education and related topics, to write on how the lives of everyday Americans were likely to change. Kronholz, a veteran foreign correspondent, epitomized the "whatever it takes" attitude that permeated the *Journal*'s reporters and editors on September 11.

She had no sources in intelligence. Nonetheless, Kronholz steeled herself for the task at hand.

I had a lot of sources in child psychology etc so I started there. Then I got to thinking about how I loved going to the Capitol and strolling around — how accessible it was to visitors. So I started making some more calls about what would change in society. That became the focus of my reporting.

Kronholz did most of the heavy lifting on her story, *"Hour of Horror Forever Alters American Lives,"* aided by Christina Binkley in Los Angeles and Clare Ansberry in Pittsburgh, as well as a stream of emailed memos from the paper's network of journalists.

I had so many [emailed memos] that I hadn't the time to read them all — or even open all the emails — but I incorporated as many as I had time to read and edit in.

One I remember clearly, because it brought me to tears, was from someone in NY who had gone to a blood-donation center, where people were lined up to give. Of course, the blood wasn't needed because there weren't many injuries that required that kind of attention, but people waited and donated anyway.

Murray tasked Bryan Gruley, a senior staffer who oversaw one of the bureau's pods, with what was possibly the most intense assignment of all. It fell to him to recount the day's events and capture its profound emotional force by curating the well over 100 incoming emails and story drafts that arrived fast and furious.

Most of the emails and memos, albeit significantly abbreviated, made it in one form or another into Gruley's front-page roundup — *"Nation Stands In Disbelief And Horror: Streets of Manhattan Resemble War Zone Amid Clouds of Ash"* — or other stories published on September 12. And they kept on arriving in D.C. and at his desk long after the presses began rolling.

Gruley relayed the trauma of the Australian couple who had only relocated to New York and an apartment near the Twin Towers a month earlier. They were holding their two children, ages 3 and 5, and frantic to find an escape route.

A Roman Catholic priest, laying on a stretcher in Battery Park, recounted that he'd been buried and had to dig his way out. He paused to spit, and out came a wet, gray wad of ash.

A 24-year-old taxi driver hoped it was all a bad dream and he'd wake up from it. "Guys were on their knees crying, begging me to give them a ride away."

"Everywhere you turned, there was someone taking bodies out of the rubble," one firefighter lamented. Another sobbed aloud: "My company is dead, they're all dead."

A spokesman for the Westmoreland County public-safety department in Pennsylvania confirmed that its emergency call centers received a call from a man aboard the doomed United Flight #93 over Pittsburgh at 9:58 a.m. The caller, who was locked in a bathroom, repeatedly stressed that the plane had been hijacked. "[This is] not a hoax."

Gruley concluded his 2,800-word story with a few vignettes from Washington D.C.

By yesterday evening, military vehicles were patrolling the city, and police had cordoned off a three-square area near the White House.

In Arlington, Va., abutting Washington, fishermen plunking for catfish at a marina near the Pentagon said they could feel the heat from the explosion. The White House, the Capitol, and the Treasury and State departments were evacuated shortly after the crash at the Pentagon. "Get out! Get out!" police yelled as they swept through federal buildings. As legislators streamed out of the Capitol, the memorial chimes across the street played "God Bless America."

———————————

By the time Paul Steiger reconnected with Alan Murray, there was little of substance for Steiger to do other than marvel at how well Murray had picked up the baton and run with it.

Throughout the day and well into the night, Murray was in close contact with Marcus Brauchli, the national news editor who was planning and coordinating the entire menu of news coverage from his Brooklyn home, and Jim Pensiero, who had taken charge of the copy desks and composition efforts in South Brunswick.

That day's contributions from the three editors, none of whom were high enough in stature to appear on the *Journal*'s daily masthead, were unquestionably the cornerstones that allowed the *Journal* to publish on September 12.

Like their counterparts in South Brunswick and bureaus around the country, most of the D.C. staff worked overtime, taking a pause periodically to update their spouses on their status or to arrange for childcare. While early in the day family members were concerned for the safety of their loved ones in the D.C. bureau, by evening the conversations were mostly about logistics: when will they be home, how will they get home, and the like.

One of the more unusual family reunions that took place that night was between Carla Anne Robbins and her husband, Guy Gugliotta.

Who had the more demanding day?

Gugliotta, who years earlier had reported from the Persian Gulf region during the Gulf War and later covered Capitol Hill for *The Washington Post*, was well-established on the Science beat for the Post in 2001.

When the Post decided to go to press with a special early street edition of the newspaper on September 11, the Post's editors assigned Gugliotta to write the lead front-page story, "N.Y. Skyscrapers Collapse After Hijacked Planes Hit."

Why they selected Gugliotta is a bit unclear, although, given the chaos of the day, it certainly helped that he was a veteran journalist, a fast writer, and, perhaps most important, he was in the newsroom and available.

The Post's special edition carried a 25-cent cover price, but primarily it was distributed free of charge.

Robbins had no idea that her husband, in the Post newsroom only a few blocks away, was chasing the same story that she and her *Journal* colleagues were tracking.

I remember I picked up the phone and I called him and I asked him to go get our then eight-year-old daughter and take her home. And he was writing. And I said, but you're covering science now.

Only that day, he wasn't.

Jerry Seib, who would succeed Alan Murray as bureau chief in March 2002 and currently serves as the *Journal's* executive Washington editor, says that on reflection, he was happy with the bureau's coverage in 2001 and is even more proud of it now.

I'm struck by how lucky we were to be so exquisitely prepared for this moment, in personnel terms. Alan wasn't just a good manager; he knew markets and the economy very well. I happened to have had a lot of reporting experience on national security, and had done a tour in the Middle East specifically. In June Kronholz and Bryan Gruley we had two of the finest feature writers of their time at the WSJ right at hand. And in Greg Ip you had one of the great analysts of economic impacts. So in retrospect, a rare case in which the stars aligned, serendipitously.

Indeed, for those in D.C., their performance on September 11 was an ordained redemption of sorts.

Before September 11, a growing number of New York colleagues and senior managers had grown skeptical — especially with the emergence of Silicon Valley as a major news hub — that D.C. remained worthy of its stature and the large number of journalists assigned to it. One reflection of the bureau's waning standing was the recurring struggle Murray had getting his group's stories onto the paper's front page.

Murray, himself, had seriously considered departing the *Journal* and journalism to accept an offer to run the Center for Strategic and International Studies, a think tank addressing the world's greatest challenges.

The second Clinton administration was not a fun time to be in Washington. The main story was the impeachment of the president because he had this disgusting affair with an intern in the White House. That's not [what] I went to Washington to cover.

That's not what got me going.

You had to do it, because it was an incredible abuse of the office. And he was going to be impeached. So we had to have reporters chasing the semen on the blue dress and all of that.

It was the only time in my journalism career when I seriously thought about leaving.

The September 11 terrorist attacks changed all that overnight.

Rather than plead with the editors in New York to run D.C. stories on the front page, they were on the phone first thing Wednesday morning, the 12th, imploring Murray and his staff to generate Page One articles.

Robbins, for example, had written or contributed to only six front-page stories between January 1, 2001, and September 12, 2001. Between September 13 and the year's end, her byline adorned ten Page-One articles.

But in the wake of 9/11, Page One byline counts didn't take on the same importance for Murray, Seib, Robbins, or the others in D.C. that they had before. In the aftermath, national security was center stage, and Robbins led much of the reporting.

We were at war. The whole country was at war. And that's all I wrote about. So I didn't denominate my life in terms of the number of front-page pieces I wrote. It was just very tragic and overwhelming, and that is what I did.

It was three minutes past 11:00 p.m. on September 11 when Alan Murray finally found a minute to reflect on what he and his D.C. bureau had accomplished. He sat at his desk, the newsroom now nearly empty, and punched out an email to his entire staff.

Folks —

Assuming the paper gets out and delivered tomorrow morning, it's going to reflect awesome work on the part of this bureau. There will be five excellent front page stories, four of which were assembled here, and much more throughout the paper. And it will reflect all the reporting and editing and help of all of you, who were so willing and eager to pitch in. It's a tragic day for the country and the world, but once again, it feels nice to work with such pros.

• Chapter Two •

"I Think We Are Going to Name Her Zoë"

The backstories of what inspires journalists to pursue the profession are countless.

Like many of the news industry's leaders in the 1990s and early 2000s, Marcus Brauchli was a "Watergate Baby," inspired by the reportage of *The Washington Post*'s Bob Woodward and Carl Bernstein, as well, in Brauchli's case, as by two local news events that arose while he was still a teen.

Brauchli was *The Wall Street Journal*'s national news editor on September 11, responsible for virtually all of the breaking news in the paper. His efforts that day, in particular, would prove indispensable to the paper's ability to publish.

Working from his home in Brooklyn Heights, Brauchli choreographed much of the staffing and reporting for the September 12 edition.

He had come a long way from the period, 26 years earlier, when he was a student at Boulder High School in his native Boulder, Colorado, the university town located 25 miles northwest of Denver along the foothills of the Rocky Mountains.

Back then, Brauchli already had a curiosity about journalism.

I read everything about that scandal [Watergate], about Vietnam, and about journalists in general when I was still in school. I even subscribed to The Wall Street Journal in high school, since it was the only national paper you could get in Boulder in the 1970s.

Young Brauchli volunteered at *Town & Country Review*, a weekly newspaper (long since defunct) that reported local news and features. He also photographed the "pet of the week" for the local humane society.

In March 1975, for a few days, Boulder became front-stage-center for a news story that rippled across the nation. *Town & Country Review* didn't let Brauchli report the event. Nonetheless, it left an indelible impression on him.

It was one of the things that got me really interested in journalism because you had all these national press [people] descending on Boulder. I was fascinated by how a local story could become a national issue.

The blockbuster story involved Boulder's newly installed county clerk, Clela Rorex, two Daves, and a horse named Dolly.

Rorex, who was 32 years old at the time, recalled her version of the entire affair for *Esquire* magazine four decades later.

It was three months into my term that the first couple came to me. They were both named Dave - Dave McCord and Dave Zamora. They had gone to the county clerk in Colorado Springs to get a marriage license. The clerk there said, "We don't do those kinds of things here. Go to Boulder."

With a population of fewer than 100,000 and residential zoning restrictions intended to prevent overpopulation, Boulder was viewed — rightly or not, as a liberal hotbed.

Rorex, who described herself as "a feminist who wore short skirts, had long hair, and was a single parent," did not rebuff the two Daves but told them she needed to consult with the Boulder district attorney's office.

I did, and a week or so later he advised me that the Colorado code at the time did not specify that marriage had to be between a man and a woman. So his advice was that if I wanted to marry them, I could give them a license...

So I issued the license, and all hell broke loose.

Most histories credit Rorex with authorizing the first same-sex marriage license anywhere in the United States, dated March 26, 1975, although other accounts contend she was the second to do so.

Rorex became an instant hero to some, a pariah to others.

She processed five more same-sex licenses before stopping in the wake of a letter issued by the state's attorney general, J.D. MacFarlane. MacFarlane, himself in office only a few months, did not order Rorex to cease. Instead, he cautioned her that the licenses would mislead same-sex couples into believing that they had rights that actually wouldn't be conferred upon them.

The media circus was still in progress when one day, Rorex peered out the window of the Boulder County Courthouse. The facility is a distinctive, light-colored, Art Deco-style stone building situated on what today is the popular Pearl Street Mall, a four-block pedestrian hub of restaurants and small retail shops.

Roswell "Ros" Howard, an elderly man, was being interviewed alongside a horse trailer.

Oh my God, I thought. He's going to try to get a license for his horse.

Indeed, he was.

Denver Westword, a free weekly paper that wouldn't begin publishing until two years later, picked up Rorex's tale in an August 2014 remembrance.

He [Howard] was an old media hack. He had done work in the media when he was younger. He was much older than I was.... and he decided to set up a photo opportunity for himself.

It was clear to Rorex that Howard had rehearsed his argument, not just for her but for the very responsive reporters gathered outside the courthouse.

If a man can marry a man and a woman can marry a woman, why can't a tired old cowboy like me marry his best friend, Dolly?

In actuality, at the time, there wasn't a statute on the books prohibiting such a union. Rorex tried in vain to reach the district attorney for advice. However, as she later recounted to *Esquire*, she came up with her own strategy to checkmate Howard's media play.

I asked him the normal questions — name, address, etcetera. Eventually we got down to the age of Dolly on the form. He said she was eight years old. So I just laid down my pencil and I said, "Oh, I'm very sorry, but I can't issue a license. She's too young, and you'll need parental permission."

On December 7, 2018, a plaque was affixed to the exterior of the Boulder County Courthouse building, now home to the offices of the county commissioners, stating that the structure had been added to the National Register of Historic Places in recognition of Rorex's role in the civil rights struggles of Lesbian, Gay, Bisexual, Transgender, and Queer people. The plaque read, in part:

The six licenses she issued were never invalidated, foreshadowing the eventual legalization of same-sex marriage by the U.S. Supreme Court in 2015.

In August 1976, Brauchli was awed once again by the arrival of the national news media. They came to cover the largest natural disaster in modern Colorado history. It was estimated that 12 inches of rain fell over the course of about four hours. The downpour flooded the Big Thompson Canyon, killing 144 people, creating more than $35 million in damage (calculated in 1977 dollars), and changing the topography of the canyon forever.

I was in Estes Park (Colorado) and ended up at the center where all the TV crews were. That's when I decided I had to be in journalism.

The choice led Brauchli on a serpentine route to being named *The Wall Street Journal's* national news editor in January 2000.

Before landing the influential post, Brauchli spent time based in Scandinavia, Hong Kong, and Tokyo, reporting from more than 20 countries, including Cambodia and the former Soviet Union. In Indonesia, he covered the violent upheaval surrounding the final days of President Suharto's autocratic reign. Years later, to illustrate the dangers that commercial vessels faced from modern-day sea pirates, he sailed in the Java Sea with the crew of a 440-foot ship on its way to Singapore.

After the February 1993 World Trade Center bombing, Lee Lescase, then the *Journal's* foreign editor, dispatched Brauchli from the Hong Kong bureau to Pakistan in an effort to gain insights into who was responsible for the attack.

[A similar assignment in 2001 cost *The Wall Street Journal's* Daniel Pearl his life when the reporter was dispatched to Pakistan in the wake of 9/11. Early in 2002, Pearl was kidnapped and gruesomely beheaded.]

It wasn't Brauchli's first visit to the South Asian Islamic republic. In 1990, he and his wife, Margaret "Maggie" Farley, also a journalist, got engaged in the scenic Swat valley in northwestern Pakistan. Brauchli returned to the country in the late summer of 1991 to report on the failed Bank of Credit and Commerce International, better known as BCCI. According to a *Journal* editorial, the collapse of the bank, founded in 1972 by Pakistani banker Agha Hasan Abedi, was the most important corruption story of the 20th century.

Crooked international bankers cast a world-wide web of influence. They bought and sold politicians around the globe, ripped off depositors for some $10 billion, laundered drug money, worked with assorted spooks and trafficked with terrorists.

In the spring of 1993, at Lescase's behest, Brauchli, the 32-year-old Asia correspondent, was riding in a hired car up the Khyber Pass toward a fortress located in Landi Kotal, a protected tribal area along the border with Afghanistan. Next to the taxi driver in the front seat was an elderly so-called Khyber Rifle, a member of a century-old paramilitary force that in modern times helped police the tribal areas of the Kyber region.

It was a requirement for Westerners, such as Brauchli, to be accompanied by a Khyber Rifle, given the general lawlessness of the Landi Kotal area, home to an assortment of international drug smugglers, militants, and terrorists who the U.S. government believed plotted the 1993 bombing of the World Trade Center.

Brauchli's guard packed a bolt-action, magazine-fed Enfield repeating rifle, which appeared to be older than the white-bearded sentry himself.

Eventually, Brauchli, a world away from his upscale Boulder, Colorado, roots, found himself knocking at the giant wooden doors of the 20-acre stronghold of Ayub Khan Afridi, believed to be the czar of Pakistan's traffickers of heroin and hashish. Afridi's compound, as Brauchli reported, was protected by battlements and steel-plated turrets with gun slits, surrounded by barbed wire and reinforced concrete walls.

When former Pakistani Prime Minister Benazir Bhutto in 1989 considered sending troops to arrest Mr. Afridi, a provincial official in nearby Peshawar says, Mr. Afridi retreated to Afghanistan and left as many as 1,000 armed defenders in his fortress.

Brauchli was carrying with him the business card of the Speaker of the Pakistani parliament, with whom he had met when reporting an unrelated story.

This guy sent me to talk to you.

Brauchli concedes that was "sort of not true," but the ruse worked. After a brief delay, Afridi's men swung open the creaking wooden doors and allowed the reporter entrance to the interior grounds, an oasis featuring football-field-length rose gardens, meticulously manicured lawns, marble floors, and heavily armed guards.

Sitting in Afridi's expansive wood-paneled dining room, the reporter and the drug lord shared a lunch of fried chicken and french fries. Afridi maintained throughout his time with Brauchli that he was innocent of any and all criminal allegations people attributed to him.

I am a good Muslim, a good man. Who can find anything wrong with my life?

It was a highly risky attempt by Brauchli to link Afridi, directly or indirectly, to the World Trade Center bombing. In that regard, his visit was unsuccessful. When Brauchli's June 3, 1993, story about his visit with the 58-year-old Pakistani was published, the *Journal* ran it on page A10.

On September 11, 2001, Marcus Brauchli's day began, as usual, walking to a nearby gym at 6:00 a.m., lifting weights, and putting in twenty minutes of cardio on the elliptical trainer. His pregnant wife, Maggie Farley, and his 17-month-old daughter, Aria, were still asleep.

The three of them lived quite comfortably on the lower two floors of a four-story, red-brick Brooklyn Heights brownstone, constructed in 1910. Their unit, 136 State Street, Apartment 2, featured hard-wood flooring, brick interior walls, ample window lighting, and a fenced backyard flush with greenery, and even a small garden pond.

Brauchli, clean-shaven, had piercing blue eyes, a rapidly receding dark-brown hairline, and a slight dimple on his left cheek that punctuated his thin lips and soft smile.

Six-foot tall with an athletic 175-pound build, the 40-year-old always dressed impeccably. He bought his British-cut custom suits from De-luxe Tailor in Hong Kong; expensive but far less costly than London's Savile Row apparel. On this day, he dressed in a gray suit, a gold-patterned tie, and a blue-striped shirt adorned with his great-grandfather's cufflinks.

On his way from the gym, Brauchli made a quick stop at a Russian shoemaker's shop to pick up the re-heeled dress shoes he intended to wear to the office. Back home, as he noted in a diary that he later shared with family members, he was waiting for his toaster to eject his wheat bread when shortly after 9:00 a.m., the phone rang.

It's funny that I don't remember the first plane crash, because by all accounts it made a very loud noise. The first sound I heard of the day's terror was in the voice of my neighbor and colleague, Adam Horvath, who called to say that a plane had just hit the World Trade Center.

Horvath, 48, was no stranger to covering dramatic events. Prior to joining the *Journal*, he worked for *Newsday*, where he contributed to two Pulitzer Prize-winning efforts for deadline reporting, including the August 28, 1991, crash of a southbound No. 4 IRT subway train that resulted in five deaths and 200 injuries. It was the worst subway derailment in 60 years.

Brauchli sifted through the toys scattered on the living room floor for the television remote, and once located, watched live coverage of the unfolding drama. Like most every other viewer, initially, he assumed it was an unfortunate accident.

I told Adam I thought we should go to the office immediately.

There was a delay, not unlike thunder after lightning, before the roar of the second plane hitting the South Tower of the World Trade Center reached Brooklyn Heights.

If there was one lesson that Brauchli carried with him from his time reporting the bloody Suharto protests in Indonesia, it was to dress down.

I ditched the suit and put on tennis shoes.

Brauchli and Horvath correctly reasoned that the subways into Manhattan wouldn't be running. So the two journalists hoofed it to the Brooklyn Bridge, whose pedestrian entrance was about three-quarters of a mile away.

Brauchli made a mental note of the many onlookers who gathered in clusters along the route, staring southeast at the spectacle. There were construction workers, police officers, men in suits, and nurses in white.

He and Horvath were maneuvering upstream against an increasingly sizable crowd headed out of Manhattan.

I tried calling everyone I could think of at the office. Couldn't get through.

Plodding forward, fixated on the flaming towers directly in front of him and able to spot the Statue of Liberty and Ellis Island off to the south, Brauchli's attempt to phone Alan Murray, the *Journal's* D.C. bureau chief, was successful.

[Murray] began talking as if we were in the middle of a conversation, saying, "We have to get someone to Westchester Airport. The plane came from there." He slowed down, realized I knew only what I'd seen, said he already had people chasing the story.... I told him I'd get back to him with our plans for production, then lost the connection...

Brauchli and Horvath had made it two-thirds of the way across the Brooklyn Bridge. Someone in the throng shouted their names. It was Steve McKee, a copy editor who earlier that summer also originated *The Daily Fix* sports column for *WSJ.com*. McKee had been evacuated from the *Journal's* headquarters and was heading toward home, anxious to reach his son who was in school.

Knowing they'd need every available staffer, Brauchli and Horvath had just about persuaded McKee to about-face and troop with them to Manhattan when the South Tower disintegrated.

...We heard people start to shout. We turned and saw the first tower of the World Trade Center collapse. You could see the top of the building, visually intact, as it fell, almost in slow motion, into the billowing clouds of dust.

The deep, nearby rumble of the building collapse was overlaid by the screaming and then the pounding of feet as thousands of crying, disbelieving people fled towards Brooklyn. One woman fainted. Others muttered, "No, no, no," unable to accept what they had seen...

We all decided to go back to Brooklyn, to see whether we could help at least get the newspaper out on our computers....

As we walked, the cloud of dust and smoke enveloped us. It was thick by the time we got off the bridge, as dense as fog and acrid.

Maggie Farley, 35, had aligned her journalism career with her husband's for almost a decade overseas — living in Hong Kong and Shanghai — before returning together to the U.S. in October 1999.

The couple met in Tokyo in December 1989. Conversant in French, Chinese, and Japanese, she read the news in Japanese for Fuji Television News — a job she landed straight out of Brown University. Brauchli was covering economics and finance from the *Journal's*

Tokyo bureau after graduating from Columbia University.

Farley and Brauchli had a great deal in common.

Both were journalists and high achievers. Both grew up in Colorado; she in Denver, he in Boulder. Both had an adventurous streak; he twice vacationed alone in Siberia, and later, as a couple, they climbed Mt. Kilimanjaro. And both Brauchli and Farley had fathers who were prominent Colorado attorneys.

Brauchli's father, Christopher, specialized in trusts and commercial real estate, and before he retired in 2014, served separate terms as president of the Boulder and Colorado Bar Associations. For 14 years, Christopher also wrote a regular column for the Boulder *Daily Camera*.

Farley's dad, J. Michael Farley, was a lifeline advocate of civil rights and fair housing. He headed a foundation that provided low-income housing. He also worked in a church soup kitchen feeding the homeless.

Christopher Brauchli and Michael Farley knew each other through the Colorado Bar Association and came to realize that they both had children working in Tokyo. (Marcus is five years older than Maggie.) Christopher wrote a letter to Brauchli encouraging him to connect with Maggie, which he did.

The two were married in Denver in December 1990, the week that the frigid winter weather dipped to a record-setting negative-25 degrees.

While Brauchli earned a paycheck from Dow Jones and *The Wall Street Journal*, Farley freelanced for the *Boston Globe* and then, in 1995, was hired by the *Los Angeles Times* as an overseas staff correspondent.

When the *Journal* transferred Brauchli stateside in 1999, the *LA Times* appointed Farley its United Nation's bureau chief, with the additional responsibility of covering Canada for the foreign desk.

Although in her eighth month of pregnancy, on the morning of September 11, Farley was not about to be a bystander to the unfolding events. By the time Brauchli retreated over the Brooklyn Bridge and reached their brownstone, she was headed out the door, sporting comfortable shoes and carrying a pack with her cellphone, a camera, notebooks, and pens.

He looked at me and said, "Don't even try. I don't want you to go." But I felt like I had to try... I felt this journalistic desperation to get to the scene.

She didn't make it far.

Farley shared her account of the day in the book *running toward DANGER*, produced in 2002 by the Newseum with Cathy Trost and Alicia C. Shepard.

Although Farley carried a press pass that typically allowed her to cross police lines, this time she was turned back at the entrance to the Brooklyn Bridge because the span was just too overwhelmed with pedestrians headed away from Manhattan.

Suddenly, the stream of people turned into a throng that looked like the "Night of the Living Dead."

Undeterred, Farley began questioning those Manhattan refugees parading across the bridge. She caught up to one man who was covered in a shroud of gray ash.

I couldn't even tell the color of his hair. He told me he was a Muslim and he was going to his mosque to pray. I walked with him and when he got there, he did his ritual ablutions, literally washing the horror and the suspicion from his skin. I was not allowed to enter the mosque, but listened to the Imam from outside the doorway, saying that the actions of the day were against the teachings of the Quran.

Farley moved to a nearby hospital and chased after a group of police officers she witnessed adorning bulletproof vests. The police were responding to reports — erroneous as they turned out — that a car with a bomb had driven into the emergency room at NYU Hospital. A Brooklyn policeman told Farley that they were checking on all emergency rooms in greater New York City.

Between interviews, Farley returned home to dispatch her reporting to her editors in Los Angeles. It helped that her friendly upstairs neighbor, Park Foreman, was an internet security consultant who made sure that she and Brauchli always had a reliable DSL connection.

From the upper floors and the roof of the brownstone where Farley and Brauchli lived, there was an unobstructed view of the World Trade Center towers. Foreman was in the living room of his unit, atop theirs, when he heard the first plane fly overhead and then sighted the North Tower aflame. Astutely, he whipped out his Sony digital video camera and ascended to the roof in time to capture exclusive video of the second plane approaching, then hitting, the South Tower.

Conveniently, Farley interviewed Foreman for the *LA Times*.

A huge fireball erupted from all four sides. Three seconds later, I felt the shock wave. My heart just went into my stomach. I saw the second tower fall. I saw it collapse. It was the scariest thing I've ever seen in my life. You could see people jumping out of the tower on fire. That moment changed my life.

Foreman's account was contained in the lead front-page story, "Terror Attack," of an extra edition that the *LA Times* published on the afternoon of September 11. The story, co-authored by Farley and Geraldine Baum, the *LA Times*'s New York bureau chief, ran alongside two dramatic full-color still shots extracted from Foreman's video footage. With help from Farley and Foreman's brother, Howell, in Atlanta, Foreman sold his video to CNN, which, as he recounted in *running toward DANGER*, began broadcasting a clip from it at about 3:00 p.m.

It was exclusive. CNN didn't run all the video I shot. Only five seconds of the airplane flying across the city, only the sensational part. They did not show the bodies.... CNN paid me a lot. It's embarrassing to say, almost a year's salary.

Operating from a single Brooklyn Heights brownstone, Foreman and CNN, Farley and the *Los Angeles Times*, and Brauchli and *The Wall Street Journal* all offered viewers and readers exclusive coverage of the terrorist attacks.

While his wife was out reporting and securing Foreman's photos for the *LA Times*, Brauchli was setting up a satellite news command center and using his apartment as a way station for Brooklyn colleagues who he was redirecting to South Brunswick.

Over the next several hours, Brauchli would receive or be copied on more than 1,000 emails and send 500 of his own — originals and replies.

It fell to Brauchli, with an assist from the *Journal*'s bureau chiefs in Dallas and Chicago, to produce the "Sked" — alternatively referred to as the "WIP" (for Work In Progress). The Sked was the blueprint for each day's newspaper, and it is how top editors steered the paper and made their choices known to the dispersed bureaus and reporters.

Given the extent of the chaos throughout the *Wall Street Journal* diaspora and the communications imbroglio they faced, it was quite impressive that Brauchli sent the Sked out at 12:56 that afternoon.

Brauchli used a steno notebook to keep track of those *Journal* colleagues who had reported in, and the numbers where they could be reached if phone service would allow. Quietly, he also maintained a list, last names only, of those who he feared might have fallen victim to the day's attacks.

The name at the top of the "Missing" list was "Steiger," the managing editor. Other names included (Rich) Regis, the senior New York news desk editor, (John) Bussey, the foreign editor, (Daniel) Hertzberg, the deputy managing editor, (Phil) Kuntz, the D.C. reporter who was overnighting in New York, and (Peter) Skinner, the senior Dow Jones executive who was among the very last to evacuate the paper's headquarters.

[In time, to Brauchli's and everyone else's great relief, all of the missing resurfaced.]

Brauchli was in steady contact with Alan Murray in D.C., Jim Pensiero and others in South Brunswick, and the senior editors who were assembling at the Upper West Side apartment of Deputy Managing Editor Byron E. "Barney" Calame.

He also became the primary liaison with Peter R. Kann, the *Journal's* publisher, and the chairman and CEO of Dow Jones, and Kann's wife, Karen Elliott House, who was president of the company's International operating group. Kann and House were in Hong Kong, twelve hours ahead, for a dinner with business and political leaders marking the 25th anniversary of *The Asian Wall Street Journal*. They had no convenient access to email.

To keep Kann and House informed, Brauchli sent emails to Philip Revzin, the Hong Kong-based vice president of Dow Jones's International group, and Revzin passed them on. Likewise, when Kann or House initiated contact with Brauchli, the emails listed the sender as Revzin.

It was 11:36 a.m. in New York, 11:36 p.m. in Hong Kong, when Brauchli emailed Kann and House to update them on his list of the missing.

As you will surmise, haven't heard from any of them since WTC collapse. But Steiger ordered the move to SB, so he may be in transit.

House, who signed her emails "KEH," replied five minutes later.

Thanks. We'd like to know when he surfaces. hope he's safe.

One of Brauchli's journalistic superpowers was that he, like Steiger, always projected a sense of calm and control. Brauchli's level-headed leadership on September 11 played a role in his favor in early 2007 when Steiger tapped Brauchli, ahead of a field of other highly qualified candidates, to serve as his successor as the *Journal's* managing editor.

Brauchli knew viscerally that with or without Steiger, the *Journal* would publish on September 12. His confidence was so strong that early that afternoon, Brauchli delegated much of what remained to be completed for the next day's paper to Pensiero and copy chief Jesse Lewis in South Brunswick so that he could already begin working on the Sked for the September 13 print edition. Before finally heading to bed, Brauchli dispatched the 9/13 Sked so that everyone could get a running start on it first thing the next morning.

Brauchli didn't sleep well that night, nor did his wife. It had been an adrenaline-fueled, demanding, nightmarish, and yet, also a professionally fulfilling day for both of them.

Even with their windows closed, Brauchli and Farley couldn't shut out the stench of the burning towers that had wafted eastward and saturated Brooklyn Heights.

On September 12, Brauchli joined his colleagues in South Brunswick while Farley, ever intrepid, made her way to Ground Zero.

First Responders had been digging with their hands and shovels all day in the rubble, hoping to uncover colleagues they thought were still alive there. By the end of the day, they had not found any survivors.

I was sitting with a few guys on pieces of debris, in a circle, silently contemplating the fact that we might not find anyone. As we were sitting there, the baby began to kick actively, and she kicked so hard, the police tags resting on my belly popped into the air.

One man started to smile a little, and when it happened again, he laughed out loud. It was a sound we hadn't heard for a couple of days. He looked at me, and said, "Life goes on. You've got to give the baby a name that honors that."

In the days that followed, as Farley recounted in *running toward DANGER*, people asked her how she felt about bringing a child into such a dangerous and cruel world.

All I could say is life continues. I think we are going to name her Zoë, which means "life" in Greek.

Zoë E. Brauchli arrived six weeks later.

———————————

"Belopotosky, Danielle" <Danielle.Belopotosky@wsj.com>

08/29/2001 10:24 AM

ToRichard Bause/Somers/IBM@IBMUS

cc

SubjectRE: ThinkPad T23

Hi Rick,

Walt will be in NYC on the 11th, but only in the morning. If you guys can
go to his hotel, and at 9am, he could do it. I believe he's staying at the
WTC Marriott. I should have the confirmation within a day or so.
Is this possible?

thanks,
danielle

-----Original Message-----
From: Richard Bause [mailto:rbause@us.ibm.com]
Sent: Tuesday, August 28, 2001 3:27 PM
To: mossberg
Cc: Belopotosky, Danielle
Subject: Re: ThinkPad T23

Walt, we'll be in New York on Tuesday. Will you be in New York on Sept. 11?
We could meet there.

Rick Bause
ThinkPad PR Manager
IBM Personal Computing Division
(914) 766-3990; FAX (914) 766-9309

• Chapter Three •

The Kingmaker

Times were different in 2001.

Office fax machines were still indispensable. Cell phones weren't smart, nor did they come with cameras. America Online was dominant, with more than 28 million members, many of them relying on dial-up connections. Apple debuted iTunes. Wikipedia was born.

BlackBerrys were essentially two-way pagers. The BlackBerry 6000 series, which offered an integrated phone, would not come along until 2002. Yahoo was the leading internet search engine. It would try, unsuccessfully, to acquire Google in 2002 for $3 billion.

Mark Zuckerberg was in high school at Phillips Exeter Academy. He and Eduardo Saverin would not launch "TheFacebook" until February 2004. Twitter arrived in March 2006. The first iPhone was released in June 2007. Zoom launched its video conferencing software in 2013.

In the pioneering days of the internet, no journalist in the country wielded more influence on the buying habits of technology consumers than did Walter S. "Walt" Mossberg, a one-time *Wall Street Journal* national security correspondent and former deputy D.C. bureau chief.

An early computer hobbyist, Mossberg funneled his obsession with all things tech into a weekly Thursday column, which debuted on October 17, 1991, under the banner "*Personal Technology*." Many people credit Mossberg with coining — or at the very least, popularizing — the term "personal technology" to cover consumer computers, software, communications devices, accessories, and the like.

By 2001, Mossberg, 57, had become, as *Wired* magazine dubbed him, "The Kingmaker"

— able to make or break new hardware and software offerings with a single review.

Manufacturers, developers, and service providers worldwide sought an audience with Mossberg to show him their wares and ask for his blessings. Bill Gates, Marc Andreeson, Andy Grove, Eric Schmidt, and, of course, Steve Jobs were among the many Silicon Valley CEOs who whispered secrets to him about themselves and their competitors.

Give him a cape and a rounded, regal purple-and-gold hat with a tassel, and Mossberg could have passed for a professor at the Hogwarts School of Witchcraft and Wizardry.

The columnist's baldpate, gray goatee, and square wire-rim glasses were almost as iconic among tech geeks of the period as were Steve Jobs's signature black mock turtleneck, Levi's 501 blue jeans, and New Balance 992 sneakers.

Walt Mossberg addressing the National Association of Business Economists on the evening of September 10, 2001, in the Grand Ballroom of the Marriott World Trade Center. The hotel was destroyed the next morning.
(Photo: Bruce Kratofil)

So many companies sought to have their paid messages appear in proximity to Mossberg's columns that the paper struggled to find room for all the advertisers that wanted in. Historically, the *Journal* eschewed star reporters, preferring the paper to be viewed collectively as the star. But Mossberg shattered the mold.

In 1997, the magazines of Time Inc., then overseen by Norman Pearlstine, a former *Wall Street Journal* managing editor, made a run at Mossberg, waving big money his way to woo the columnist to its family of publications, including *Fortune*, *Money*, and *Time*.

To keep Mossberg in the fold, the *Journal* ponied up a king's ransom that made him the highest-paid reporter on the paper's staff, earning more than evan Paul Steiger, the managing editor. The *Journal* also showered Mossberg with lofty perks, including support staff, a unique employment contract, and a suite of offices (for him and his assistants) in the D.C. bureau.

One of the benefits of Mossberg's employment contract was that it allowed him to give paid speeches — something verboten to most *Journal* reporters — so long as he didn't accept money from the companies he directly reported on.

So it was that Mossberg found himself on the evening of September 10, 2001, in the Grand Ballroom of the Marriott World Trade Center addressing a group of 300 men and women in attendance at the 43rd Annual Meeting of the National Association of Business Economists (NABE). It was the same conference that Jon Hilsenrath, the *Journal*'s economics reporter, planned to attend the next morning, until he was caught in the maelstrom of the attack on the Twin Towers.

Ordinarily, Mossberg charged $10,000 or $15,000, plus expenses, to present a talk. But for this group, he agreed to a lower fee, $5,000, along with the promise of a comfortable suite at the Marriott, located just across West Street from *Journal*'s main newsroom.

Mossberg took the Acela to Penn Station on Monday, September 10, and figured he'd catch the noon train back on Tuesday, the 11th.

His plan was to sleep later than usual on the morning of the 11th, enjoy a full breakfast at the hotel — compliments of NABE — and then drop by the *Journal*'s newsroom. He'd visit with Stephanie Capparell, who edited his columns, perhaps Steiger if he was around, and any other friends he might spot. Mossberg would then catch a cab to Penn Station and be back in D.C. in time for dinner with his wife, Edie.

But for a quirk of fate, Mossberg might have perished along with no fewer than 50 other people inside the Marriott (mostly firefighters) when his room was buried under millions of pounds of concrete, glass, and other debris from the collapse of the South Tower.

Danielle Belopotosky worked for Mossberg in D.C. as his reporting assistant. The 29-year-old had no significant journalistic responsibilities, but she was intelligent and organized. Mossberg relied on her to receive, inventory, and return the flood of high-tech product samples that companies sent his way.

Belopotosky also managed Mossberg's calendar and made his travel arrangements. It was she who scheduled a meeting between Mossberg and a team of IBM public relations and product managers. The company had a new line of ThinkPad laptops that they were anxious for the columnist to inspect.

IBM was one of the companies that generally impressed Mossberg, so he welcomed their visits once or twice a year.

I used to be quite positive about the ThinkPads. I gave them pretty good reviews. They were rugged. They had great keyboards. The company was pretty innovative and would come up with interesting things.

Rick Bausé, the lead public relations manager for the ThinkPad, reached out to Mossberg by email in late August 2001 to request a product showing in D.C. on September 10.

Sorry, Rick, but I'll be in NYC. Can you work out an alternate arrangement with Danielle?

The new plan, Bausé recalled, was for him and his colleagues to meet Mossberg at the Marriott World Trade Center on the morning of September 11.

If we had not changed the venue, we would have been in Lower Manhattan that morning.

Rather than have the IBM team meet him at his hotel, Mossberg suggested that they connect at the company's 590 Madison Avenue building, located at the corner of 57th Street. Although it meant sacrificing his relaxing morning at the Marriott and skipping his visit to the *Journal* newsroom, Mossberg reasoned that IBM was a much closer to Penn Station and the Acela back to D.C. than was the Marriott in Lower Manhattan.

Their Midtown meeting was confirmed for 9:00 a.m.

Although Mossberg had paid multiple visits to New York City over the years and received a master's degree from the Columbia University School of Journalism on the city's Upper West Side, he wasn't a confident Manhattan commuter.

I don't like to be late for meetings. If I was going to somebody's building for a meeting, I was always early so that I would be on time.

I knew the traffic at eight to nine in the morning was going to be terrible. So I decided to leave the Marriott at 8:15 a.m. and give myself 45 minutes.

Mossberg had been staying in a suite on the hotel's 21st floor, one flight below its penthouse. The Marriott had 26 suites and 817 standard rooms. The columnist rode the elevator down to the lobby, suitcase in tow, and checked out. He stepped through the revolving doors facing West Street and caught a taxi uptown.

That was the angel on my shoulder.

Traffic was surprisingly sparse, and Mossberg arrived even earlier than he expected. He got out a block-and-a-half from the IBM building and walked the remainder of the way.

He didn't know it at the time, but he, like tens of thousands of others who planned to leave Manhattan Island to commute home later that day, would soon have to navigate a gauntlet of gridlocked streets, blockaded tunnels, closed bridges, delayed rail service, and padlocked airports to reunite with his panicked spouse.

At the moment, however, he was gawking skyward, taking in the grandeur of the Manhattan skyline on a beautiful, sunny morning.

I was waiting for a light to change so I could cross the street when I see this plane that seemed to be flying too low and right down Madison Avenue. I was not an aviation expert, but it seemed strange to me. I thought, "Gee, I thought you weren't supposed to fly right over Midtown Manhattan." Given that LaGuardia is always jammed and has huge delays, maybe they opened up a new flight path. That's what I literally thought.

Only later, when his 9:00 a.m. IBM meeting was disbanded, and he had joined Bausé in the PR man's Ford Explorer trying to find a way north out of the city, did Mossberg fully comprehend that the low-flying plane he had seen when he was heading into the IBM building had been zeroing in on the North Tower of the World Trade Center.

Bausé and Mossberg crawled through traffic. Third Avenue was effectively a parking lot. Drivers and their passengers, unable to advance, got out of their cars and exchanged stories, congregating in small clusters. Eventually, with the help of a pushy food truck driver who led the way, inch-by-inch, Bausé and Mossberg found themselves crossing the old Willis Avenue Bridge, a one-way north passage over the Harlem River at the crown of Manhattan.

Constructed in 1941, the swing bridge was popular with bicyclists and pedestrians but carried minimal vehicular traffic. On September 11, when Mayor Rudolph Giuliani ordered all bridges closed in and out of Manhattan, somehow, the Willis Avenue Bridge was overlooked.

Driving across the span with Mossberg from Manhattan into the Bronx, Bausé's SUV was sandwiched between hundreds of people making the crossing on foot.

Miles later, Bausé and Mossberg found themselves headed north on the Major Deegan Expressway just past Yankee Stadium. Ahead was a crystal clear blue sky.

In his rearview mirror, however, Bausé glimpsed a soul-stirring sight: roiling black smoke where the World Trade Center and Marriott hotel once stood.

4:0

SKED FROM BUREAUS OUTSIDE OF WASHN

ISLAMIC-AMERICAN, which would explore their recations to the day;s events, any worries that it will distrub religious and ethnic hramony, and any adverse reactions the; might be seeintg today, chicago has offered to help. any other contributions would also be appreciated. BOSTON handling

Corporate reaction—Joe White coordinating, DX

Writing/Reporting the shutdown of the air traffic system. CX coordinating. Carey,Spurgeon.Callahan

HIJACK—Breakdown of the airport security system, hijacking of American, United airlines. Dallas coordinating

Shutdown of markets.Kilman.

Oil prices respond. Barrionuevo, HU

EVACAUATE—Cities, buildings evacuating. LA coordinating.

AIRCARGO -- The shutdown of U.S. skies paralyzes FedEx Corp., United Parcel Service Inc. and the U.S. Postal Service. By tomorrow afternoon, UPS could have more than 10 million packages piled up. 10 inches, Brooks, AT

MONEYFLOW by Mollenkamp, Pinkston, and Brooks--The potential effects on the flow of money--both by the air delivery of checks and computers--at the Atlanta Fed, Bank of America, First Union, and AirNet Systems.

FEDERAL: Chris Oster checking on Centers for Disease control. Will Pinkston checking on other federal institutions.

• Chapter Four •

"I Don't Want My Life to Be Dust"

Good Morning, Moss Haven was broadcasting the day's weather forecast as Karen Blumenthal looked on. It was 69°F in Dallas at 8:00 a.m., but temperatures were expected to climb to a high of 84°F.

Blumenthal was standing in the library of her sixth-grade daughter's elementary school as the student presenters segued to the Tuesday lunch menu. Chicken — bites, tenders, patties, and nuggets — was a staple, as was pizza, cheeseburgers, salad, and, of course, mac & cheese.

Blumenthal, who had light hazel eyes and chin-length hair, parted to the left, always seemed to be smiling. When her cell phone rang, she broke away from the juvenile newscast and a conversation she was having with a friend to take a call from her mother, Beverly. Her mom was practically shouting into the receiver.

Where are you? Turn on the radio! A plane just flew into the World Trade Center.

In her fifth year as Dallas bureau chief for *The Wall Street Journal*, Blumenthal had her doubts.

Surely, she is mistaken. Surely, she heard something wrong. But I'm not going to argue with her or start rumors in the middle of an elementary school library.

Making her excuses, Blumenthal dashed to her car to catch the adult news on the radio. Her recollections of that day are captured in an unpublished account that she wrote years later.

The Dallas bureau, a 40-minute drive west via I-30 from American Airlines' global headquarters in Fort Worth, was a central hub for the *Journal's* worldwide airline industry reporting. Blumenthal knew that coverage of the biggest airline story since Kitty Hawk — four hijacked passenger planes used to devastating effect as lethal missiles — would fall heavily on her shoulders.

The timing was less than ideal.

The *Journal's* lead airline and travel reporter, Scott McCartney, who arguably had the best sources of any mainstream reporter on the beat, was attending a conference in Seattle examining what had been the industry's biggest preoccupation until that morning: air traffic control congestion and the resulting gridlock.

McCartney was still asleep in his hotel room when Blumenthal called on her way into the bureau's downtown office.

Now I was shouting, telling him what happened and some of what we needed to do right away. "See what you can find out, and keep me posted," I barked. And then, quite unprofessionally, "I love you."

Blumenthal met McCartney in 1978, her sophomore year at Duke University. A freshman, he walked into the office of *The Chronicle*, Duke University's independent student newspaper, where she was serving as editor of the paper's weekly magazine. In 1979, the same year that she was promoted to editor-in-chief, they began dating.

Abby Blumenthal, the couple's now-adult daughter, 21 years later recounted her parents' early interactions.

My mom gave my dad his first assignment, and the joke was that [it] continued for about 40 years.

McCartney showed early promise, despite making spelling and stylistic errors.

Finally, she just hauled off and threw a stylebook at him, which I guess got his attention.

In return, McCartney, who succeeded Blumenthal as the editor of *The Chronicle*, snared her heart. The two married in Dallas in August 1983. She was 24; he was 23.

McCartney's love and respect for his wife were unbridled. He was raised in the Episcopal Church; she was brought up Jewish. A rabbi and a minister jointly presided at their wedding.

Neither McCartney nor Blumenthal saw their interfaith marriage as an obstacle. But she was committed, when the time came, to raise their two daughters Jewish.

As McCartney told a religion writer for *The Dallas Morning News*, the more time he spent attending temple with his wife and children, the more comfortable he became.

It was my spiritual home. I really thought of myself as Jewish.

As it turned out, however, the religious authorities — even at his Reform congregation — drew the line between "feeling" Jewish and "being" Jewish.

So McCartney committed to the required two years of classes and intense study necessary to convert officially. In the same way that both he and Blumenthal threw themselves into their jobs, McCartney took his Judaism very seriously. In April 2013, just shy of 20 years after he married Blumenthal, McCartney became president of Temple Emanu-El, the oldest and largest Jewish congregation in Dallas. His wife recognized the humor of it.

I still think it's crazy. I never dreamed I would be the wife of a temple president. I'm married to a guy named McCartney.

Journalism couples are pretty common in the profession. Whether they meet in college, the newsroom, or covering the same stories, reporters and editors have been drawn to one another since the marriage of ink and type.

Less common, however, was the situation that Blumenthal and McCartney faced. After working several years as a reporter in *The Wall Street Journal*'s Dallas bureau, Blumenthal had been hired by *The Dallas Morning News* to be its business editor. McCartney, meanwhile, continued as a *Journal* staff reporter in its Dallas bureau. In essence, wife and husband were rivals.

To keep the peace, the rule in the Blumenthal-McCartney household was that anything work-related was to remain off-limits for discussion at home.

That pact, however, was seriously tested one Saturday in the fall of 1994 when Blumenthal answered their home phone. On the other end of the call was a senior-level corporate source who she knew well. However, the executive was not calling for her but for her husband.

McCartney met with his contact over breakfast the next morning, and Blumenthal could sense that her husband was on to something important.

So I come home with this huge scoop. I get the story done about 10 o'clock at night, and I walk into the living room, and she's sitting there just staring straight ahead, her arms folded. We ended up staying up all night trying to figure this out.

At the office on Monday, McCartney asked Kevin Helliker, then the *Journal*'s Dallas bureau chief, to be assigned a new beat, one that wouldn't put him in competition with his wife. Helliker did McCartney one better. With the encouragement of managing editor Paul Steiger, Helliker rehired Blumenthal to the *Journal*, allowing her to work alongside her husband.

———————————

Blumenthal was a multi-talented journalist; a great editor, manager, reporter, and a rising star. Lindsey Rupp, a news editor at Bloomberg News who years later came to know Blumenthal when they both served on the board of the Duke *Chronicle* publishing company, described her friend.

I think the most amazing thing about Karen is that she's this incredible badass, like she just was so tough and so sharp and fearless. But she was also somehow incredibly warm, as she was this doting mom and she adored her husband, Scott.

In the spring of 1996, Blumenthal was placed in charge of the *Journal's* Dallas bureau. Her province eventually extended to covering eight states and supervising a dozen reporters, including McCartney.

On September 11, with the *Journal's* New York newsroom rendered unoccupiable and the usual lines of editorial authority frayed, Blumenthal stepped into the void. Outwardly, she appeared calm and in control, as she always did. But her stomach churned with fear, fretting for the safety of her *Journal* friends in Manhattan who were caught in the epicenter of the attacks.

With systems and personnel in Manhattan indisposed, the Dallas bureau took on additional responsibilities. The *Journal's* New York and New Jersey engineers, at least those technicians who were available, shifted some critical computer operations to Dallas, along with control of the newsroom's essential email network.

Since phone service on the East Coast was spotty at best, the ability of the *Journal's* dispersed editors and reporters to communicate with one another, coordinate plans, and file stories and memos rested heavily on the email framework.

Now stationed in Dallas, the *Journal's* email functioned that day. Sometimes.

Other times, the system went down or operated slowly. There would be no incoming messages, then suddenly, a burst of delayed correspondence would arrive. Complicating matters, reporters by the dozens began to relay their whereabouts, asking how they might help and expressing their gratitude on hearing that their colleagues were safe. Because so many of the journalists repeatedly hit "reply all," the email chain became unwieldy and eventually clogged the entire system.

Before Marcus Brauchli, the paper's national news editor, was able to situate himself in his Brooklyn Heights home to take charge of that day's "Sked" — newspaper slang for the list of stories slated to run in the next edition — Blumenthal had taken it upon herself to compile one for Dallas and the domestic bureaus, other than Washington, D.C.

Deciphering Blumenthal's lineup, it indicated that Gary Putka, the paper's Boston bureau chief since 1993, would orchestrate coverage of how Islamic Americans were reacting, with help from the Chicago bureau, where her former Dallas bureau chief, Kevin Helliker, was now in charge.

Joe White, the Pulitzer Prize-winning Detroit bureau chief, and his crew would be responsible for reporting on the corporate reactions to the terrorist attacks.

Susan Carey, who was based in Chicago and often collaborated with Scott McCartney when it came to tracking the airline industry, would report on the shutdown of the air traffic system, along with Windy City colleagues Devon Spurgeon and Patricia Callahan.

McCartney, who was curating emails from reporters around the country, would write the lead airline article from his hotel roost in Seattle.

His story, "*U.S. Airport Security Screening Long Seen as Dangerously Lax*," co-authored with J. Lynn Lunsford in Los Angeles and David Armstrong in Boston, would be the first to correctly theorize what happened aboard the hijacked airliners:

Pilots and airline officials believe it is likely the hijackers disabled or killed both pilots in each of the three planes that struck the twin towers of the World Trade Center and the Pentagon, and then flew the planes themselves into the structures.

Scott Kilman, who often wrote about agriculture from Chicago, was recruited to write about the shutdown of the Chicago Board of Trade and the Chicago Mercantile Exchange.

The closure of the New York exchanges shut down the Chicago futures markets, creating a situation in the Farm Belt not seen since the Chernobyl nuclear plant explosion in April 1986: nobody knew the price of a bushel of U.S. grain yesterday.

Alexei Barrionuevo, who covered global energy from the *Journal*'s Houston bureau, a part of Blumenthal's domain, would size up the impact on oil prices.

In Los Angeles, veteran aerospace/aviation reporter Andy Pasztor phoned his bureau chief, Jonathan Friedland, at home shortly after 6:00 a.m. Pacific to clue him in on the developing story. Friedland was watching CNN when the second plane hit the South Tower. His thoughts immediately turned to how he would harness the bureau's staff to help cover the breaking story.

Blumenthal's Sked listed the Los Angeles bureau as responsible for coordinating the paper's coverage of closures of businesses and high-rises across the country. Disney World in Orlando was evacuated. Disneyland in Anaheim, California, never opened. The Transamerica Pyramid in San Francisco was cleared as a precaution.

Even as Blumenthal was meting out and tracking assignments, one of her reporters ran into her office, gasping.

There's a report that a hijacked plane may be headed here.

The Dallas bureau was located on the 50th floor of the 56-story Renaissance Tower, the second-tallest skyscraper in the city. Soon every business in the high-rise, except the *Journal*, would shut down, leaving the hallways dark and the downstairs restaurants shuttered.

But Blumenthal and her team didn't consider reporting and organizing coverage from their homes as a viable alternative. So they persevered in place.

In the Los Angeles bureau, Friedland and two of his top reporters, Rebecca Smith, who kept watch on the energy industry, and John Emshwiller, an expert on white-collar crime, produced the Page Two-story (along with Barrionuevo in Houston), "Energy Firms Act to Protect Their Systems."

Energy companies that control the nation's electricity and natural-gas supplies as well as big oil companies went on heightened alert to safeguard the system from possible attack.

Across the country, utility emergency control centers came to life and extra security patrols were initiated. But with thousands of miles of pipelines and transmission lines, it was largely a symbolic effort. With energy markets suspended and trading floors closed in New York and Houston, the biggest impact was financial.

What the public didn't know, and wouldn't learn for more than a month, was that Houston-based Enron was teetering on the verge of collapse. As Friedland recalled, Smith and Emshwiller were hot on the trail of one of the largest corporate cons in American history when they had to temporarily set aside their pursuit to help chronicle the aftereffects of 9/11.

We were locked and loaded.

Smith and Emshwiller's first Enron story did not run until Wednesday, October 17, 2001, followed by a nearly non-stop series of exposés. Within a month, Enron's stock lost more than 75% of its value, and in early December 2001, the seventh-largest Fortune 500 company, with $101 billion in revenue, filed for bankruptcy.

Jeffrey K. Skilling, the former Enron chief executive, was eventually convicted of 18 counts of fraud and conspiracy and spent more than 12 years in prison. Kenneth L. Lay, the company's founder and chairman, was found guilty of six counts of fraud and conspiracy and four counts of bank fraud. Lay died about a month after his trial in 2006, and his conviction was vacated.

Had the September 11 terrorist attacks not occurred, the *Journal* likely would have broken the Enron story sooner. However, it's debatable whether that would have cushioned the blow to the investors, vendors, and employees who were walloped by Enron's malfeasance.

In their 2003 book, *24 Days*, the two journalists wrote that the lies Enron told destroyed not only it and the accounting firm Arthur Andersen but also the lives of thousands of employees and the integrity of American business.

Nonetheless, the Enron flimflam paled in comparison to the ruination caused on September 11.

Blumenthal rounded out her Sked for the next day's paper with assignments for Atlanta bureau reporters Rick Brooks, Chris Oster, Carrick Mollenkamp, and Will Pinkston.

When McCartney completed his September 12 draft, he sent it on to Blumenthal to edit. It was long by the paper's standards, and McCartney was worried about its verbosity. As she later wrote, Blumenthal was bemused by her husband's concerns but understood their basis.

The Journal measured its stories in inches, fifty words to the inch, and it was stingy with even the most important breaking-news stories. Old-timers used to joke that the second coming of Jesus would have to be told in twelve inches, or 600 words.

Blumenthal assured McCartney that, on this day, he'd receive a reprieve.

She lobbied the editors in New York to feature McCartney's dispatch on the front page, which they did. The exclusive was one of ten stories the *Journal* included in its successful nomination package for the 2002 Pulitzer Prize for Breaking News.

McCartney, with a ruddy-cheeked complexion, is a strapping man of Scottish descent who grew up in Boston and, in his college days, could well have passed for a linebacker with the Duke Blue Devils.

His article submitted, and now in the hands of others, he sat in his confined hotel room, littered with food service items which he hadn't allowed housekeeping to collect, and watched as New York City Mayor Giuliani held a news conference.

The number of casualties will be more than any, any of us can bear ultimately.

McCartney finally let the day's events sink in. He collapsed on the bed, sobbing.

Karen Blumenthal stood only shoulder-high to her husband, but she kept her emotions in check on September 11.

Scott McCartney and Karen Blumenthal at Dallas Love Field Airport in 2019
(Photo by Justin Clemons. Courtesy of Scott McCartney)

In mid-afternoon, she phoned her babysitter, who was looking after her and McCartney's thirteen and eleven-year-old daughters. In her written account years later, Blumenthal shared the conflict she felt between her parenting and news instincts.

More than anything, I wanted to be with my girls, but that would have to wait.

That evening, at 8:30 p.m. Eastern, President George W. Bush addressed the nation from the Oval Office.

Today, our fellow citizens, our way of life, our very freedom came under attack in a series of deliberate and deadly terrorist acts. The victims were in airplanes or in their offices: secretaries, businessmen and women, military and federal workers, moms and dads, friends and neighbors.

Thousands of lives were suddenly ended by evil, despicable acts of terror. The pictures of airplanes flying into buildings, fires burning, huge — huge structures collapsing have filled us with disbelief, terrible sadness, and a quiet, unyielding anger. These acts of mass murder were intended to frighten our nation into chaos and retreat. But they have failed. Our country is strong.

At about the same time President Bush was speaking, Blumenthal finished up at the office, making sure the stories she had overseen were done. Then, she headed home.

I was drained and distracted. I thanked our babysitter for staying late and supporting the girls, and went to hug my oldest, Abby. She was grim, but okay. She didn't want to talk just yet.

Blumenthal sat with her youngest daughter, Jennifer, who was ready for bed but not for sleep.

"I don't want to be like that," she cried....

"Like what, Jen?"

"Dust — they're dust!" she said, sobbing now. "All those people! I don't want to end up like that. I don't want my life to be dust!"

Blumenthal tried to reassure her daughter. The bureau chief's words that night, retold a decade later in her written memoir, were meant to offer hope in the wake of 9/11. But they could well also have served to comfort Jen, her sister, Abby, and their father, Scott, when unexpectedly, on May 18, 2020, at age 61, Blumenthal died of a heart attack.

In my awkward adult way, I tried to reassure her. People who were loved and cared for were never dust, I promised. They would always be real and whole to those [who] knew them and remembered them. It might be hard to understand now, I tried to explain, but as journalists, we would tell and retell their stories so that we would know them for the people they were and not just for how they died....

On September 11, 2001, I promised my young daughter that we would not forget, that the lives that were lost that day would never be dust. Even after ten years, we are still telling their stories and ours. And we will keep telling them, to honor and remember those who died and to try to ensure that we will never have another day like that again.

Alan, et al.:,

I'm in jersey city at a school. evacuated from nyc. it was a panic. no phone lines are working. please reply and let me know you got this. got a fair amount of good witness stuff. let me know what to do. i can file from here. try my cell phone: some people could get calls into their cells, but not out.

-- phil

• Chapter Five •

"Take Me to Washington, Whatever It Costs"

On any normal day, Phil Kuntz might rightly have been accused of impersonating a police officer, potentially a class "E" felony that can land offenders in jail for up to four years.

But this was the morning of September 11, 2001, and "New York's Finest" had more pressing matters to attend.

Kuntz, a reporter for *The Wall Street Journal*, was desperately trying to get a restaurant at the southern tip of Manhattan to open its locked doors and allow him and other choking pedestrians in.

As instructed by police, a swarm of thousands, including Kuntz, had fled the World Trade Center and dozens of hotel and office buildings in its vicinity, heading south. Under the circumstances, most of them did so relatively calmly.

That changed, as Kuntz recounted in a memo he emailed to colleagues later that day, when the throng arrived at the boardwalk facing New York Harbor.

Things started to get really scary when we reached the southern end of Battery Park. There was no place left to go and it seemed like the smoke and ash might smother us.

Their best hope was American Park at the Battery, a restaurant along the water's edge that billed itself as an urban oasis and offered sweeping panoramic views of the Statue of Liberty, Ellis Island, and the big boats sailing past.

Through the windows of the glass-enclosed dining room, Kuntz could see a small group of the restaurant's staff fixing the china and cloth place settings, and they clearly could see him and the others — covered in grey dust and trying to shield their mouths and noses with their shirts or whatever else they could find.

But pound as Kuntz and the others alongside him might on the restaurant's massive windows and glass doors, the alarmed employees refused to let the outsiders in.

In his memo, Kuntz confessed his feint.

I screamed at the apparent manager of the eatery that I was a police officer and ordered him to open the door. Nice try. He still refused.

Some people alongside Kuntz in the crowd didn't take "no" for an answer. Grabbing chairs from the restaurant's two wraparound terraces and the nearby park, they slammed the metal seats into the glass door, to no avail.

Out of nowhere, a young man made his way through the crowd carrying a big claw hammer. Where he found the forged steel implement is a mystery.

He yelled for everyone to stand back and then whipped the tool into the glass, smashing it. The stranger and Kuntz kicked in the shattered remnants and led the multitude storming the restaurant.

American Park, which opened in 1998, sat on land owned by the New York City Department of Parks and Recreation. Before a major interior redesign by architect Larry Bogdanow — whose best-known projects included Union Square Café, Savoy, and the Cub Room — the building served as a maintenance and storage facility.

The sprawling food-service complex often hosted special events, able to accommodate at least 1,200 guests in its upstairs banquet space and many more in its stylish main-floor restaurant and cocktail areas. There is no record of how many people poured into American Park after Kuntz busted in, but based on his description, it's reasonable to assume the number was at least several hundred.

Once inside, the staff members of American Park changed their tune.

The restaurant workers were great, passing out water and drinks. The manager later apologized, saying he was unsure what to do and wanted to prepare the restaurant for the huge crowd, which included numerous school children, babies, and toddlers, and several dogs.

The diners who until that day had sustained American Park would never return. In the aftermath of September 11, the restaurant was used variously as a command post for the authorities, a police precinct, and a shelter providing meals.

Unable to meet its lease commitments, the Department of Parks and Recreation eventually evicted American Park.

Hanging chads were the reason that Phil Kuntz was in Manhattan in the first place.

The 41-year-old, clean-shaven reporter could have passed for a decade younger, with bushy brown hair drooping down over his forehead and wire-rimmed glasses that exaggerated the intensity of his piercing brown eyes.

Ordinarily, Kuntz worked from the paper's D.C. bureau, where he earned a reputation as a prize-winning investigative reporter and a news editor adept at coordinating editorial projects.

After the Supreme Court ruled in *Bush v. Gore* on December 12, 2000, to halt the selective manual recount of Florida votes — effectively tipping the electoral college vote to George W. Bush — a consortium of eight news organizations banded together to undertake a painstaking review of 175,010 disputed presidential ballots.

With the help of a small army of screeners from the nonpartisan National Opinion Research Center at the University of Chicago, the news organizations examined each punch-card ballot to determine whether its chads were dimpled, detached at one or more corners, or cleanly punched.

Kuntz had been assigned as *The Wall Street Journal*'s liaison to the consortium, which included journalists from *The New York Times*, *The Washington Post*, The Associated Press, Tribune Publishing (the *Chicago Tribune* and *Los Angeles Times*), *The Palm Beach Post*, the *St. Petersburg Times*, and CNN.

It took more than nine months and cost close to $1 million, but the project was completed, and the news organizations were preparing to publish and broadcast their findings on Monday, September 17, 2001. Each news organization would be free to report the results as it saw fit. Kuntz was in New York on September 11 to meet with *Journal* editors and the graphics team to determine how the business daily wanted to play the consortium's conclusions.

(As *The Wall Street Journal* would later report, the exhaustive analysis by the eight news organizations found that even if all the disputed ballots had been counted, Bush would still have won Florida by 493 votes, only 44 votes fewer than the official victory margin.)

Kuntz spent the night of September 10 at the Marriott Financial Center, now known as the Marriott Downtown. The 32-story hotel is located at 85 West Street, between Albany and Carlisle Streets, two blocks south of the World Trade Center site.

Unlike Walt Mossberg, the D.C.-based personal tech columnist who overnighted in the World Trade Center complex itself, Kuntz hadn't yet left his hotel room when the first plane hit the North Tower. In fact, he was still asleep.

From Room 2702 on the 27th floor, Kuntz had a view facing north toward the World Trade Center. He was awakened by the loud explosion and felt the percussion of the first plane.

I immediately saw debris raining down outside my window - huge chunks as well as a storm of office paper and toilet paper. I could see the building on fire. Several small fires broke on the roof of the building next door, apparently caused by the falling debris. There was debris all over the street and flying through the sky. Then, as I was looking out the window [I] saw two huge fireballs explode from the second tower.

The inferno in South Tower was raging roughly 350 yards away from Kuntz's bed.

Kuntz phoned the D.C. bureau to appraise his colleagues of the situation. Over the hotel's public address systems, guests were first advised to stay in their rooms, then soon after, to use the stairs to gather in the lobby.

When I got to the lobby, I thought to myself, you know this is probably going to be a pretty big story, so I'll probably have to stay here again tonight.

Kuntz checked his suitcase at the bell desk and pocketed the receipt. Before the police commanded everyone in the lobby to evacuate altogether, Kuntz began interviewing fellow guests.

Dawn Wanamaker, 45 of Brooklyn, said she was in the parking lot at 90 West, preparing to enter the building to start her day as a Morgan Stanley customer service rep. She started to run and was hit above her left eye by a piece of debris. "There were body parts in the street," she said, a bandage over her wound and blood smeared on her gray blouse. "I saw somebody's hand and foot in the street. There was flesh all over the street."

The notes from Kuntz's interview with Wanamaker, emailed to *Journal* editors later that day, never made it into the paper, nor did his outdoors interview with Stefan Wambach-Olariu, who recounted gazing up to see "a big huge plane" fly right into the South Tower, followed by a deafening boom.

But Kuntz's street interview with 31-year-old James Cutler, an insurance broker, landed at the very top of the lead front-page story in the September 12 edition of the *Journal*. Compiled from hundreds of email memos he received that day, including Kuntz's account, D.C. reporter and editor Bryan Gruley wrote the roundup: "Nation Stands In Disbelief And Horror - Streets of Manhattan Resemble War Zone Amid Clouds of Ash."

[Cutler] was in the Akbar restaurant on the ground floor of the World Trade Center when he heard "boom, boom, boom," he recalls. In seconds, the kitchen doors blew open, smoke and ash poured into the restaurant and the ceiling collapsed. Mr. Cutler didn't know what had happened yet, but he found himself standing among bodies strewn across the floor. "It was mayhem," he says.

Cutler added that even though he was a Gulf War veteran, he'd never seen anything like that, but Gruley didn't include the remark in his final version.

Kuntz, too, was witnessing the unimaginable, as he wrote in his emailed recap.

Shortly after I interviewed [Cutler], I walked a bit east to get a better view of the damage to the two buildings. There was fire billowing out of both, and the second building to be hit had a huge gash in the side of it.

Hundreds of people were nearby gaping at the buildings when the first one collapsed. It was the most unbelievable sight I've ever seen. I was probably about five blocks away. The woman I was standing next to and I just spontaneously started hugging each other for comfort. It was horrible beyond description watching that thing fall.

Still interviewing those nearby as he proceeded south toward the American Park restaurant, Kuntz joined a chorus of evacuees — including a copyright lawyer named Trebor Lloyd, who he interviewed — in shouting for everyone to walk and remain calm.

David Dolny, a New York City Department of Transit employee who Kuntz encountered at the American Park restaurant, told the reporter that just a week earlier, he had seen his 18-year-old daughter off to a year of study in Israel and had been worried about her safety, not his.

Everton Reid, 34, an engineer with the Long Island Railroad, knew the girders of the Twin Towers wouldn't survive the intense heat. When the first tower began to crumble, Reid expected the worst.

This is it. I thought I was going to be dead.

The interviews with Lloyd, Dolny, Reid, and others, like the ones he conducted with Wanamaker and Wambach-Olariu, never were published. But they are testament to the resoluteness that Kuntz and his colleagues, including Jon Hilsenrath and John Bussey, displayed in pursuing the 9/11 story despite the personal trauma and danger they faced.

About an hour after Kuntz crashed the gate at American Park, he was evacuated once again. This time, the police were ordering people to board New York Waterway ferries that had been conscripted to transfer those stranded at the tip of Manhattan for the short ride across the Hudson River to Jersey City. There were no docks in Battery Park for the boats to land. Instead, the ferries would pull up as close to the shore as possible, and those already on board would stretch out their arms and help pull the awaiting passengers onto the boats.

Kuntz recalled his experience in his email memo to colleagues.

The scene from the boat was incredible. The Towers were absent from a skyline I've admired my whole life, including on vacation just two weeks ago. There appeared to be considerable collateral damage to the what I think was the World Financial Center. (I think it was our building, but I'm not sure.) One corner of the building, from about the 11th floor down, was badly damaged.

It was, indeed, *The Wall Street Journal's* severely battered headquarters that Kuntz eyed as he studied the brand new Manhattan skyline.

Disembarking from the ferry in Jersey City, Kuntz was as bewildered as many of the Ellis Island immigrants who arrived over the decades not more than a couple of miles from where he was now wandering aimlessly.

Still a dusty mess, he had no idea where to go, what to do, or how to communicate with his colleagues in the D.C. bureau. He knew they likely feared he was dead.

His cell phone was useless. The last they heard from him was hours earlier, when he was still in his hotel, well within the range of the collapsing South Tower.

Rescue workers at the dock handed Kuntz and his fellow evacuees bottles of water and wet towels.

He must have walked in something of a daze for nearly an hour before coming upon a school just shy of three miles from the iconic Colgate Clock, facing the Hudson River near Exchange Place in Jersey City.

Adults and children were gathered outside the schoolhouse, staring in the direction of the massive cloud now filling the eastern sky where the World Trade Towers stood only that morning. Kuntz approached one of the adults.

I'm a journalist with The Wall Street Journal. I have nothing but the clothes on my back and my notebook. And I've got to get to an email or a phone right away because my office knows nothing about what happened to me.

Kuntz was directed to Karen Jones, principal of the Golden Door Charter School, who graciously ceded her office to him and allowed him unrestricted access to her desktop computer, email account, and phone.

It was from Jones's office that Kuntz let his concerned colleagues know he was alive.

I just emailed everybody whose e-mail I could think of off the top of my head. And I said, I'm here. I'm in Jersey City. I'm at a school. This is the principal's email. I'm sitting in her office and I'm going to type up my notes. Standby and I'll send them as soon as I can.

I got this flood of emails back saying, "Oh, thank God, we all thought you were dead."

At 2:11 p.m., Kuntz transmitted a nearly 1,400-word memo to the D.C. bureau, chronicling his experience and the interviews he conducted with Cutler, Wanamaker, Wambach-Olariu, and the others. Only later would he learn that some of the children and teachers at Golden Door Charter School had lost family members in the terror attacks.

Having filed his report, someone from the school gave Kuntz a ride to his brother's home in nearby Weehawken, New Jersey. In the evening, Kuntz watched the replay of Mayor Giuliani's somber press conference.

... We will strive now very hard to save as many people as possible and to send a message that the City of New York and the United States of America is much stronger than any group of barbaric terrorists, that our democracy, that our rule of law, that our strength and our willingness to defend ourselves will ultimately prevail.

And I'd ask the people of New York City to do everything that they can to cooperate, not to be frightened, to go about their lives as normal. Everything is safe right now in the city. And the people who are doing the relief effort need all of the help they can get.

The next morning, September 12, Kuntz was anxious to return to the D.C. bureau. The news consortium's release of the data on the final Florida count would have to be postponed. Kuntz and the other syndicate members were preoccupied covering the aftermath of the terrorist attacks. It would take another two months for the nine news organizations to disclose their findings.

No trains or airplanes were operating. But once more, Kuntz would not take "no" for an answer. He flagged down a taxicab.

Take me to Washington. Whatever it costs, I'll pay it.

Still photos from "Wall Street Journal: Events of 9/11" video, circa early 2002
(Courtesy of Freedom Forum)

• Chapter Six •

The Flying Wallendas

The atmosphere of an adrenaline-fueled newsroom on deadline is hard to comprehend if you've never had the responsibility for "locking up" the print edition of a daily newspaper, especially one as widely read and influential as *The Wall Street Journal*.

Transmitting all the content to the printing plants — including articles, photos and graphics, advertisements, and the markets' tables — resembles a reality game show where contestants must juggle multiple complex tasks in a continuous race against the clock, leaving little margin for error.

Two hours until the presses run. Ninety minutes. One hour. Thirty minutes. Five minutes. Now or never.

A small battalion of unheralded journalists — copy editors and desk editors — review the content received from reporters, bureau chiefs, and wire services, checking the text for accuracy, thoroughness, internal consistency, style, spelling, and grammar. When necessary, these intermediary editors rewrite the incoming stories or toss them back to the reporters for revisions.

As deadlines approach, the flow of articles becomes a cascade. The desk editors, not the reporters, write each headline, governed by the assigned news "real estate" that the stories will occupy: Page One, column six; Page Three at the top; Page Twenty-Seven, a single column running below the fold, and so on.

Even while the process is whirring on, news is breaking. Fresh articles need editing, while edited articles require freshening.

The ultimate length of each story is determined by the space allotted by senior newsroom supervisors. The size of the so-called "news hole" fluctuates daily, determined, in part, by the number of advertisements that will appear in the next day's edition, and thus the over-all number of pages. If the available space is too tight, the copy desk will trim the stories, or kill them outright, to fit.

For decades in the second half of the 20th century, once the copy was finalized, it would be transmitted by satellite or fiber-optic cable to *Wall Street Journal* composing rooms located in printing plants that dotted the country. There, the stories, headlines, and graphics would be exported on long strips of coated paper, which compositors would cut and glue onto full-page templates in preparation for printing.

By September 2001, however, the classic composing rooms had been mothballed. They were replaced by sophisticated pagination software that enabled the desk editors to compose every story on their computer screens in a what-you-see-is-what-you-get fash-ion.

With the push of a button, the desk editors transferred the pages to the *Journal*'s pre-press team, which performed a final quality-assurance check before transmitting the finished pages to the company's 17 printing plants. Once at the press sites, the pages were imaged to metal plates, mounted on the presses, and soon used to produce the next morning's paper.

The process was no different on the evening of September 11; only the number of desk editors on hand was a fraction of the usual contingent. Most of the regulars assigned to the domestic edition typically began their workdays around 2:30 p.m. and were still at home when the Twin Towers were hit and disintegrated.

With bridges, tunnels, and commuter services shut down, they had no way to make it to South Brunswick if they were even aware that the *Journal* had established a backup newsroom there.

Almost all the copy editors who did get to South Brunswick lived in New Jersey and were able to make it to the backup site where a few small training rooms were being retrofitted to put out the paper. South Brunswick managers requisitioned computers from non-news departments, and the company's IT staff stripped them down and reloaded them with the newsroom's pagination software.

Some of the desk people felt shell-shocked by what they had witnessed in person or on television, but the production schedule offered no leniency for personal trauma or exten-uating circumstances.

Everything was running behind, except for the deadline clock, which ticked ahead unin-terrupted.

Who was in charge?

No one.

On what was arguably the most important news day since the December 7, 1941, attack on Pearl Harbor, *The Wall Street Journal* faced a serious leadership vacuum.

As previously noted, Peter Kann, the paper's publisher, and his wife Karen Elliott House, a senior Dow Jones executive, were in Hong Kong.

The *Journal's* four deputy managing editors — Stephen J. Adler, Barney Calame, Daniel Hertzberg, and Joanne Lipman — whose names appeared daily on the newspaper's masthead, were marooned in New York, as was Page One editor Mike Miller.

Paul Steiger, their boss and the paper's journalistic North Star, was missing. He was last seen before the collapse of the South Tower on the plaza outside of the paper's 200 Liberty Street headquarters enlisting any staff members he was able to locate to make their way to South Brunswick. It was a mission which he, himself, was unable to complete.

To be clear, no one told Frank James "Jim" Pensiero to step in for Steiger. He just did and, under the unprecedented circumstances, no one questioned his authority.

Pensiero was 48 years old and had rarely been front-and-center during his 17-year career at *The Wall Street Journal*. He was of medium build with a wide oval face and hazel eyes framed by large square glasses. He had a mop of dark hair brushed to the right and dipping onto his high forehead.

The son of an RCA public affairs executive, Pensiero had worked in the news business since the summer before his seventeenth birthday. As a copy boy at *The Evening Bulletin* in Philadelphia, reporters would shout "Boy!" and Pensiero would obligingly grab their carbon-copied, typewritten stories and run them to the appropriate editing desks.

Along the road to joining the *Journal* as a copy editor in August 1984, Pensiero worked for a succession of small-town, then larger news outlets, including Time Inc. and The Associated Press.

Similarly, at the *Journal*, Pensiero ratcheted his way up the newsroom ranks, primarily editing copy and overseeing others who did likewise. His best preparation for September 11 may have been the two years he spent from 1986 to 1988 as night editor, running the entire nightside news operation after all of the regular newsroom honchos had departed for the day.

Pensiero was well-liked, good-humored, and conscientious. But at a paper brimming with journalistic all-stars, few, if any, of his peers would have selected him in an office pool of those most likely one day to succeed Steiger on a permanent basis.

Back in January 1997, Steiger tapped Pensiero, ten years his junior, to serve as a consigliere of sorts, managing the $100 million-plus newsroom budget, negotiating contracts, helping to determine what each editor and reporter would be paid, and serving as the principal newsroom liaison to the Dow Jones technology, production, and advertising teams. Crucially, those who worked in technology were responsible for the hardware, software, and communications systems that were the backbone of the daily paper.

While Dow Jones was a leader in developing the satellite technology, methods, and infrastructure that allowed it to deliver the morning *Journal* coast-to-coast, and even to Alaska and Hawaii, the company was a straggler when it came to modernizing its newsroom operations.

The Wall Street Journal newsroom culture resisted change, continuing, for example, to rely on typewriters and pencil edits long after many other dailies had embraced word processors and digital editing terminals.

For decades, the *Journal* relied on a tried-and-true production system made by CSI (Composition Systems Inc.), which replaced the antiquated typewriters and pencil-edit process, but still required staff in the printing plants to compose the pages manually.

Even as personal and professional versions of QuarkXPress and Adobe PageMaker software gained popularity in the 1990s for their effortless ability to allow users to generate print-ready page layouts, Dow Jones and the *Journal* remained rigidly loyal to CSI.

Eventually, the higher-ups at Dow Jones relented and hired Electronic Data Systems to build a proprietary solution, known as the Global News Management System (GNMS), that was to be the Swiss army knife of pagination systems. Instead, it turned into a $65 million Edsel.

The slew of features that were supposed to make GNMS an editor's godsend instead made it difficult to wrangle. The D.C. copy desk spent weeks trying to edit deadline articles on GNMS. It was a mess. Often, the befuddled journalists were forced to revert to the doddery CSI to get out the paper.

Until year-end 1999, Cathy Panagoulias served as the *Journal*'s national editor, supervising the news desk and copyediting operations. It was during her tenure in that post that GNMS came online and rapidly drove her editors and the paper's remote bureau chiefs batty.

Full-faced, with curly black hair, wire-thin eyebrows, and rimless eyeglasses, she was as protective of cub reporters as a mother lioness. Yet, Panagoulias brooked no arguments from colleagues who attempted to contravene her editorial judgments with well-crafted, but in her mind, specious rhetoric. She frequently responded to their rationales in no uncertain terms.

You are fullashit.

Years later, writing about her career with the *Journal*, colleague Jared Sandberg saluted her ability to upset the conventional order of things.

[Panagoulias's] singular trait was her ability to nurture at one moment, stalk and kill the next. Instead of sucking up and managing down by fear, she kowtowed to defenseless interns and tormented upper management, often for the good of the paper, mostly for the fun of it. The clatch of twentysomethings was her pride; the latter, her prey.

While studying history and Mandarin at Cornell University, Panagoulias served as managing editor of the *Cornell Daily Sun*. After graduation, she was hired by the *Journal* in 1976 and soon dispatched to Hong Kong, working on the copy desk of *The Asian Wall Street Journal*.

On her path to becoming national editor, Panagoulias worked in a variety of supervisory roles, including layout editor, that prepared her well for the challenges that arose on September 11. Her talent and management skills were unassailable.

Panagoulias was one of the few senior editors besides Pensiero who understood production.

As she saw it, GNMS, which had been in development for nine years, was effectively obsolete on the day it was introduced into the newsroom because it could not design pages electronically.

For weeks on end, the paper's editing team missed their deadlines because — to the extent that GNMS operated — it crawled along like a tortoise. Panagoulias resolved to put GNMS out of its misery. For her unyielding effort, she would eventually earn the nickname "Xena: Warrior Princess."

Some of Panagoulias's senior management colleagues were too deeply invested in GNMS — literally and figuratively — for her to execute a straight-on assault. Instead, she elected to attack GNMS's many flaws by installing a Quark pagination system in a carefully planned Trojan Horse operation.

Panagoulias assured the GNMS chorus that the use of Quark was only an experiment, intended solely for application to the paper's two daily foreign pages. The remainder of the paper would continue to be produced using GNMS, she maintained.

When John Bussey, the foreign editor, saw that with Quark he could control his pages unaided — and with lightning speed no less — he was sold. Bussey helped Panagoulias convince Steiger to ditch GNMS entirely.

Upper management could not have been too happy. In Dow Jones & Company's 1998 annual report, the company attributed much of its multi-million dollar technology charge to the write-off of GNMS.

While GNMS added some increased functionality to the news staff's desktops, the system that was built was too complicated to effectively prepare the pages for printing. The company decided it was more cost beneficial to invest in a new pagination system using current off-the-shelf technology rather than to invest additional resources in fixing the GNMS system.

Although Panagoulias merited credit, Dow Jones didn't publicly commend her for her campaign to replace GNMS or for helping to find a system, eventually, to replace it.

With GNMS decommissioned, Panagoulias and Pensiero went on the hunt for software that would work like Quark but could be adapted to the rigorous specifications of the *Journal*. One of the paper's bureau chiefs happened upon just such a system at a digital publishing trade show.

Hermes was a new pagination and editorial production system designed by Unisys. Named for the messenger of the Greek gods, it had the necessary speed and flexibility to serve the *Journal's* needs.

Pensiero won permission to purchase Hermes, and soon he and Panagoulias began installing the new system. Pensiero worked most closely with the Dow Jones and Unisys tech teams, while Panagoulias concentrated on helping the newsroom staff adapt and configure Hermes for the *Journal's* needs.

The paper's D.C. bureau was so elated when Dow Jones finally pulled the plug on GNMS that staffers pitched in and sent Panagoulias a scarf from Hermés, the French luxury goods company.

And to thank the entire Dow Jones and Unisys technology team, the news department hosted a gala at the Windows on the World restaurant on the 106th floor of the World Trade Center's North Tower.

Geographically, Dow Jones's sprawling South Brunswick office complex is located on a 206-acre campus, 50 miles southwest of the *Journal's* Manhattan headquarters. It is light-years away when juxtaposed with the concrete and asphalt urban surroundings — not to mention the massive devastation — that characterized Lower Manhattan in the wake of 9/11.

The campus's original two-story Indiana limestone building, built by Dow Jones, began in 1964 as an 80,000-square-foot research and administrative center perched on a high rise of land along busy Route 1, about a 15-minute drive from Princeton.

Over time, the size of the South Brunswick tract was expanded and the number of buildings and their functions grew. By 2001, the site consisted of five connected buildings totaling 420,000-square-feet of workspace, 3,000-plus parking spaces, a satellite earth station, and a printing plant that serviced subscribers in New Jersey, metropolitan New

York, and Philadelphia.

Most *Journal* reporters and editors had never visited the South Brunswick outpost prior to September 11, and many of them were unsettled by its pastoral setting. Well-manicured lawns abounded, allowing for picnics, outdoor barbeques, and friendly interdepartmental softball games. Canada geese splashed about in the estate's pond, eventually growing so numerous that the company bought a pair of border collies to chase them off the main lawn. The on-site forest served as a natural bird habitat, and walking trails offered employees a chance to be at one with their idyllic surroundings.

On 9/11, and in the days that followed, the number of people converging on South Brunswick swelled with each passing hour. Refugees from 200 Liberty — journalists, technicians, executives, and security personnel — as well as vendors and outside consultants, all began to pour in.

Resident South Brunswick staffers took up posts at the facility's various entrances and parking areas to help bewildered migrants find their way to their makeshift stations.

Though most of those on hand would never receive a byline in the paper or much of any acknowledgment outside the confines of Dow Jones, hundreds of employees deserved recognition for their FEMA-worthy efforts to find office space, technology, supplies, food, and even clothing for the incoming throngs.

The influx of personnel proved a boon for area hotels and motels, which were transformed into corporate dormitories for the large contingent of Dow Jones exiles for whom a daily, hour-plus commute back to Manhattan, Brooklyn, or Connecticut was a bridge — quite literally — too far.

In a November 2001 handout, the Dow Jones public relations team endeavored to honor some of these otherwise inconspicuous staffers by recounting their contributions on 9/11 and during the days and weeks that followed. The PR broadsheet was designed to replicate the look of the *Journal's* front page, complete with a *What's News* two-column section, *The Outlook* in the mock-paper's fifth column, and three main features, left, right, and in the center of the page.

Art Quimby and Melanie Brown browbeat suppliers to get more PCs, no mean trick when planes weren't flying. Tom Ennis organized staffers who set up phones and networking equipment. Phyllis Carey and Claire Frazier worked to get the hundreds of desks and chairs. Construction manager Fred Cooper got additional power to handle the huge load needed by the new computers. John Coston organized an efficient van service to shuttle news staffers to and from the train station and Brooklyn.

The South Brunswick complex was cavernous. It was divided into sections labeled 1 through 76, and for some inexplicable reason, the sectors were not sequential. The newcomers relied on signs, posted on virtually every wall, directing them: "Vans to the hotels." "Shuttle to the train." And so on. Even so, one day, a senior editor got lost and missed a *WSJ.com* news meeting.

Kristine Farr worked for Eurest Dining Services, which operated Dow Jones's two South Brunswick cafeterias. On September 11, Kristine marshaled a Eurest crew in an effort to feed the rapidly expanding swarm. As the public relations handout recounted:

... the central Dow Jones larder was quickly depleted. Worse, Kristine discovered with dismay, all food deliveries had been stopped because of the emergency. So she sent her cooks to raid the refrigerators of other Eurest clients nearby, most of which had closed down. At Princeton Plasma Physics Laboratories, for example, Kristine's staffers found a treasure trove of corned beef. Which is why, that long night of Sept. 11, News and IT people chowed down on Reuben sandwiches.

Cathy Panagoulias, whose term as national editor had been completed 21-months earlier, served as a newsroom general without portfolio on September 11, doing and directing whatever was needed. Officially, she was an assistant managing editor responsible for screening prospective reporters, editors, and interns.

It was Panagoulias who asked Farr to find "lots of protein, no junk food" for the journalists who were arriving hungry and would need fuel to work late into the night. South Brunswick managers who had learned over the years that Panagoulias acted decisively and quickly, lined up at her desk awaiting orders.

She ordered up more desks, televisions, and phones. During a lull, the managers showed her a large room filled with cubicles. She told them to rip out the dividers and start setting up an open newsroom that could hold 100 desks with computers because that room was going to become the *Journal*'s temporary headquarters starting on September 12.

Eyeing newsroom personnel covered in ash and dirt, Panagoulias instructed staffers to find an open Kmart and purchase clean clothes and toiletries for those who would be staying in South Brunswick for the night. Matter of factly, Panagoulias queried male staffers on their preference.

Boxers or briefs?

With Mike Miller, the regular Page One editor, stranded in Manhattan, Pensiero tapped Lawrence Rout, a seasoned *Journal* reporter and special sections editor, to serve as Miller's stand-in. It was an assignment Rout would acquit flawlessly.

Reflecting on his extended South Brunswick layover, Rout's observations were included in the company's November 2001 broadsheet PR handout.

Watching the tech group put the newsroom together reminded me of the scene in "The Sting," where the con men are all feverishly setting up a fake betting parlor before Robert Shaw gets there. Suddenly — where there was nothing — there's a bustling gambler's paradise.

That's the way it was in South Brunswick, as the techs were opening up boxes, hooking up computers, getting phones working. Suddenly — where there was nothing - there's a newsroom. But unlike "The Sting," this wasn't a fake, and everything really worked.

Earlier that day, Jim Pensiero waited nervously outside the entrance to 200 Liberty Street, as he had agreed with Steiger that he would. He was unsure of what to do.

Not fifteen minutes earlier, peering out the newsroom's 9th-floor windows that overlooked the World Trade Center, there seemed no imminent threat to the *Journal's* headquarters or the many people who worked in the World Financial Center.

Pensiero had arrived from his home in northern New Jersey at 8:00 a.m., an hour-and-a-half earlier than usual, in order to complete some administrative work before most of the dayside staff wandered in at the usual time, between 9:00 a.m. and 9:30 a.m. Pensiero's wife, Karen Miller, who also worked for Dow Jones, had the day off and so would attend to the morning care of their two young children.

Walking the corridor to his office, Pensiero observed that John Bussey was already in to file his early-morning foreign markets reports for CNBC. Steiger arrived at his 9th-floor corner office facing the Hudson River at about 8:30 a.m. A few other staff members were also at their desks.

When the first plane hit the North Tower, Pensiero took little note. On reflection, he thought that maybe he heard the crash but shrugged it off as typical New York dissonance.

It was his wife, Karen, who on the radio first learned about the unfolding disaster at the World Trade Center. She phoned Pensiero to alert him, as had Steiger's wife, Wendy Brandes, who had reached her husband only a few minutes earlier.

Both men separately raced across the newsroom to gape out the east side windows, which faced the blazing North Tower.

Over the years, the *Journal* had developed contingency plans and run backup drills to ensure that the paper could be produced uninterrupted in the event that its New York headquarters became temporarily unavailable. Those plans anticipated a short-term disruption caused by a power failure or hurricane, but never a terrorist act that would shutter the 200 Liberty Street office for nearly a year.

Before the *Journal* converted to newsroom pagination, the plan was for key editors and newsroom staff to make their way to the Dow Jones printing and composing plant in Chicopee, Massachusetts, roughly 150 miles northeast of the World Financial Center. On several occasions, *Journal* personnel were bused on weekends to Chicopee to test the facility's preparedness.

However, once the Hermes system was installed, the South Brunswick complex became the *Journal's* primary backup site.

South Brunswick was only 50 miles from Manhattan and, along with administrative employees, housed the company's technology and engineering staff. The campus was also equipped with a satellite uplink which allowed the news team to transmit pages to the company's other printing sites.

Like they had in Chicopee, the *Journal's* editing and news production staff had run weekend drills in South Brunswick prior to 9/11. During the exercises, they worked from two training classrooms designed to instruct employees on how to use Hermes and to test the system.

As Steiger's liaison to the technology and production teams, Pensiero was familiar with the people and facilities in South Brunswick, perhaps more so than any other newsroom leader.

When Steiger, his eyes still fixed on the smoldering North Tower, asked Pensiero about where best to direct the *Journal's* staff in the event that 200 Liberty Street would need to be evacuated. Pensiero unhesitatingly replied that South Brunswick was the only solution.

We can edit and paginate if we can get our editors and graphic artists to South Brunswick and if the backup newsroom is activated and ready to run.

Steiger instructed Pensiero to make sure that South Brunswick was prepared, just in case.

It was not yet 9:02 a.m. when United Airlines Flight #175 would plow into the South Tower, but Steiger and Pensiero were well along in designing a stand-by plan.

When the second plane struck, this time Pensiero felt the *Journal's* offices shake and almost simultaneously heard the violent impact. Although both World Trade Center towers were visible from the *Journal's* offices, the newsroom was located closest to the South Tower.

Steiger now felt certain that the *Journal* facilities would be evacuated. Neither tower had fallen, but given the global prominence of the Twin Towers, the certain loss of life, and the enormity of the damage, the managing editor already was envisioning running a six-column headline across the front page of the next day's paper.

Back in his office, Pensiero set about alerting the South Brunswick tech folks that, indeed, he and his colleagues were headed their way. Simultaneously, Pensiero composed an email to D.C. Bureau Chief Alan Murray, National News Editor Marcus Brauchli, and other key lieutenants, apprising them of the situation and letting everyone know that he, Steiger, and all others were abandoning the New York newsroom.

The public-address system at the World Financial Center, at first, announced that there was no need to evacuate. Now the PA system blared the message that everyone should get out.

Steiger dropped by Pensiero's office to let him know that he was headed off to search for his wife, who worked at the Lehman Brothers offices situated down a long central passageway on the north side of the World Financial Center complex.

Once I'm sure Wendy is safe, I'll meet you on Liberty Street, and we can go to South Brunswick together.

Pensiero nodded his acknowledgment. He didn't realize it, but that would be the last he'd see of Steiger that day.

A Dow Jones security guard shooed Pensiero out of his office just as the editor pushed the send button to distribute his email alert to the *Journal* troops. Surprisingly, the guard, who, like Pensiero, clearly was not anticipating the impending tsunami of destruction, told the editor that it was okay to take the elevator down to the lobby level.

On the outdoor plaza, Pensiero impatiently scanned front and back, left and right, trying to spot Steiger approaching their meetup spot. Sirens wailed. EMS workers and firefighters filled the plaza and the streets. Emergency vehicles were everywhere.
A police officer, in a friendly manner, asked Pensiero to move along.

Where you're standing isn't safe, and it could interfere with rescue efforts.

Pensiero shuffled about ten feet south when a second officer again urged him to leave the area.

A co-worker from employee relations who happened on Pensiero told him she had seen a large burning airplane-tire in the street. He watched as an injured stranger was taken into an ambulance. Still no Steiger.

In a reconstruction of his day that Pensiero crafted a month later, he wrote of his dilemma.

My inner conflict got worse: Paul had ordered me to get to South Brunswick and get our backup newsroom [working]. He also asked me to wait for him… I was becoming increasingly afraid as I watched the horrific scene unfolding before me…

Ultimately, Pensiero decided to find a boat to convey him across the Hudson River to New Jersey.

Paul will have to meet me there.

Pensiero was on one of the last ferries to leave the boat basin that was located just west of the World Financial Center. Had he missed the water taxi, the *Journal* very well may not have printed the next day.

Indeed, his was just one of a few dozen "but-fors" that day that would have vanquished the *Journal* had fortune not fallen the paper's way.

Pensiero's boat was just pulling into the Jersey City dock when the South Tower collapsed.

I can't believe what I'm seeing.

An older man in a business suit openly wept. The others, including Pensiero, looked on in stunned silence.

Pensiero planned to take the PATH rail service to the commuter parking lot in Harrison, New Jersey, about ten miles from his home. He had parked there that morning before catching the train to work. He planned to retrieve his car and then make the one-hour drive to South Brunswick.

But the nearest PATH station was closed. As he walked in search of an available station, a fighter jet roared overhead.

Eventually, Pensiero did find his way onto a westbound PATH train, picked up his car, and headed for South Brunswick. He tried to reach his wife from payphones and with his cellphone. But the calls would not go through.

As he drove south on the New Jersey Turnpike and the Garden State Parkway, Pensiero eyed waves of emergency vehicles across the divide headed north toward Manhattan. In his October 2001 chronicle of the day, he recalled the scene vividly.

The Turnpike was closed northbound at Exit 11, where it intersects with the Parkway. The view from that intersection was deeply distressing. Both towers were gone, replaced by a thick plume of grayish-black smoke. I had witnessed a mass murder, and now I was trying to get to work.

Thanks to the heads-up from Pensiero, the resident team in South Brunswick knew relatively early on the morning of September 11 that soon they would be overrun with needy, impatient outsiders determined to transform their tranquil, orderly office compound into a serviceable, albeit chaotic, newsroom.

Before the first castaway arrived, additional on-site training rooms were converted to editorial pods — a News Desk, Overseas Copy Desk, Edit Page section, quarters for

Barron's, and for the Graphics department.

The collection of rooms and workstations, located in what had been the relatively underutilized "Building 4," was quickly nicknamed "The Bunker."

The team in South Brunswick — Bland Smith, Cheryl Badger, Jim Champion, Deb Carlino, Karen Kennedy, Gary Goyden, John Lynch, Gary Cender, Dave Dunn, and dozens of other staffers — were expecting an onslaught. But for an eerie period, no one arrived.

Then, at last, Jesse Lewis, who drove to South Brunswick from his home in Fanwood, New Jersey, walked through the door and the frenzied race to the publishing finish line began.

Lewis was an unflappable, professorial-looking journalist, who made everything he did look easy, and for him, it usually was.

In 1998, as a contestant on *Jeopardy*, Lewis won $12,600 and a trip to Portugal. Five-foot ten and about 195 pounds, he had inquisitive dark eyes reflected behind large-rimmed glasses and a full head of curly, short-cropped black hair.

As the paper's global copy chief, Lewis, 45, supervised the staff of 40 to 50 people who edited the U.S. edition on a typical workday. Unlike other senior editors who had ersatz roles, Lewis performed his regular duties on September 11, albeit with far fewer assistants.

When Hermes was introduced into the newsroom, Lewis chose to customize the new system himself instead of delegating the task to deputies. As a result, he possessed an encyclopedic knowledge of every idiosyncrasy of Hermes and knew how to adapt the system to function under the extreme conditions of the extraordinary day.

His admirers later joked that Lewis was so well-versed in Hermes that he could have produced the September 12 edition from his kitchen on a laptop.

Eight years earlier, Lewis was working in the *Journal*'s 200 Liberty Street headquarters when, shortly after noon on February 26, 1993, a 1,200-pound bomb planted in a rented Ford Econoline van in the B-2 level of the parking garage beneath the World Trade Center exploded. The terrorists' aim had been to topple the North Tower onto the South Tower. While the bomb caused significant damage, injuring more than 1,000 people — mostly from smoke inhalation — and killing six, the structural integrity of the towers was not compromised.

On September 11, Lewis was headed out his front door, planning, as usual, to commute to work by train, when his wife summoned him back to watch the drama unfolding on television. He immediately recalled the chaos that ensued in Lower Manhattan in the aftermath of the 1993 bombing, which closed the Twin Towers for a month and was a commuters' hell.

Well, I'm not going to be working there today.

Lewis deduced, correctly, that the *Journal* would rely on the South Brunswick backup site to produce the next day's paper. He made the 45-minute drive from Fanwood, a 1.3 square-mile borough in Union County, to Dow Jones's New Jersey facility in his green Jeep Grand Cherokee. Although he couldn't spot the enflamed Trade Towers from the road, he learned from WCBS NewsRadio 880 that the South Tower had imploded.

Pensiero was the next news-side staff member to arrive, meeting up with Lewis at about 12:15 p.m.

Days and weeks later, in public relations dispatches and other pronouncements, the *Journal* would take pride in the fact that there was never any doubt that it would publish a September 12 edition. But that is not entirely accurate.

While Lewis began configuring Hermes, Pensiero surveyed the hastily activated workstations that were at the ready but unoccupied. He was keenly aware that the version of Hermes that editors in South Brunswick would need to rely on to edit and compose the paper had been upgraded only two days earlier and was still glitchy. Indeed, only that morning, before all hell broke loose, Andrea Carabillo, an on-call Unisys employee and Hermes expert, had been summoned in the predawn hours to 200 Liberty Street to troubleshoot a malfunction.

Pensiero weighed the odds.

We still have a good shot at producing a Journal if we can get ourselves organized... Like an army retreating from defeat to a prepared position, we at least have a place in which to carry on the fight. We have the right tools; now we just need the right people.

Each exile who trickled in had his or her own tale.

Lawrence Rout, the newsroom veteran who would serve as that day's Page One editor, likened his experience on landing by ferry at the Jersey City boat dock to a zombie movie.

People were walking and walking...but there was nowhere to go.

Without intent, he found himself at the foot of a stairwell leading to a PATH station. He descended.

A train was idling in the station but without passengers.

A conductor, who spotted him, called out asking if he wanted a lift to Newark.

So the two of them, absolutely alone, rode a PATH train to New Jersey's largest city, from which Rout was able to catch a commuter train to Princeton Junction, about six miles from the Dow Jones campus.

Sheila Courter, a news desk editor who lived in Westfield, New Jersey, had filled in for a vacationing colleague on the 200 Liberty Street night news desk on September 10. Headed home from Lower Manhattan around midnight, she drove past the Twin Towers and gazed up at the monoliths, whose floors and rows of on-and-off office lights resembled morse code.

Courter, who was training for the New York City Marathon, was up early on September 11, running with a group of neighborhood friends on a high school track when word reached them that a plane had crashed into the World Trade Center.

Like most everyone who heard the news before they saw live, on-the-scene television coverage, Courter assumed it had been an accident involving a small plane. Nevertheless, instinct kicked in, and she immediately headed for South Brunswick after a quick stop at home to pack an overnight bag, just in case.

In Maplewood, New Jersey, Cathy Panagoulias was on autopilot, trying to wake up with her usual morning routine — coffee, shower, two fried eggs, more coffee, makeup, even more coffee — when her brother called from Lower Manhattan and told her husband, Dan Margulis, to stop Panagoulias from getting on the train to New York because he had just seen a plane fly into the World Trade Center.

Panagoulias, whose practice for more than a decade had been immediately upon waking to monitor television news and read the dailies, had forsaken the habit once she was no longer national news editor. She and her husband rushed to the television just in time to witness the second plane hit the South Tower.

All she could think of at that moment was the 1974 disaster movie, *Towering Inferno*, which as a 21-year-old, she had screened twice because the film featured two of her teen heartthrobs, Paul Newman and Steve McQueen. She intuited immediately that the Twin Towers would topple.

At the end of the movie, Fire Chief Steve McQueen turned to Newman and said something like, "When are you going to learn? We can't save these buildings if they are more than six stories high."

Calculating that the *Journal*'s headquarters would sustain serious damage once the Twin Towers fell, Panagoulias began to count on her fingers how many editors she knew who both lived in New Jersey and had been trained to use Hermes. When she got to a dozen, she reasoned that might be enough to get a newspaper published at the backup site.

Panagoulias grabbed the paper printout of staff home and cell phone numbers that she kept in her commuter backpack and began calling copy editors to urge them to get to South Brunswick. She didn't mention to anyone that she hadn't been able to reach Pensiero or Steiger or Brauchli and had no idea what had happened to them. Nor did she tell them that when she called South Brunswick, a panicked technology expert told her that no one from 200 Liberty had made contact since the first tower fell.

As if it had been prearranged, which it hadn't been, Panagoulias's doorbell rang. It was Elyse Tanouye, the *Journal*'s senior pharmaceutical reporter, who lived only a few blocks away.

She was one of the few people who knew my shameful secret that I didn't drive. She asked if I needed a ride to South Brunswick. I said yes.

Since Tanouye's husband had the family car, Elyse rented one, and together she and Panagoulias collected other Maplewood-area *Journal* staffers and carpooled to South Brunswick.

It was past 1:00 p.m. when more people began to straggle in. Bart Fraust, one of Lewis's two deputies, found his way to an editing terminal. Ken De Witt, the editorial technology director for the paper's editorial page, made it, as did the editorial pages' Paul Gigot and William McGurn, albeit a bit later.

By 1:30 p.m., Pensiero had assumed the role of field marshal in the battle to publish.

On the inside, Pensiero was stressing. He understood the role he assigned himself, the momentous nature of the day's events, and the imperative that the *Journal* publish, not just for the sake of its readers, but to send an unambiguous message that the paper and the country would not be bowed by terrorism.

When two newsroom stalwarts arrived in the South Brunswick training rooms — Rout, the special sections editor, and Lawrence Ingrassia, a 23-year *Journal* veteran who oversaw the *Money & Investing* section — Pensiero heaved a sigh of relief.

I wanted to cry on seeing them, but I wasn't quite ready to show my emotions.

Others, too, wanted to cry, scream, break down, throw objects, get drunk, and leave. But no one did. These journalists, technicians, and support personnel did not put their lives on the line like the hundreds of first responders who ran into the World Financial Center when everyone else ran out. But their same sense of duty and pride compelled each of them to block out their emotions and focus on the job at hand.

Pensiero, coordinating with Brauchli, Murray, and the paper's global bureaus, emailed everyone who was at work a "story budget," listing the coverage planned for the September 12 edition and who was responsible for each article.

The stand-in managing editor received an email from Steiger, the actual managing editor, in the early afternoon. Steiger explained that he had been caught in the cyclone of dust and left without the ability to phone. He told Pensiero that he was safe at home in his Upper East Side apartment and planning to seek out his four deputy editors. Steiger said he aimed to make it to South Brunswick still that day. But that was not to be.

Pensiero continued to administer essential newsroom activities. He alerted all editors and reporters to file their stories by 6:00 p.m. Eastern, with the aim of locking up the early edition of the paper by 8:30 p.m., about an hour past the regular time.

On a normal day, the *Journal* printed a Two Star, Three Star, and Four Star edition, each with respectively later deadlines. To this day, sharp-eyed readers can determine which version they have in hand by looking just under the "THE WALL STREET JOURNAL." nameplate that appears at the top of the front page and counting the number of stars to the left of the date.

The Two Star was aimed at the most remote delivery locations — such as rural areas where papers were delivered the next day by the U.S. Postal Service or, in some cases, including Hawaii and Alaska — where there was no nearby printing plant and the papers had to rely on airline transportation to reach awaiting delivery trucks.

Because of its early deadlines, the Two Star seldom included news from the West Coast, which was particularly conspicuous to Two Star subscribers as news emanating from Silicon Valley grew in importance.

Wall Street Journal lore has it that following complaints from readers that the paper's One Star edition was a day-old by the time it was delivered, some big shot at Dow Jones resolved to address the discontent by simply adding a second star to the otherwise unchanged edition so that all readers believed at least they weren't getting the earliest edition.

By 5:00 p.m., about 40 staffers — counting WSJ News, WSJ Editorial, and WSJ Ad Services — had run the gauntlet and were in South Brunswick laboring to produce the next morning's paper. That amounted to less than one-seventh of the New York-based staff, leaving the unspoken question: Who among the absent had survived?

In his October 2001 account of the day, Pensiero recalled the atmosphere as the first deadline approached.

Little by little, we gained better control of the situation. The rooms became quiet and intense, the way it gets on deadline on any other day.

Around 7:00 p.m., too late to make the Two Star, John Bussey, who had been caught in the maelstrom of the collapsing World Trade Center towers, wandered into the makeshift newsroom, still limping. Like a genuine war correspondent just back from the front, he was wearing his 'battle fatigues' — dress shirt, dress slacks, a loosened necktie, all covered in soot, as were his hair and face.

In his head, as he made his way to South Brunswick, Bussey had begun drafting a first-person account of his harrowing escape.

Panagoulias gave him the terminal she had been using to track stories and watched him type with a calm intensity. He showed her the first few paragraphs, and she told him to keep typing.

As Bussey continued, Rout conferred with Steiger by phone. The two editors, along with Pensiero, squeezed as much as they could of Bussey's article into a replate of the Two Star, whose first run was already coming off the printing plant conveyor belts. For the Three Star, they wedged his entire 40-inch story inside the paper. And for the Four Star, they made room for Bussey's account "The Eye of the Storm: One Journey Through Desperation and Chaos," to begin on the lower left-hand column of Page One.

The 32-page paper produced that night was only two sections instead of three. There were no pages of financial tables as the markets were closed. The second section, *Money & Investing*, would feature a black-and-white AP photo of the two stricken towers. Running photos in the *Journal* was a rare occurrence in those days.

The paper's Ad Services team pulled most of the advertisements that were originally slated to run on September 12 to protect its advertisers from appearing crass in promoting commerce on such a solemn occasion. In their place, the *Journal* ran house ads for itself or its Dow Jones siblings, including *Barron's* and *The Wall Street Journal Online*.

Beyond the short staffing and all of the other obvious emotional and time-pressure shoals that the *Journal's* news desk had to navigate, it faced another obstacle that only copy editors would readily recognize.

Many parts of the daily *Journal*, especially the three features that ran on the front page and the cover pages of the two other sections, were written and edited well in advance, freeing editors to handle strictly breaking news. But on September 11, virtually every feature and story was breaking news, reported and edited under enormous deadline pressure.

Moreover, with few exceptions, the articles slated to run in the September 12 edition were "virgin," meaning that the desk editors had no prior reporting foundation from which they could crib context and boilerplate paragraphs to expedite the fact-checking process. The *Journal* had never before written about terrorist attacks that fell iconic buildings, struck at the Pentagon, used civilian planes as offensive missiles, left thousands dead, and tugged at the heart of the nation.

The Hermes pagination system proved indispensable. It could have delayed the entire process had bugs surfaced. But they didn't.

Luck also favored those in South Brunswick who needed Hermes to edit and compose the September 12 edition.

Many of the *Journal*'s vital operating systems were resident in the 200 Liberty Street headquarters, including Hermes. However, because Hermes had been elevated to a newer version, Hermes 5.5, on Sunday, September 9, 2001, the tech team responsible for its operations transferred the complex program to servers in South Brunswick, the designated backup site.

It was standard protocol, whenever a system upgrade occurred, to verify that the backup system also worked properly. Had the terrorist attacks never occurred, Hermes would have been run from South Brunswick for a week or two of live inspection and then again operated from 200 Liberty.

The fact that Hermes 5.5 was already installed and operating smoothly in South Brunswick saved valuable time. If it was still based at 200 Liberty, it is not clear that the transfer would have worked, given the chaotic circumstances.

Even without Hermes, it's possible the tech team in South Brunswick would have still rigged a makeshift system functional enough to produce a bare-bones paper. At the very least, however, the paper would likely have been delayed and missed delivery windows, if it was able to print at all.

The Three Star edition closed at about 10:15 p.m. on September 11. The Four Star, which was distributed to major urban areas located in close proximity to Dow Jones's 17 printing plants, closed at about 11:40 p.m.

At the end of the day's marathon, when the Four Star was finally on the presses, Panagoulias found herself alone, walking the endless, dimly lit walkways that ran between buildings in South Brunswick. She was exhausted.

I saw this man walking toward me who had an uncanny resemblance to George Clooney. He had on the whitest shirt, but he was all disheveled, and he seemed to be smiling and trying to make eye contact with me. I was just beginning to process the lunacy of the day and how nothing would ever be the same for The Wall Street Journal.

For a moment, I thought I was hallucinating. Was I dead? Is this Heaven and is this George Clooney?

It was neither Clooney nor heaven, but rather Richard Zannino, 42, who had joined Dow Jones earlier that year as an executive vice president and the company's chief financial officer. Zannino would go on to serve a short-lived tenure as the CEO of Dow Jones.

Zannino had observed Panagoulias and the others laboring to put out the paper and wanted to acknowledge her efforts.

Hi, I'm Rich Zannino, and I want to thank you for your work today.

Indeed, Panagoulias, Pensiero, Lewis, Rout, Ingrassia, Bussey, and the others departing South Brunswick for a shower and a bed, be it in a nearby hotel, a colleague's house, or their own home, had pulled off the impossible. It was a profound moment for each of them and one that Panagoulias felt Steiger deserved much credit for, even though he hadn't been with them in New Jersey.

The magic of that day was that Paul Steiger had spent his entire tenure at the Journal hand-picking and developing a team of editors that performed better for him than they would ever perform without him.

He nurtured, challenged, mentored, manipulated, and rewarded each of us in a way that was particular to each of us, and each of us would have killed for him. We knew what he expected of us because he told us almost daily: we understood how he thought about journalism because each day in the top editors' news meeting he led by example, raising issues about particular stories. In those meetings, the story list was a jumping-off point to discuss all the tools of the trade: sourcing, ethics, fairness.

We were all different. We didn't all like one another. We all had big egos. But we were unified in our desire to meet his high standards.

So on the morning of September 11, when we couldn't find him or communicate with him, when we couldn't communicate with one another, when some of us thought he was dead, we each did our job, knowing the other top editors if they weren't dead were doing their jobs (and if they were dead their deputies would take over), and somehow we would produce a paper that would make Paul Steiger proud. Paul Steiger's editors were like the Flying Wallendas — each one had an individual journalistic daredevil act that could be performed without a safety net because Paul had spent years developing each daredevil.

Without diminishing the cataclysmic wounds inflicted on the nation on 9/11, for most of those assembled in South Brunswick, September 11 was then and would prove to be in the years to follow, the journalistic apex of their careers.

They had done all they could. Now, as the clock struck and passed midnight, it fell to the printing plants and, most especially, to the delivery truck drivers to complete the mission.

• Chapter Seven •

"-30-"

A good editor is someone who cares a little less about the author's needs than the reader's.

Dene October
University of the Arts London

While many employees of Dow Jones and *The Wall Street Journal* suffered physical and emotional infirmities in the aftermath of September 11, only one — Richard Regis, a senior news desk editor — became seriously ill and eventually died of his exposure to the World Trade Center's deluge of debris.

In early July 2020, 215 people, primarily former colleagues, joined a Zoom video conference to celebrate the life and mark the passing of the newsman, who expired five weeks shy of his 68th birthday.

The Zoom call was notable for two reasons.

First, Regis — and almost everyone who knew the deskman always called him by his surname — had retired from the *Journal* three-and-a-half years earlier. Most of those on the call had, themselves, moved on from the paper.

Second, during the 34 years that Regis worked at the *Journal*, he was regarded by many colleagues as a gruff and intense editor, known for his steely gaze and "no b.s." directness.

Regis: *Where's your copy?"*

September Twelfth

Reporter: *It's coming.*

Regis: *So's Christmas.*

Even veteran reporters initially cowered before Regis.

The Zoom call began with a greeting by Regis's adult daughter, Nora, and the streaming of a photo and video montage of Regis's personal life, extending from his chubby baby photo to his marriage to Janet "Jan" Brandstrader — a long-time Dow Jones staffer, to the birth of Nora, and into his retirement years.

Matt Murray, the cherubic editor in chief of the *Journal*, spoke next. Wearing an open-necked white dress shirt and serious brown-framed eyeglasses, Murray told the digitally assembled audience that it fell to him to talk about Regis as a journalist.

He was an intimidating presence. I can attest the first time you met him or saw him could be a little bit terrifying.

His phone would ring. He'd pick up and bark, 'News Desk, Regis.' He'd listen, and with his back ramrod straight, he would turn to his keyboard and start typing.

Murray came up through the *Journal*'s ranks as a reporter and later spent time working alongside Regis on the national news desk. On the Zoom tribute, Murray reflected on the unsung role such editors play.

Editing within the context of a newsroom is rarely seen as particularly glamorous. Reporters tend to look down on editors. You can feel sorry for them a little bit. Newsrooms are pretty famous for running on ego and adrenaline, usually measured in bylines. And editors are often seen as the supporting players in that drama, or even worse, as obstacles.

While the death knell tolled for Regis on September 11 when — unbeknownst to him — he aspirated detritus from the Twin Towers, it took an excruciating 18 years, nine months, and a day for his sentence to be executed.

The resplendent life and career of Rich Regis were such that he left an indelible impact on those who knew him, at work and especially at home.

I am on the record as him being the absolute best dad in the entire world.

That said, Nora and her mother do acknowledge that Regis's outer shell was brusque. However, once you penetrated the surface, what lay beneath was charming, loyal, risible, worldly, and imbued with the work ethic, integrity, and encyclopedic institutional memory of a consummate journalism professional.

Murray's "disclaimers" about Regis's temperament and the underrated role of copy editors aside, the editor in chief explained what most of those on the Zoom tribute already knew and why they felt compelled to share their fond memories of Regis.

Rich was also an incredibly generous soul [with] a very self-aware sense of humor, who was very amused by the daily carnival and maybe the sharpest renaissance mind in the world.

He was the sort of person we all went into journalism to meet. I'm only really one of hundreds who was made better by his character and talents over many decades.

———————————

Over the years, the configurations of *The Wall Street Journal's* editing desks under the command of Cathy Panagoulias varied, as did the editing roles that Regis filled. Significantly, during her tenure as national editor, Regis was her deputy, sitting side-by-side and effectively serving as the paper's night editor.

It was a period of the globalization of many industries, as international trade, the internet, and the rise of China as the world's factory radically changed how companies and their stocks were viewed by investors. As such, Panagoulias and Regis — in coordination with John Bussey, the foreign editor — oversaw a great deal of the *Journal's* international dispatches.

After Regis died, Panagoulias wrote a letter to his daughter to share work-related anecdotes that Regis — who was of that generation of men who didn't talk about work at home — had never divulged.

[Regis] was a rock star ... The guy (and most editors were guys) who has your back, who types faster than you can think, who thinks more clearly than you about what you actually want to say, and helps you say it accurately and grammatically. He remembers what you wrote last time and puts in the relevant background this time. He catches when you don't know the difference between millions and billions; he saves you from looking like a fool all the while teaching you not to be one next time ...

Regis was the standards bearer. He knew the rules, and he enforced them. The years 1995-2000 were a time of explosive news. The stock market was booming as emerging technology killed some companies and created new ones. We demanded our reporters break news; we drilled into them that the most coveted news they could break involved mergers and acquisitions. When Giant Company A decided to take over Giant Company B, billions of dollars would change hands, and the newspaper that had that story first would remain a must-read for every Wall Street investor. News of these deals became known often late in the evening, when I had left for the day, and Regis was on duty.

Even when his fingerprints were all over an edited story, Regis never took a byline. Panagoulias recalled to Nora that her father presided over the merger mania that swept Wall Street in the mid-1990s and early 2000s. Among the largest deals that the *Journal* hustled to cover were Exxon's 1998 acquisition of Mobil, Pfizer's purchase of Warner-Lambert in 1999, and America Online's ingesting Time Warner in early 2000.

Superstar *Journal* reporters, members of the paper's "A" team of scoopmeisters, relied on Regis to have their backs and process their stories at warp speed when only minutes remained to get their late-evening scoops into the final editions of the paper.

Regis's cadre, Panagoulias wrote, included Steven Lipin, who broke innumerable exclusives covering M&A from 1995 to 2000; Jeff Cole, the dogged aerospace correspondent who once hid in the bushes outside a restaurant to snare an interview with the CEO of an airline in takeover talks; and John J. Keller, the telecom reporter who regularly demonstrated that he had AT&T's number when it came to snooping on the influential conglomerate and its competitors.

It was awesome to see Regis coordinate with these stars. I would joke that they were his Jedi knights ... and he was their King.

When Panagoulias first met Regis, he reminded her of the young Al Pacino.

Regis was always a sharp dresser whose voluminous head of jet-black hair, strong jawline, thin lips, and piercing dark eyes attested to his ancestral roots in Turin, Italy. At five-foot eight, Regis was an inch taller than Pacino but several stones lighter than the Academy Award-winning actor.

Regis met Jan Brandstrader, his wife-to-be, at Dow Jones. Both were hired in the early 1980s by Joe Guilfoyle, a venerable editor. Guilfoyle started at Dow Jones as a teenage messenger boy in the mid-1920s. After a distinguished reporting career at *The Wall Street Journal*, he became the managing editor of Dow Jones News Service, the real-time newswire nicknamed the "Ticker."

Brandstrader was hired to generate scripts for *Wall Street Journal Radio* and subsequently spent many years writing for the print edition of *Barron's*. Regis began on the Ticker and moved to the *Journal's* copy desk in 1982.

Guilfoyle's style and Regis's no-nonsense, tough-guy approach mirrored one another. In his 1986 book, *Worldly Power: The Making of The Wall Street Journal*, Edward E. Scharff described Guilfoyle's trademark persona.

Though now nearing sixty, Guilfoyle retained the air of a street fighter, and he terrified those who worked for him.

Regis, like Guilfoyle, was born to be a journalist. At three, using the comic sections of the city's newspapers, Regis taught himself to read. As a child, he was unbridled, as his wife detailed in a February 2021 well-turned email to the author.

Rich's education was punctuated with frequent trips to the principal's office. In fact, he had his own seat there, which meant when other kids showed up, the principal would make them move because Regis was a regular.

The only son of George Regis and Rose Cairo, young Regis grew up across the street from St. Columba's Church, a Roman Catholic parish on West 25th Street, and attended its elementary school.

To punish him for talking in class, the nun would make him sit with all of the girls in the back of the room. That only landed the girls in the principal's office with him.

George Regis, a stalwart New York native who earned his living making dice, let his son tag along as he frequented some of the city's most popular sports venues and bars. In September 1957, five-year-old Regis and his dad were among the 38,000 boxing fans packed into Yankee Stadium to watch the brutal 15-round bout between middleweights Sugar Ray Robinson and Carmen Basilio. Basilio won the match in a split decision.

The elder Regis introduced his son to his friend Jack Dempsey, the legendary heavyweight boxing champion (1919-1926), on one of the father-and-son's many visits to Toots Shor's, a restaurant, lounge, and celebrity haunt frequented by the likes of Mickey Mantle, Yogi Berra, Jackie Gleason, Don Ameche, and even Chief Justice Earl Warren of the U.S. Supreme Court.

Regis always had an ear and a love for music. At age 14, with the connivance of his music teacher and unbeknownst to his parents, the future journalist would occasionally play the saxophone at a strip club on 42nd Street. Regis spent many weekends in the late 1960s at the 2,654-seat Fillmore East, the so-called "Church of Rock and Roll." Located in the East Village, the venue featured performances by rock legends, including Jimi Hendrix, the Grateful Dead, Janis Joplin, The Who, and Santana.

His long-suffering mother once wailed to his father that "he is going to get mugged taking the subway home at all hours." Here is how his father comforted her: "What? Are you kidding? everyone on the train thinks he is the mugger."

Regis attended Hunter College of the City University of New York, tuition-free. Shortly after graduation, he went to work for *The Staten Island Register*, a now-defunct hyper-local weekly community newspaper. At the *Register*, he flourished, covering New York City politics and winning multiple awards for his reporting.

Ironically, Regis won recognition for his coverage of the long-term effects of Agent Orange on Vietnam veterans. The defoliant chemical, used to clear dense vegetation for military operations, claimed the health and lives — even decades later — of many of the U.S. military personnel who came into contact with the tactical herbicide during the war years.

To this day, first responders and others overrun by the clouds of World Trade Center dust and debris, like Regis, are dying from their 9/11 exposure.

Regis interviewing New York Governor Mario Cuomo for *The Staten Island Register*
(Photo courtesy of Steve Zaffarano)

Like John Bussey, *The Wall Street Journal* foreign editor who ran into the paper's head-quarters at 200 Liberty Street after the first plane hit the World Trade Center when almost everyone else was evacuating the building, Regis ran toward the *Journal's* head-quarters after the planes hit, thinking he would be needed.

He never actually made it inside.

Daily, Regis commuted by train and subway the 40 miles to Lower Manhattan from his home in Croton-on-Hudson, a village in Westchester County. A magnet for creatives, the 4.8-square-mile enclave, part of the town of Cortlandt, at one time was also the domicile of Alan Abelson, the acerbic *Barron's* editor and columnist; muckraking journalist Upton Sinclair, author of 1906's *The Jungle*; and Roger Kahn, who wrote the 1972 elegy to the Brooklyn Dodgers, *The Boys of Summer*.

On September 11, Regis got as far as the Brooklyn Bridge subway station before the trains stopped running, and he was forced to make his way on foot. He surfaced at 9:10 a.m., according to a precise timeline that Brandstrader subsequently reconstructed.

Regis saw the smoke shooting from the two towers and instinctively raced toward the office, knowing it would be a hectic day.

Normally, the brisk walk would have taken him 15 minutes or less. But as Regis proceeded down Broadway, he was slowed by the tide of pedestrians pushing toward him. He headed south, below the World Financial Center to dodge the crowds and the falling debris, and then U-turned north, back to the *Journal*'s headquarters. The area surrounding Trinity Church at Wall Street and Broadway, he thought, resembled a war zone.

When he finally arrived at the World Financial Center at 9:45 a.m., he was locked out.

Tough as he was, Regis was traumatized watching falling, burning people jump to their deaths. Brandstrader recounted her husband's experience in her timeline.

One woman's dress was on fire. She crashed through the awning at the Marriott. It took [him] a while to realize that the garbage on the street was bodies. A cameraman was sitting on the ground crying with his camera beside him.

Regis recalled that Dow Jones had an emergency policy that instructed all personnel, if ever evacuated, to gather on the esplanade to the south of the company's headquarters, located between 200 Liberty Street and the Hudson River. So he headed there.

The veteran desk editor must have been surprised when, breaking through the cacophony of noises, he heard voices calling out to him from the massive Gateway Plaza apartment complex nearby.

Gwendolyn "Wendy" Bounds, a *Journal* news editor, and Kathryn Kranhold, a reporter, shared a rental on the 10th floor of one of Gateway Plaza's towers. Their unit afforded a clear view of the Twin Towers.

Bounds was in the shower, and Kranhold was busy getting ready for work when the first plane struck. The noise didn't seem extraordinary to them. They assumed an upstairs neighbor had dropped something heavy.

Erle Norton, a former *Journal* reporter who lived in the same complex, only on a low floor of a different tower, phoned his two close friends and explained that a plane had crashed into the World Trade Center.

In signed affidavits, written in June 2003 to aid Regis's application for 9/11 survivor benefits, the two women recounted the events of that morning.

Bounds: We heard another roar over our heads as we watched on TV, the second plane flew in and hit.

Kranhold: At that point we grabbed our cell phones and reporters' note pads, fled down the stairwells, and went to Erle's second-floor apartment nearby.

Bounds: Within a few minutes one of us saw Richard Regis outside, walking away from the Trade Center and toward the river. We yelled for him to wait, and Kathryn, Erle and I joined him.

Kranhold: Our focus as we talked with Richard was two-fold: How to get away, and how to get out the story of the attack.

A few minutes after we had joined Richard, we heard an enormous roar as the first tower fell, and we all began fleeing south along the river.

Bounds: I heard a deep guttural noise that, in retrospect, I realize was the sound of the first tower collapsing. At the time I didn't know what it was. The air became thick and acrid with dust, smoke, ash, and debris. Visibility quickly dropped to a few feet.

Kranhold: I used the handrail along the Hudson River to make my way south. It was like being in a snowstorm of ash, and everyone was quickly covered in whitish soot. Richard was totally covered and looked light gray.

Bounds: Soon I saw Richard, still walking calmly to the south, head tucked down. I was having difficulty breathing through the thick dust and smoke, and he gave me a handkerchief and showed me how to tie it over my face.

Kranhold: It was a tremendous comfort to me that Richard was with us at that time. The scene was totally chaotic, and Richard's calm, no-nonsense approach to the unfolding tragedy was helpful that morning as people fled with their children and their pets in their arms.

At this point, roughly 10:10 a.m., *Wall Street Journal* editors and reporters were setting up shop where they could. Some were able to escape Manhattan for South Brunswick, where the paper was assembling an improvised newsroom. Others were working from their homes and apartments or gathering at the residences of colleagues. A few found workable facilities elsewhere.

Since none of them had heard from Paul Steiger, dread began to fall over the *Journal* diaspora — like a dark cloud gathering before a thunderstorm — that Steiger was dead or gravely injured.

Barney Calame, a deputy managing editor and one of Steiger's oldest and best friends, was one of the most concerned. He sent a hastily written email at 10:14 a.m. to Mike Miller, the paper's Page One editor, and other senior staff.

Mike, you should be seeing my email to steiger querying him as to where we should go. I can't raise him on his cell phone. pensiero amd steiger were the office when the planes hit, but i can't get either of them on the phone yet.

Before phone service went down, Steiger had agreed to meet his wife, Wendy Brandes, who worked nearby at Lehman Brothers, on the Hudson River esplanade.

In his 10th year leading the paper, Steiger stood his ground on the plaza outside the *Journal's* headquarters, hunting for members of his team and urging them to make their way across the Hudson to New Jersey. Amidst the confusion that arose when the South Tower fell, and unable to catch a water transport, Steiger headed south toward Battery Park while Brandes fled north.

That's when Steiger crossed paths with Regis, Bounds, Kranhold, and Norton. The group didn't remain together long. The latter three split off, leaving Regis and Steiger headed for the tip of Manhattan Island.

Beyond survival, Steiger's and Regis's goals diverged. Steiger was anxious to communicate with his wife and resume his command of the paper. Regis was laser-focused on locating Nora, then 15 years old, who attended Loyola School, a private Jesuit high school located at 83rd and Park Avenue.

Fulfillment arrived for both men in the form of a Metropolitan Transportation Authority bus, one of many which Mayor Giuliani conscripted to carry evacuees out of Lower Manhattan.

Given the crush of people testing the limits of the southern waterfront to contain all of them, Steiger was surprised by how few people joined him and Regis on the MTA bus. The driver made his way up the FDR Drive, then proceeded north on First Avenue, dropping Regis close to Nora's school and Steiger near his 86th Street apartment.

Matthew Bolton, then the dean of students at Loyola School, signed an affidavit attesting to what he witnessed, as had Bounds and Kranhold.

At approximately 11:30 am on September 11, 2001, Mr. Richard Regis entered Loyola School ... He looked strikingly different from how I remembered him. He was coated in what appeared to be white dust or powder. It covered his hair, face, and suit. His pupils were dilated and his skin looked ashen, which I do not believe was merely a function of his being covered in the dust. I recalled from my medical training that both of these symptoms are associated with the onset of shock.

Mr. Regis's demeanor reinforced my concerns about his going into shock. He seemed dazed and was not able to articulate clearly what he was doing at the school. I believe he said some-thing to the effect of "I'm Nora's father. I walked all the way here." He did not call me by name, and I could not be sure whether he knew that we were already acquainted. I asked him if he was all right. He seemed unsure of how to respond, and he may have said that he did not know if he was all right.

Bolton didn't want Nora to see her dad in his unsteady state and wondered if Regis had the capacity to get them both back to Croton-on-Hudson safely. The school administra-tor shuffled Regis off to a seat in a quiet, cool room. Regis said he hadn't had anything to eat or drink that day.

While most other parents picked up their children, Bolton held Nora back until her father — after resting, eating, and drinking — appeared more composed.

Regis did make it home and, true to his nature, was back on the job, working from South Brunswick, New Jersey, the next day.

———————————

There is a debate among journalism historians and scholars about the origins of the symbol "-30-" — signifying the end of a news story or feature. The colophon was ubiq-uitous in newsrooms for decades, especially when reporters still pecked out their articles on a typewriter.

Indeed, when Regis was first hired at the *Journal* in 1982, pencil-editing copy, many reporters — especially in the bureaus outside of New York — still crafted their stories on manual typewriters in triplicate, using carbon paper. After a bureau chief edited the articles, the stories would be handed to a typist who would punch them into a two-way telex and transmit them to New York for additional handling.

The mythology surrounding the "-30-" is rich. As the *American Journalism Review* noted in a 2007 feature, it possibly dated back to when journalists wrote their copy in longhand — X marking the end of a sentence, XX the conclusion of a paragraph, and XXX, the completion of the story. Because XXX in Roman numerals is 30, that *might* explain how the symbol came to be widely embraced.

Although almost certainly apocryphal, a more colorful theory is that "-30-" was adopted after a dedicated telegraph operator remained glued to his keyboard to transmit a breaking news story that stretched on and on. The hapless journeyman, his duty done, collapsed. When he did, by coincidence, he struck two keys on his teletype, dispatching the 3 and the 0.

———————————

Within days of his return to work, Regis's health began to deteriorate. He was hospital-ized with a severe case of vasculitis and subsequently suffered significant organ failures.

He was administered last rites on several occasions.

More than a year passed before Regis was able to return to *The Wall Street Journal*, during which time his former responsibilities were assigned to others. Those who knew Regis best recognized that he was not the same. Regis was given tasks that his superiors felt were less demanding but would hopefully allow him to keep his sense of purpose and dignity. He and Brandstrader knew, however, that effectively he had been demoted.

Regis's health never fully recovered. As time passed, he experienced a steady progression of ailments.

By late 2005, unable to navigate the walking required of a commuter, Brandstrader drove Regis to work daily.

No one could figure out why he was in such pain. We were just about to try extreme pain control measures such as nerve blocks and nerve ablation when we went to Dr. J. Robert Seebacher, who told us that his back was not the problem. The high-dose steroids administered to quell the autoimmune response post 9/11 resulted in significant osteoporosis. The diagnosis was aseptic necrosis of the hips.

Regis was hospitalized for a double hip replacement.

In 2015, his bones brittle, Regis was carrying dinner dishes upstairs when he fell backward from the fourth step up and broke his back in three different spots. Brandstrader tended to him for seven weeks at home.

I lost a dress size running up and down those stairs.

Regis, being Regis, pressed on.

Other *Wall Street Journal* reporters and editors had previously battled back from significant illness or injury. Most remarkably, perhaps, was John McWethy, who headed the paper's Midwest Bureau. In February 1971, he was in a serious car accident that left him a quadriplegic. McWethy, working from a specially equipped wheelchair and using prosthetic hands, returned eight months later and continued on the job for another six years.

But in the pantheon of no-quit, dedicated, convalescent *Journal* editors and reporters, Regis certainly earned a place of distinction and the admiration of his colleagues.

As October 2016 came to a close, Regis and Brandstrader weighed a buyout offer from Dow Jones.

... we have begun an extensive review of operations as part of a broader transformation program. There will be, unfortunately, an impact on the news department staff in this process. In order to limit the number of involuntary layoffs, we will be offering all news employees around the world — management and non-management — the option to elect to take an enhanced voluntary severance

benefit.... We are seeking a substantial number of employees to elect this benefit...

Gerard Baker
Editor in Chief

Brandstrader and Nora urged Regis to accept.

Regis had edited somewhere in the vicinity of 35,000 stories, groomed dozens — if not hundreds — of colleagues, worked for seven managing editors and five Page One editors.

Reluctantly, he agreed that it was time.

The company held no fancy going-away party. Regis and some of the others who had also accepted the buyout gathered with colleagues at Hurley's Saloon, a restaurant and bar located in Manhattan's theater district, and toasted to the next chapter in their lives.

Between taxes and medical bills, Regis's payout from Dow Jones didn't leave much of a retirement cushion. He went on disability and eventually Medicare. His monthly supplement amounted to less than $100.

In 2017, he and Brandstrader traveled to Europe, visiting London, Milan, Venice, Florence, Rome, and his ancestral home of Turin. Brandstrader planned their trips carefully to accommodate Regis's physical limitations. Notwithstanding, his health continued to deteriorate. In Florence, Regis spent nine days bedridden. In 2018, in Scandinavia, he required a wheelchair to get around.

At the end of May 2020, Regis began to exhibit alarming signs of illness. A lifelong wordsmith, he struggled to express himself. He had no appetite. Perhaps most telling of all, his hair, always well-coiffed, went untended.

With New York City experiencing more than 1,300 fresh coronavirus cases daily, Brandstrader had to settle for an initial telemed visit. COVID or not, the physician instructed her to bring him to the hospital.

Regis was admitted on the afternoon of June 1 and was intubated the next morning.

For all the time Regis had spent in hospitals and visiting doctors since September 11, no one had ever offered a convincing explanation as to why he suffered so many health complications, while the others who were with him that morning — including Paul Steiger, Wendy Bounds, and Kathryn Kranhold — coughed out the dust they had inhaled in short order and quickly recovered.

This time, the doctors determined that Regis had sepsis-related pneumonia. A physician found the infection was resting on small silicone tubing lodged deep in his airway.

On 9/11, without realizing it, Regis had aspirated remnants of the World Trade Center, each about the size of the crown of an adult tooth. Much, if not all, of his debilitating ailments over the years likely resulted from his immune system responding to the unseen foreign objects in his lungs.

Why the seeds of his nearly two-decade health nightmare were not discovered in the immediate wake of his 2001 bout with vasculitis or the dozens of ensuing medical examinations is a grim reminder that physicians are fallible, and something almost two decades later that Brandstader struggles to comprehend.

The doctors knew he had a spot on his lung, but since it never changed size, they didn't go in to see what it was. I am still in shock about this. •

That said, Nora Regis credits her father's physicians for pulling him back from the brink in 2001.

We did have 20 amazing years with him that seemed impossible when he was going through organ failure that first year. A very [large] part of his living so long has to do with his doctors.

Brandstrader and Nora were expecting Regis to be released on June 12. They had been unable to visit him during his hospitalization because of the pandemic restrictions.

Very early that morning, Regis repeatedly tried to phone his wife's cell phone, but she was asleep and missed his calls. When she finally picked up, he was unable to speak. During that call, the Brandstrader's landline rang. It was a physician from the hospital notifying her that Regis had had a setback and was back in the ICU, intubated, yet again.

Regis had not allowed the nurses or attendants to separate him from his cell phone. Although he could not speak, he wanted to be with his wife — even in silence. So Brandstrader stayed on the phone with her husband for two hours until she and Nora were able to arrive at the hospital.

Brandstrader and Nora had no explanation for his final setback. Perhaps age, and all the years of battling sickness, finally wore him down.

Nora remembers that they stayed with her dad for about an hour. And that was it.

We thought he was going to be released from the hospital into a rehabilitation facility. But instead, he died.

Regis only had about nine percent lung capacity shortly before he died. Doctors ascribed his severe COPD as stemming from his presence on September 11 and stated so on his death certificate. Nevertheless, Regis never received a cent of compensation from the 9/11 fund.

On June 13, the day after his passing, the 9/11 Responders Remembered Park — which on granite walls engraves the names of first responders who died of illnesses related to September 11 — paid tribute to Regis on its Facebook page.

Friends - Another Hero has passed!

The post went on to note that many people lost sight of the fact that journalists were not only at Ground Zero on 9/11 but also worked from Lower Manhattan for days, weeks, and months preparing follow-up stories.

On our wall in our park, there are a handful of these very brave men and women who put themselves at risk to tell the stories of those lost and those who were searching. For that, we mourn with Richard's wife Janet and his daughter, Nora....

Richard, sir, your journey is complete and you are now with God's Army of 9/11 angels, and you will be writing stories for an eternity!

The names on the memorial, which is located in Nesconset on Long Island, are not alphabetical. PAUL A MCMANAMAN FDNY • LT JOHN ROWLAND NYPD • JERRY D JOBE FBI • LOUIS J MASSA CONSTRUCTION • RICHARD REGIS WSJ • and more than 1,500 others.

As a journalist, Regis was never a sentimentalist. Many of those former colleagues who paid tribute to him noted in their Zoom eulogies that Regis would have edited out the more fawning parts of their remarks.

As for Regis, he sent his colleagues a farewell email when he retired in 2016. Such goodbyes, which are common at the *Journal*, are often laden with memories of career achievements, nods to mentors and colleagues, and details of what's on tap for the future.

Regis's email valediction was bare; how one would imagine he would have liked his obituary to read:

> *From "Regis, Richard"*
> *Date: December 15, 2016 at 6:08:15 PM EST*
> *To: WSJ ALL US*
> *Subject: -30-*

The body of the email was left blank.

• Chapter Eight •

Project 2002

For Rebecca Distler, September 12, 2001, promised to be an extra special day. Not only was the sixth-grader turning eleven years old, but she had just started at a new school.

Rebecca told her mom, Joanne Lipman, a senior editor at *The Wall Street Journal,* that she'd like refrigerator magnets for her locker.

Growing up in East Brunswick, New Jersey, Lipman was a serious student of the viola, playing in a string quartet and subsequently studying at the Yale School of Music. In one of Lipman's earliest front-page stories for the paper, published October 7, 1983, she wrote a humorous first-person account of spending a day as a street musician, playing in Times Square, in front of the New York Stock Exchange, and in the concourse of the World Trade Center.

The story's denouement was that Lipman earned more fiddling on a per-hour basis than she was making as a reporter.

Ten-year-old Rebecca was now the one taking violin lessons.

Before work on the morning of September 11, Lipman was browsing the aisles of the Lechters Housewares store located on the concourse of the World Trade Center. When she spotted a violin-shaped magnet, she knew it would be perfect for Rebecca. The novelty had a button in the middle that, when pushed, played a little tune. Lipman pressed it idly while waiting to check out.

I hope this will be a gentle reminder to Rebecca to practice for her violin lessons.

For good measure, Lipman also grabbed a magnet in the shape of a flip mobile phone.

It happened that on her way into Lechters that Tuesday morning, Lipman ran into Joe Dizney, the paper's design director and one of her best friends.

Before the day would end, they would both play key roles in producing the next day's edition of the *Journal* after its nearby newsroom was destroyed.

Lipman and Dizney had been meeting daily for the better part of the past year in a cloistered conference room at the paper's headquarters, where they were working on a top-secret restyling of the *Journal*, the first in 60 years. Each morning, he would stop by Lipman's office first thing, coffee and muffin in hand, and check in.

Dizney joined Lipman at the cash register. The two planned to walk together through the World Trade Center concourse and over one of the West Street pedestrian bridges to the World Financial Center.

As they waited to pay, they could hear a commotion coming from the corridor. The two witnessed a security guard shooing a crowd of people toward the Church Street exit on the east side of the Trade Center complex.

The Lechters cashier was concerned.

Everybody's running. Maybe we should get out of here.

Lipman pushed the two magnets forward.

Once again, the anxious cashier looked apprehensively toward the concourse.

We've got to leave.

Lipman was and is an exceptionally congenial individual, but she didn't rise to the upper echelons of the journalism profession without knowing how to stand her ground. All the more so when the cause was Rebecca's birthday.

Lipman rolled her eyes at the nervous cashier. After all, she and Dizney hadn't heard anything. The commuters being steered to the exits looked more annoyed than worried. She figured whatever it was, it was most likely a false alarm.

Ring this up first. I'm not leaving until I pay.

Lipman handed the cashier a $20 bill to cover the two five-dollar magnets. Adding in the 83 cents in sales tax, the cashier returned $9.17 and a receipt. It was time-stamped 8:55 a.m., nine minutes after American Airlines Flight #11 struck the North Tower, 90-plus floors above Lechters.

The cash register stub was one of the last, if not the very last, receipts to be generated in the World Trade Center complex before the concourse and everything above and in proximity to it was annihilated.

Lipman and Dizney surfaced on Church Street. Always elegant, Lipman, 40 years old, slender, and fit, was wearing a skirt suit and high heels.

When she'd entered the World Trade Center complex, it had been a picture-perfect, late-summer morning. Now it was snowing. In Lipman's 2013 biography of her childhood music teacher, *Strings Attached: One tough teacher and the gift of great expectations,"* co-authored with Melanie Kupchynsky, Lipman recounted the apocalyptic scene that she and Dizney encountered.

At least it looked like snow, as pulverized plaster drifted down from a brilliant blue sky, pinging metallically when the flakes hit the sunglasses perched on top of my head. Hundreds of papers — blank financial order forms — were wafting through the air. Above us was the unimaginable sight of the World Trade Center on fire, smoke billowing out of an ugly gash in the upper floors. In front of us, cars were pulled up at crazy angles on the sidewalk, abandoned. One was crushed by a giant chunk of concrete. There must have been sirens, and maybe there was shouting, but it was as if it were a dream: every sound was muffled and every action in slow motion.

The scene turned ghastly when Lipman and Dizney — trying to make their way to the office — turned onto Liberty Street, at the south end of the World Trade Center complex. Liberty Street ran east-west from Church Street to the West Side Highway and its pedestrian overpass to the World Financial Center tower housing the *Journal*'s newsroom.

On a typical day, walking from Church Street to the bridge took five minutes at best.

This day, however, would take infinitely longer, and the memories of what they witnessed would remain with them for a lifetime.

Everything on Liberty Street was aflame. Rows of burning airline seats were spread out in the middle of the road, along with what looked like a jet engine. Lipman and Dizney moved one block further south to Albany Street, which runs parallel to Liberty Street.

Human carnage, raw and red, was splattered thickly across the pavement and the sidewalks. We picked our way through an indescribable hell, our heads down, stepping gingerly and trying not to look at the gruesome vista spread out in front of us. When we reached the West Side Highway, across from our building, we swerved to avoid a headless corpse on the sidewalk that someone had inadequately covered with a restaurant napkin. Waiting at a red light, we stood next to a businessman with a head wound streaming blood onto his white shirt collar.

When the second plane, flying just overhead, hit the South Tower at 9:02 a.m., Lipman and Dizney were staggered.

The crash was like a sonic boom, a deep, deafening, cataclysmic eruption that went on and on, layer after sickening layer of destruction... Like everyone else there, I assumed I was about to die.

In September 2000, Joanne Lipman was promoted to deputy managing editor, sharing the title with Stephen Adler, Barney Calame, and Daniel Hertzberg. Her elevation made her the highest-ranking woman on the newsroom's organization chart and one of the few women in any senior newsroom position at the *Journal.*

When Paul Steiger, the managing editor, was away, it was Calame who was left in charge. Often, even when Steiger was on site but otherwise engaged, Calame ran the entire paper.

Every evening, one of the four deputy managing editors would be responsible for conducting a final review of the next day's edition before the presses began to roll.

As a teen, Lipman often would join her father, a business executive, on bus commutes from East Brunswick to Manhattan, reading his copy of *The Wall Street Journal* along the way. She took a liking to the paper, especially the quality writing on Page One, and set her mind to working for the paper someday.

It was my goal in life.

As a junior at Yale, Lipman interned for the *Journal*, which proceeded to hire her in New York shortly after her graduation in May 1983. Laurence G. "Larry" O'Donnell was the managing editor at the time. Shortly thereafter, Steiger returned to the paper as an assistant managing editor, working for Norman Pearlstine, who succeeded O'Donnell in September of that year.

Steiger, who also graduated from Yale, had been hired by the *Journal* in its San Francisco bureau in 1966. He left the business daily two years later to join the *Los Angeles Times*, where he distinguished himself. Steiger later became a D.C.-based economics and finance correspondent. He was serving as the *Times*'s financial editor when Pearlstine wooed him back to the *Journal.*

Steiger and Lipman, in time, would transform the paper in ways that it's unlikely either of them could have imagined in their first few years on the *Journal*'s staff.

Initially, Lipman was assigned to cover the insurance industry and real estate, neither of which was considered a prestigious beat. Nonetheless, she impressed Steiger with her ideas and writing skills.

Lipman broke from the pack in 1989 when Pearlstine and Steiger tapped her to create a regular advertising column, conceived in large part to draw readers and advertisers away from the rival *New York Times*.

The *Times*'s reign as the paper-of-record covering the advertising business was deeply entrenched, dating back more than 50 years. Beginning in October 1966, its stewardship fell to Philip H. Dougherty, who, writing a daily column, became a highly influential figure in the advertising world.

Dougherty's column was considered a must-read by Madison Avenue's cognoscenti. At his peak, he helped make or break the careers of key advertising executives. He also served as a semi-official barometer of the creative success, or lack thereof, of major advertising campaigns.

When Dougherty died in his sleep on September 27, 1988, at age 64, it left a void in the world of advertising journalism.

Lipman soon filled the vacuum.

Her four-day-a-week column was a departure from what Dougherty had done. An aggressive and well-sourced reporter, she was driven to break news. Rather quickly, Lipman won over Dougherty's influential readers and the lucrative advertisers that his column had attracted.

She became a *Journal* star, punctuated by her winning the prestigious John Hancock Financial Services Award for Excellence in Business and Financial Journalism.

Lipman's fast-track career almost derailed with the birth of her two children — Rebecca in September 1990 and Andrew in October 1992.

I was having a hard time being away from home. I would have quit if I could have afforded to, or gone part-time.

She shared her struggles with Steiger, who wasn't about to lose one of his most promising editors. He recalled his response, which not only kept her on the staff but led Lipman to much greater achievements at the paper and in her post-*Journal* endeavors.

I said, "No, Joanne, you're not going to quit. You're going to become an editor, and that will allow you to get control of your schedule."

Steiger reached out to John Brecher, his Page One editor. It was Brecher who led the team of elite journalists that had oversight of the three daily features that ran on the paper's front page: Two comprehensive stories, known in *Journal* jargon as "leders," that appeared in the right-hand and left-hand columns, and the so-called "A-hed," the quirky fourth-column story that mostly eschewed serious topics. (The "A-hed" was supposedly so named because, in the eyes of some, the stacked headlines that ran above the article had a passing resemblance to the capital letter A.)

John, have I got a deal for you. You're going to get Joanne Lipman. But there are a couple of provisos. She's going to work from home every Friday unless she has a story going for Monday, and you're going to be really sensitive to her needs to be doing childcare stuff and various other similar things, because you know she'll work from 10:00 at night to 3:00 in the morning if she has to [in order] to close the gap.

Brecher was delighted. He was already an admirer of Lipman's writing. Moreover, he and his wife, Dorothy Gaiter, who also worked for the *Journal*, had children of their own and could readily relate to Lipman's struggle to manage both kids and career.

Lipman remained on the Page One staff for five years, editing, and conceiving major news and feature stories. One series of articles that she nurtured, written by Ron Suskind about inner-city honor students in Washington, D.C., won the 1995 Pulitzer Prize for Feature Writing.

Steiger's admiration for Lipman continued to grow.

Joanne became one of the greatest editors we ever had.

The Wall Street Journal was published in a single section from its founding in July 1889 until it added a second section in June 1980. Beginning in 1988, the *Journal* expanded to three sections, Monday through Friday.

The first section delivered major corporate and economic news, as well as the Editorial and Op-Ed pages. The second section, dubbed *Marketplace*, encompassed news and features on careers, entrepreneurship, personal technology, law, health, and other matters directly affecting readers' working lives. The third section, *Money & Investing*, provided comprehensive content for both personal and professional investors.

The Friday editions of *Marketplace* featured weekend-oriented coverage, including an expanded personal finance column, a residential real estate page, and articles on sports and travel. The content was designed not merely to help readers navigate the "business of life" but also to attract more consumer-oriented advertisers.

In 1996, the *Journal* began planning a fourth section to appear on Fridays. The as-yet-unnamed addition ultimately became *Weekend Journal*. Steiger turned to Lipman to flesh out the concept and oversee the project.

At the time, the paper was heavily reliant on financial advertisers, technology ads, and corporate imaging messages. Although the dot-com bubble was generating plenty of ad lineage from investment banks and newly public companies, wiser heads at Dow Jones recognized the sensibility of broadening the paper's base of advertisers. Hence, *Weekend Journal* would focus on readers' passions, including entertainment, food and wine, cars, style, art, sports, and real estate.

On the day that *Weekend Journal* debuted, March 20, 1998, Lipman wrote a "Welcome" letter to readers.

In the 15 years I've been with the Journal -- as a real-estate reporter, creator of the Advertising column and a Page One editor -- I've watched the paper evolve along with our readers. The Journal has always been essential reading when it comes to daily business. Now we hope we can become just as essential in helping you manage your personal business.

Besides, I can't even count the number of times that I've heard, "The paper would be perfect, if you just added a sports page and a crossword puzzle."

Well, now you have both.

The immediate success of *Weekend Journal* accelerated Lipman's ascension as a star.

Roughly the same time that *Weekend Journal* went live, the senior executives at Dow Jones turned their attention to a much more ambitious project, a three-year, $232 million overhaul of the entire paper. The initiative involved the installation of new printing presses and related production facilities, designed to increase the daily page capacity of the *Journal* from 80 pages to 96 pages and to triple the number of pages containing color — including for the first time, on the front page — from eight to 24.

Dubbed "Project 2002," the plan was to roll out the "new" *Wall Street Journal* in April 2002, including the first redesign of the front page since 1941, and the addition of a new section, *Personal Journal*, to run each Tuesday, Wednesday, and Thursday.

Appointing Lipman to oversee the design elements of "Project 2002" and to develop the editorial vision for *Personal Journal* was an easy choice for Steiger and his bosses, following closely on her success with *Weekend Journal*.

Lipman assembled a tiny team to create the prototypes for the enhanced *Wall Street Journal* and *Personal Journal*. She looked to Dizney, and his key lieutenants, David Pybas and Dona Wong, to take the lead on the redesign. In addition, she retained the well-known newspaper and magazine designer, Mario R. Garcia, and one of his senior people, Ed Hashey, to assist.

Sequestering themselves in an 11th-floor conference space away from the main newsroom, only Lipman, Dizney, Steiger, and a couple of others had the special key card needed to unlock the room.

They jokingly referred to their workspace as the "Skunk Works," a reference to the secret R&D team at Lockheed Aircraft Corp. that during World War II, working from an odorous rented circus tent, rapidly developed a jet fighter for the United States.

So thorough were their efforts to keep their project under wraps that the Lipman team did not network their computers with those of their *Journal* colleagues, keeping all of their work strictly localized on their computer hard drives.

Lipman and Dizney considered and focus-group-tested various concepts, especially what the new front page might look like. As they pared the field, what emerged was a subtly fresh look, featuring color and including an update to the iconic "The Wall Street Journal." nameplate. Their new logo retained the superfluous period that has adorned the newspaper from its first day of publication and remains a fixture to this day. The iconic period makes no sense, of course, since "The Wall Street Journal" is not a declarative sentence requiring a punctuation mark.

[Design and grammatical historians note that many newspaper nameplates during the 1800s and a good chunk of the 1900s placed periods at the end of their titles, including *The New York Times*, which waited until a February 1967 redesign to put an end to its period.]

When Lipman began work on "Project 2002," the *Journal's* existing design relied on entrenched templates that provided virtually zero flexibility to accommodate variances. As Lipman discovered, even minor tweaks required a major effort.

Every little change was a completely different animal, even though to the naked eye, it looks like a very small change. [It was] the same as if you had torn out the whole thing and did it all over again.

Design reconfigurations also required adapting the content. One example was the paper's daily front-page "10 point" column. The decades-old feature provided a short summary and menu of the day's most important business and finance stories.

As part of Lipman and Dizney's new format, the six columns on the front page were each narrowed slightly, which meant that the copy editors who crafted the daily "10 point" would have fewer characters with which to brief subscribers.

To gauge reader preferences, Lipman and Dizney hosted three focus groups, the last of which they conducted in San Francisco the weekend before 9/11.

On their return to the office on Monday, September 10, Dizney recalled he and Lipman were upbeat.

We were feeling very proud of ourselves.

The walls of their small conference room were draped in page prototypes.

Reflecting on all the work the pair had put in and the many, many iterations they had developed, Dizney felt a foreboding that he couldn't explain.

For some reason, I wanted to back this stuff up, you know, just in case. I burned it to DVDs

— everything I had — and took the copies home.

The next morning, as Lipman and Dizney were picking their way through pools of blood and piles of ash, debris, and body parts, it did not immediately dawn on them that much of what they had labored on for more than a year remained locked away in their fortress-like conference space, offline, and now utterly inaccessible.

September 11 would prove a considerable setback to "Project 2002," but thanks to Dizney's sixth sense, at least the team wouldn't have to start again from scratch.

───────────

The thought kept running through Lipman's head.

I've got to get to the office. I've got to get to the office.

Lipman's and Dizney's recollections of their exact locations when the second plane hit and what transpired in the immediate aftermath differ.

According to Lipman's version, she and Dizney had navigated across the West Side Highway to the south side of 200 Liberty Street, where the building's parking garage entrance was located. When the second plane crashed into the South Tower, catty-corner to their position, Lipman recalled that instinct kicked in.

It was just primal. Everybody ran and flattened themselves against a building. It was not a conscious thing.

Dizney remembered it differently, placing the two of them still on the World Trade Center side of the West Street, where they braced against the 39-story Deutsche Bank Building.

Which version is correct is a distinction without a meaningful difference.

What they both agree on is that their subsequent attempt to return to the office proved fruitless because the *Journal's* building was already locked down. So the two joined a parade of others — including some of their colleagues — walking west toward the Hudson River promenade and then uptown past both blazing towers.

───────────

Joe Dizney and his wife, Jessie Woeltz, resided on the fourth floor of a nine-story, early 20th-century Greenwich Village apartment. Located on 6th Avenue near Washington Square Park, their home was roughly two miles from the World Financial Center.

Streams of pedestrians, some covered in soot, also were maneuvering to the Village and points north. Military helicopters circled overhead. Dizney watched as one chopper landed in a park. Soldiers in full camouflage carrying semi-automatic weapons jumped out. A woman on a bicycle pressed aggressively through the crowd against the flow, furiously ringing her bell for those walking to clear a path.

The air was choked with the stench of smoke and concrete dust. People were lined up at payphones by the dozens, hoping to reach their loved ones because most cell phones proved useless. On the streets, strangers huddled around vans and other vehicles, listening to radio news coverage of the terrorist attacks. It's how Lipman and Dizney first learned that the Pentagon also had been hit.

Lipman and Dizney made it safely to his apartment just as the South Tower fell.

Although telephone landlines continued to operate on September 11, the circuits were overwhelmed. Try as she might, Lipman was unable to reach her husband, Thomas Distler, an entertainment attorney, to let him know she was safe and uninjured.

He was convinced for that first hour-and-a-half or two hours that I was dead. He was sure because he saw what was going on and he couldn't reach me.

Somehow, Lipman managed to get a call through to her parents in New Jersey, and she implored them to contact her husband and alleviate his fright.

At Dizney's and Woeltz's apartment, Lipman was first able to monitor the rapid-fire exchange of emails that was taking place between the various dispersed *Journal* editors and reporters, many of whom were filing personal accounts of their travails as well as raw reports of interviews they had conducted with eyewitnesses and survivors.

Lipman wanted to get home, and she wanted to join her fellow deputy managing editors who were assembling at the Upper West Side apartment of Barney Calame, not far from her apartment on 87th and Broadway.

Fortunately for Lipman, she and Woeltz had similar shoe sizes, so Lipman borrowed a pair of sneakers and began the several-hour walk on her own from Greenwich Village to her apartment.

Lipman saved her debris-coated high heels as a remembrance, although she never wore them after September 11.

She also made sure that she wouldn't be caught flat-footed going forward.

After 9/11, everybody I knew went out and bought a pair of "fleeing sneakers" to keep in the office in case we ever had to flee again.

A screenshot from a YouTube video recorded by the National Press Foundation in early 2002. Shown are (l-r) Steve Adler, Joanne Lipman, Paul Steiger, Dan Hertzberg, and Barney Calame.
(Mike Miller, the Page One editor, is not in the frame.)

The video, titled "A Tribute To Paul Steiger," was filmed in Calame's dining room. It was a reunion of the six editors who gathered there on the afternoon of September 11 to help produce the next day's edition
(which is displayed on the table).

• Chapter Nine •

"If Not Today, When?"

For the record, Barney Calame maintains that he did *not* cry when his close friend and boss, Paul Steiger, finally contacted him by phone early in the afternoon of September 11. He does acknowledge that he was emotional.

I was really broken up. I was really worried. I was afraid he was dead because the last report had him outside the [Journal's offices] directing traffic. And now it was 1:30 or 2:00. And so the truth was, I was afraid he was dead.

Calame and Steiger traced their friendship back to 1967 when Calame worked in the Los Angeles bureau of *The Wall Street Journal* and Steiger, three years younger, was a 25-year-old cub reporter in the paper's San Francisco office.

The two met and periodically collaborated on stories when Steiger was loaned to Los Angeles as a temporary fill-in. Both men, who were the most junior members in the bureau, hit it off, as did their wives socially.

Calame and Steiger traveled different paths to *The Wall Street Journal* in New York and, as it were, to Calame's apartment on September 11. For many years, Calame and Steiger found themselves employed by competing newspapers.

Two years after joining *The Wall Street Journal*, Steiger left the paper for the *Los Angeles Times*. He spent a total of 15 years with the Southern California daily, including seven years covering economics in Washington, D.C.

Calame transferred from Los Angeles to Washington to cover labor, where he, Steiger, and their wives again saw each other socially.

From Washington, Calame did a stint in Pittsburgh as the *Journal's* bureau chief, and eventually returned to Los Angeles to run the bureau there.

When Steiger completed his time in D.C., he too returned to L.A. to become the *Times'* business editor.

Whether working for the same newspaper or competing dailies, the two men remained good friends. When Steiger was promoted to managing editor of the *Journal* in 1991, he asked Calame to be his deputy, the position Calame still held on September 11, 2001.

Calame and his wife, Kathryn, a professor of Microbiology and of Biochemistry & Molecular Biophysics at Columbia University's medical school, lived in a so-called "Classic Seven" apartment on the Upper West Side.

Their prewar unit consisted of a living room, a formal dining room connected to the kitchen through a glass-paned door, three bedrooms, two bathrooms, and a maid's room and bath just off the kitchen that he used as a home office.

As the attacks on the World Trade Center evolved, Calame's goal was to find Steiger and drive a group of editors in his car over the George Washington Bridge into New Jersey and make their way south to the *Journal's* administrative offices in South Brunswick. He knew that South Brunswick was the fallback facility that had been designated for just such an emergency, and emails he monitored that morning from his colleagues made it clear that Steiger — before he went missing — was encouraging everyone who could get to South Brunswick to do so.

A couple of other *Journal* staffers who lived nearby met up at Calame's apartment and planned to catch a ride with him.

At 11:45 a.m., Calame emailed the paper's senior staff, subject line "Getting Organized."

I'm at home in Manhattan and haven't had contact with Steiger, Pensiero, or Hertzberg. Bill Godfrey says Pensiero is enroute to SB. Here's what I do know:

We are setting up a newsroom in S.B. Building Three. If you can get there safely, please go.

Editors in Manhattan who can't get to SB because of closed bridges and tunnels should plan to work remotely until transportation works....

Please don't send any reporters into the area south of Canal until we know it's safe to report there.

More info as soon as possible.

The Calame apartment was reasonably well-suited to serve as a satellite "office," given the limits of remote technology at the time. His unit was spacious. His shiny mahogany dining room table was easily converted to a workstation capable of accommodating his colleagues and their work sprawl. He had a laptop and a desktop computer, an inkjet printer, two phone lines, a functioning BlackBerry for sending and receiving text messages, and a decent internet connection.

The early arrivals at his apartment included his fellow deputy managing editors, Steve Adler and Dan Hertzberg, and Page One editor, Mike Miller. They'd be joined a bit later by Joanne Lipman, who first stopped at home to hug her husband and children, whom Distler had picked up from school.

The four men were in frequent contact with Jim Pensiero and the other senior staffers who were setting up the makeshift newsroom in South Brunswick; Marcus Brauchli, the national news editor, who was coordinating coverage from his home in Brooklyn; and Alan Murray, the D.C. chief whose team was responsible for much of the front-page content and major inside stories.

When the phone rang, just past 2:00 p.m., it seemed as if everyone froze.

Hello?

It's Paul.

Paul?

Paul Steiger.

We thought you're lost. I thought you might be dead.

Well, I'm not lost.

At least that's how Steiger recollected the beginning of his phone conversation with Calame. Then, according to Steiger's version, which he later recounted to *The New York Times* and others, Calame broke into sobs.

Steiger very well could have been crushed by the World Trade Center fallout or taken seriously ill from the lungs-full of nasty smoke that he inhaled. He escaped the conflagration covered from head to toe in soot. Sound in body, he had witnessed death and carnage that he still wishes he could unsee but never will.

Unbowed, Steiger made it to his Upper East Side apartment that day and was now checking in, ready to resume command of his widely dispersed crew of reporters, editors, designers, and production staff.

The George Washington Bridge had closed to traffic. The surface streets in Upper

Manhattan were gridlocked with vehicles trying unsuccessfully to escape the city, so Steiger vetoed any attempt he and his fellow editors might have made to drive to South Brunswick. Instead, he declared, they would work from Calame's apartment.

After a shower and a change of clothing, Steiger hailed a cab and arrived at Calame's apartment. Originally, Calame planned to drive to the East Side to retrieve Steiger.

But I crashed our car in the gridlock on Central Park West, parked it, and walked back to our apartment for the rest of the evening.

The senior newsroom managers of *The Wall Street Journal*, each of whose name appeared daily on the paper's masthead (except for Mike Miller), was now laboring on the most critical news day of their careers not from their well-appointed 9th-floor, state-of-the-art offices in Lower Manhattan, but from a dining room, featuring floral wallpaper, an antique rug, potted plants, and a wall shelf displaying some of Kathryn Calame's antique plates and glassware.

Those who could fit, at times, squeezed into the maid's quarters — teeming with shelved file folders and back editions of the *Journal* — to read Calame's desktop computer screen over his shoulders or sit at the keyboard to correspond with their remote colleagues.

In truth, there was only so much the six editors could accomplish. Had it been a regular weekday, at best, they would have been only peripherally involved in putting out the September 12 edition, leaving most decisions and tasks to the hands-on teams that functioned perfectly well without their direct involvement.

By the time the Calame apartment brain trust convened and was fully engaged, roughly 2:30 p.m., many of the most important decisions had already been made by the triumvirate of Jim Pensiero, Marcus Brauchli, and Alan Murray, and their assignments were well along the way to being completed.

Everyone in the *Journal* universe was greatly relieved that Steiger had risen from the presumed dead. His reappearance was a rare piece of good news on an otherwise dismal, emotional day.

Steiger, Calame, Lipman, Adler, Hertzberg, and Miller fielded whatever questions came their way and reached out to various editors and others to offer their help. Calame's son, Jon, made a pizza run, keeping the six well-fueled.

Steiger was in particularly close contact with the South Brunswick contingent because the team there had the responsibility for editing, laying out, and getting the content to the printer.

Steiger was insistent that the paper use a six-column front-page headline. There was one big problem, however. The *Journal's* tightly designed front-page template had no elasticity to accommodate his desired two-line, all-caps headline running from left-to-right across the entire top of the first page.

Indeed, multiple editors in South Brunswick pleaded with Steiger to drop the headline idea. They were short-staffed as it was, and no one there felt comfortable trying to redesign the classic *Wall Street Journal* front page on the fly.

Steiger was unmoved.

If we're not going to put a banner headline on the paper today, when are we going to do it

Joe Dizney, circa 2002
(Courtesy of Joe Dizney)

Enter Joe Dizney. He had stayed behind in his Greenwich Village apartment when Lipman pushed on.

Years later, he would be formally diagnosed with post-traumatic stress disorder dating back to that morning. At the moment, he was glued, almost hypnotically, to his sofa, staring at the endless loop of television coverage of the two towers' collapse.

It eventually dawned on Dizney that his building had an unobstructed view of the Trade Towers site from its rooftop, so he made his way up and absorbed the grim scene.

Downtown is just such a mess. I have to do something.

Trying to reconstruct his actions almost two decades later, Dizney was unsure whether the idea of walking to the paper's Midtown advertising offices to lend a hand was entirely his, or whether someone, perhaps Jim Pensiero in South Brunswick, had requested that he go.

The advertising office, a four-minute walk from Times Square, was at 1155 Avenue of the Americas, near the corner of 44th Street. It was located on the fifth floor of the 41-story, granite-clad high-rise above the distinctive, hexagonal street entrance to PINK, the upscale shirtmaker and retailer.

Dizney was familiar with the office and some of the *Journal* ad executives who worked there. He first began with the paper as a freelancer and helped design some of its special Monday sections from the facility.

While the editors in South Brunswick had been resistant, when Steiger put the request to Dizney to prepare an instant template to accommodate a six-column headline, the veteran design director was sanguine.

Sure. No problem.

Dizney was fluent in the *Journal*'s typography. He served as the lead designer of the paper's *Weekend Journal* and was, as noted, deeply immersed in the "Project 2002" makeover of the entire paper and the planned introduction of the *Personal Journal* section.

Among the challenges he faced when rejiggering the front page to make room for a two-line, six-column headline was lowering the tops of the actual columns and discarding the uninterrupted top-to-bottom "silos" that normally confined each column.

The September 12 front page broke the mold. It contained six separate stories, two beginning below the fold; the two-column *What's News* menu; a special two-column box at the bottom of *What's News* indexing the 9/11-related stories that appeared inside the paper; and a small box at the bottom of the fourth column, letting subscribers know that delivery of their papers might be delayed, but the entire September 12 edition would be available for free at *WSJ.com*. The front page also ran a two-column infographic illustrating where the hijacked planes originated and where they crashed.

Dizney commandeered a standard Apple Macintosh computer from the ad sales office. He booted up QuarkXPress and rapidly created a couple of iterations for Steiger and the cohort at Calame's apartment to review. Steiger was pleased.

I looked at it, and it was great.

Dizney, perhaps overly modestly, says the instant redesign was a snap.

His new template served as a roadmap for the editors and layout personnel in South Brunswick. Once he faxed them the design and included specs such as the correct point size and spacing, it was a breeze to use.

The only remaining challenge was deciding what the six-column headline should say and ensuring that the phrasing fit the allotted space. That duty fell to the sextet of editors gathered at Calame's apartment.

The five men and Lipman realized they were crafting the heading not only for the next day's edition but also for posterity.

Just shy of 60 years earlier, Barney Kilgore and William H. Grimes, then the *Journal's* two top editors, wrestled with a similar decision: What to declare in the *Journal's* front-page, six-column headline on the day after Pearl Harbor.

Kilgore and Grimes used a three-line, all-caps banner, with a heavy focus on the business and financial ramifications.

> *U.S. Industry's Sole Objective: Arms Production Speedup;*
> *Congress Prepares To Act; Tax Bill Will Be Rushed;*
> *N.Y. Stock Exchange To Open As Usual Today, Says Schram*

[The identity of the page designer who in December 1941 stepped up for Kilgore and Grimes has been lost to time.]

Steiger, who has always struggled to accept credit for most of his accomplishments without sharing it with one or more colleagues, attributes the September 12 headline to all six editors. They settled on a hard-news approach, foregoing any allusion to the probable business and financial consequences.

I participated in writing the headline. But nearly everybody in that room and maybe somebody in South Brunswick had a hand in that headline. I think we each wrote one word.

Maybe. Maybe not.

News accounts from 2001 and 2002, when memories were fresher, credit Steiger alone as the final arbiter of the headline's wording.

Three days after the 9/11 attacks, *The New York Times* published a story by Felicity Barringer, its media reporter, describing the role that Steiger and the others at Calame's apartment played in producing the *Journal's* September 12 edition.

And it was there that they wrote and rewrote the headline, finally agreeing on "Terrorists Destroy World Trade Center; Hit Pentagon in Raid With Hijacked Jets" — Mr. Steiger's version.

Steiger himself, as quoted in 2002's *running toward DANGER*, bared his role.

I said I wanted a six-column headline on Page One, which we very rarely do. We wrote the head. I don't remember what it said. They humored me and said they liked mine the best, so that's the one we went with.

———————————

Putting the day in perspective was complicated for the senior editors gathered at Calame's apartment. Given what they had personally witnessed and experienced, it was especially difficult for Steiger and Lipman.

On the one hand, September 11 was undoubtedly the most emotionally wrenching day of their professional careers and perhaps of their lives.

But it was also one of the most rewarding. They had done what great journalists are meant to do. They set aside personal considerations and overcame enormous obstacles to pull together a quality newspaper that shouldn't have been possible under the circumstances.

Thanks to adrenaline, and in Steiger's case, plenty of Diet Coke, they found the clarity and energy to complete their tasks.

It was after 11:00 p.m., and the presses at the paper's 17 print plants were rolling when Lipman bid her colleagues adieu and made her way home.

Before retiring, she wrapped all the gifts she had purchased for Rebecca's 11th birthday, including the two magnets she bought at Lechters. And then, exhausted though she was, she baked her daughter a birthday cake.

———————————

• Chapter Ten •

"Where Have You Been?" She Meowed

If cats could talk, one can only imagine what 14-year-old Stoli might have said on the morning of Wednesday, September 12, when her roommates Gwendolyn "Wendy" Bounds and Kathryn Kranhold finally returned to their Gateway Plaza apartment to retrieve her.

Would the feline have berated Bounds and Kranhold for leaving her behind in their darkened 10th-floor unit that shook with thunderous noises and reeked of smoke and embers? Or, would Stoli have thanked them for using their journalistic pluck to evade the numerous barriers and the security personnel who labored to keep residents such as Bounds and Kranhold from returning to the immediate vicinity of the smoldering remains of the World Trade Center towers?

Bounds and Kranhold were a subset of a subset of New York-based *Wall Street Journal* reporters and editors. Only a fraction of the *Journal*'s newsroom staff had arrived at the office on the morning of September 11 or was in the immediate vicinity before the terrorist attacks. Within that group, a much smaller slice of employees lived within a short walk of the *Journal*'s World Financial Center headquarters. Without warning, this group of journalists found themselves in exile from both their workplace and their homes.

Bounds had just turned 30. She joined the *Journal* in 1993 out of the University of North Carolina at Chapel Hill, where she served as editor-in-chief of the journalism school's magazine, *The UNC Journalist*.

From early on, *Journal* editors admired Bounds for her skill at recognizing and writing great stories. For example, post-9/11, her do-it-yourself features about the home improvement projects that she undertook caused Larry Rout, one of her editors, to quip:

She's not only a great reporter; she can put up drywall and install a whole new floor for you.

On September 11, 2000, a year-to-the-day before the World Trade Center attacks, Bounds co-authored a farewell to the Broadway musical "Cats," which was ending its record-setting run after 7,400 performances.

Bounds, who first attended a performance of "Cats" on the night of her 14th birthday, saw it eight more times, including the play's final curtain call at the Winter Garden Theatre.

Five-foot ten, with big chocolate-brown eyes, a sparkly broad smile, and shoulder-length buttery blond hair blended with honey highlights, Bounds was telegenically attractive. Indeed, later in her career, she would serve as host of *WSJ.com*'s daily streaming video news and features program, *Lunch Break*, as well as become a regular on-air contributor to *ABC News* and *Good Morning America*.

The daughter of a North Carolina veterinarian, Bounds first worked for the *Journal* from its Pittsburgh bureau. She joined Joanne Lipman's *Weekend Journal* team in the early summer of 1999. She was working for Lipman in September 2001, editing pages for the early prototype of *Personal Journal*, scheduled to debut in April 2002.

Bounds and Kranhold had been a couple for two years. Kranhold, a dozen years older than her partner, joined the *Journal* in August 1996 after spending a decade reporting for *The Hartford Courant*. Kranhold was Nordic in appearance. She had soft, ice-blue eyes and a friendly dimpled smile. Her hair was medium-brown and featured blond highlights. She stood shoulder-to-shoulder with Bounds.

For much of 2000, Kranhold focused her reporting on the high-profile antitrust trial of the world's two largest auction houses, Sotheby's and Christie's.

Two days after the terrorist attacks, Kranhold and Bounds would detail their post-9/11 rescue mission of Stoli in *The Wall Street Journal*.

Bounds would also include a fuller version of the story in her 2005 book, *Little Chapel on the River*. The nonfiction book — profiling a country store and Irish pub in New York's Hudson River Valley — was an outgrowth of her search for a place to live after her Gateway Plaza apartment was wrecked.

As noted in Chapter Seven of this section, Bounds, Kranhold, and their friend and former *Wall Street Journal* reporter Erle Norton ran into Richard Regis and Paul Steiger, but then parted company and headed south, still largely unaware of the extraordinary chain of events that was taking place.

Believing that she'd be home in time for dinner and to care for Stoli, Bounds had evacuated wearing open-toed black sandals. Kranhold left her glasses behind, with no precedent to inform her that her eyeglasses would have been much easier to clean than the contacts she was wearing.

Like Jon Hilsenrath, the *Journal* economics reporter who was staggered by the scores of abandoned shoes he witnessed along the West Street bike path, Bounds and her two companions were struck by the abandoned baby carriages that littered the waterfront pathway running from Gateway Plaza to Battery Park.

Another image that remained fixed in Bounds's memory was of businessmen, in boxer underwear, scurrying past while carrying their briefcases tucked under an arm. Apparently, these executives were in such a hurry to escape with their paperwork that they didn't take the time to put on trousers.

The collapse of the first tower left Bounds disoriented, as she wrote in her book.

I am suddenly alone several hundred feet down the river. Did I run? I must have run.

Bounds had reached the very edge of Lower Manhattan when the second tower crumbled.

Aircraft storm low overhead, and not knowing they are our own military, the noise is terrible. I start to step over the railing, ready to face the Hudson River rather than whatever that noise brings. Kathryn grabs my arm and pulls me back.

The chaotic scene was similar to Phil Kuntz's encounter outside the nearby American Park restaurant, with desperate people setting aside the niceties of everyday life and doing what they felt they must do to survive.

Bounds looked on as the panicked mob overtook the cart of a food vendor, grabbing water to wash their eyes and drinks to clear the ash in their throats. When the cart owner tried to collect money for the items, he was thrown to the ground by a burly man wearing an NYSE smock.

You do not charge anyone for anything.

A moment later, Bounds slipped into the crowd and purloined a bottle of lemonade.

Out of necessity, good journalists develop a "can-do" attitude, or perhaps more accurately stated, a "will-do" attitude that carries over to their personal lives.

It's what caused Joanne Lipman to insist that she pay for the refrigerator magnets she had selected for her daughter's birthday before leaving the Lechters Housewares store at the World Trade Center. It's what drove Philip J. Connors to feel his way in the dark along the subway tracks between the Franklin Street and Chambers Street MTA stations in his quest to reach the *Journal*'s newsroom. And it was what inspired Bounds and Kranhold, breathing through their shirts and a handkerchief, to find an egress from the increasingly crowded and shambolic commotion they found themselves facing, pressed against the seawall at the tip of Manhattan Island.

The most obvious escape route would have been to join the masses funneling into the underpass leading east from West Street to the FDR Drive. But the prospect of being stuck, or worse — buried underground — caused them to veto that path.

Then, as Bounds recapped in *Little Chapel on the River*, she, Kranhold, and Norton spotted a food vendor pulling away in a silver truck.

Quickly, we scramble over road barricades, dodging the barefoot mothers clutching their children, filthy businessmen tapping fruitlessly on their cell phones....

It is Erle who knocks on the locked passenger door.

"Can we please have a ride with you?" he yells into the closed window. The driver hesitates. All around him, people are fleeing. He does not want his truck overrun.

"Please, sir," Erle pleads. "There are only three of us."

The driver, George Apergis, relented. He unlocked his door and, with the wave of a hand, beckoned the three journalists to hop aboard quickly. While they were getting settled amid still-hot stove burners, Apergis rolled over a median and, briefly driving off-road, made his way onto the FDR Drive.

On the highway, the food truck crawled forward, closely surrounded by pedestrians headed uptown.

With Apergis's consent, the three journalists took to handing out Gatorade, Pepsi, and bottled water to those walking alongside the food truck. For Bounds, it was an emotional salve.

We are glad for the task, for the sense of purpose it offers.

Apergis wouldn't accept payment for the drinks, even though some of the pedestrians offered it. He was one of the thousands of ordinary heroes who stepped up on September 11 for no reason other than the goodness of their hearts.

It took an hour for the food truck to travel to the Upper East Side — roughly seven miles north — where Apergis dropped off his hitchhikers. Grateful, Bounds credited him both in her first-person *Journal* article on September 14 and in her book three years later.

Newly homeless, Bounds and Kranhold needed a place to shower, eat, sleep, and file their story notes, not necessarily in that order. (At the time, Norton was East Coast managing editor of CNBC/MSN Money.)

Bounds recalled that the three of them were near *Journal* editor Laura Landro's apartment, so they tried there first. But the doorman informed them that Landro was away.

We were like, where will we go?

Then they remembered that they were also near another colleague's home, Sally Beatty, who lived in a 73rd Street apartment between Second and Third Avenue. So they walked there.

I can't even imagine what her doorman must have thought when we were there and called up to her. And she opened the door. I can't remember whether she started crying or not, but she was just so happy to see us.

Beatty's second-floor unit in the 10-story prewar building proved a comfortable shelter from the day's storm. But even as they settled in that evening, dining on seared tuna and consuming more than a few glasses of wine, Bounds, Kranhold, and Norton knew in the back of their minds that the following day they would be returning to the war zone.

Early on the morning of September 11, one-and-a-half-year-old Anne Beatty's eyes were fixed on the television and *Sesame Street*. Anne particularly liked Elmo, the furry red Muppet with a falsetto voice who always referred to himself in the third person and whose trademark laugh — *Uh-ha-ha-ha-hee-hee* — helped sell a ton of Tickle Me Elmo plush toys.

Anne's mom, Sally, welcomed Elmo's presence as she rushed to get ready for work at *The Wall Street Journal*, where she covered the television industry for the paper's *Media & Marketing* section. Ordinarily, Beatty's husband, Bill, would tend to Anne in the morning until their nanny arrived.

But on this day, Bill was in Miami, so Elmo and *Sesame Street* owned the television screen instead of Beatty's regular CNBC morning programs.

Beatty was already running a few minutes late when Bill phoned from Miami.

Hey, you need to turn on the television.

Elmo yielded to CNBC anchor Mark Haines and live video showing smoke rippling from the North Tower.

Soon after, Beatty recognized the voice of her colleague John Bussey, the *Journal's* foreign editor, who was on the 9th floor of the paper's newsroom just across the street from the World Trade Center. Bussey was providing live audio updates for CNBC of what he was witnessing.

Anybody who's interested in seeing this, I would advise staying far from the building. This is still ... large pieces of debris, huge chunks of metal falling down. And these pieces of metal are smashing against, nearby these fire trucks. So this is kind of a disaster that's still unfolding. Steer clear of the place.

Beatty heeded Bussey's warning.

That's when I realized, okay, so no one's going into work.

Like virtually every other displaced *Journal* staffer that morning, Beatty did what she could to contact her editors — or whichever editor she was able to reach — and determine the game plan for the day.

She phoned Lisa Vickery, a deputy editor in the *Media & Marketing* section. Beatty didn't report directly to Vickery, but the editor was someone who always seemed to know what to do when no one knew what to do.

Beatty and her *Media & Marketing* colleagues were instructed to reach out to the companies they covered to determine how the terrorist attacks impacted them.

Beatty interviewed Erik Sorenson, president of MSNBC, and Brian Lewis, a spokesman for Fox News. She also touched base with a spokeswoman for CNN, which had replaced regularly scheduled programming on its two sister channels, TBS and TNT, with wall-to-wall coverage of the attacks.

———————

Sally Beatty referred to Martin Peers, a colleague of hers in the *Media & Marketing* group, as her "office husband" because the two of them were great friends even though they were nothing alike.

He's kind of grumpy and serious. I'm a little less grumpy and less serious.

Concerned about Peers, who she knew commuted daily from New Jersey, and fearing he might be stuck somewhere on the subway, Beatty emailed her friend on his BlackBerry, encouraging him to work from her apartment.

She was correct in her hunch that Peers had been underground when the planes struck the World Trade Center.

After an early breakfast that morning at a Central Park South restaurant with John J. Sie, CEO of Starz Encore Group, Peers caught a subway to Times Square, where he intended to transfer to the West Side lines. His train wasn't moving, so he shifted to a different line that started to operate. It quickly came to an hour-long standstill, advanced once more, then quit in the vicinity of Houston Street.

I remember that somebody came on and made this announcement. "There's nothing left for you downtown. We're going to get you off."

Metropolitan Transportation Authority personnel ran planks between a series of head-to-tail subway trains, allowing Peers and his fellow passengers to reach the nearest station and return to street level. He found himself surrounded by police blockades, having no firm grasp of what had transpired.

Peers approached one police officer and identified himself as a journalist.

I have to go down to my office.

The cop replied with the same spine-chilling message that Peers had heard on the subway.

What are you talking about? There's nothing left.

Peers was standing in front of the Federal District Court at 40 Centre Street (Foley Square) along with a pack of onlookers who were frozen in their tracks, staring southwest at the rising pillars of smoke where the World Trade Center had stood less than an hour earlier.

A [second] cop came up and shouted: "They've hit the Pentagon and Pittsburgh and the Trade Towers. You're standing next to two federal buildings... Move away from here!"

Peers took Beatty up on her earlier offer and made his way to her Upper East Side apartment, arriving at about the same time as Bounds, Kranhold, and Norton. At 2:56 that afternoon, pecking out a short memo of what he had witnessed on his BlackBerry, Peers transmitted it to the *Journal*'s news editors.

From Beatty's apartment, Bounds and Kranhold phoned their parents in North Carolina and California, respectively.

The two uprooted women encamped in the bedroom — pale yellow, with a pretty pink and yellow bedspread — of young Anne Beatty to file their accounts to the *Journal*. Bounds and Kranhold also crashed in Anne's room overnight, while Norton slept in a small spare room.

In her book, Bounds described her and Kranhold's mindset that evening.

Today and tomorrow are all we think about. It does not occur to us to wonder where we will go after that.

Wendy Bounds and Kathryn Kranhold had no specific plan of action when they set out on Wednesday morning, September 12, to retrieve Stoli, assuming she had survived the previous 24 hours alone in their apartment, as unpleasant as the experience might have been. The two women stopped at a nearby store to pick up candles and dust masks.

Norton joined Bounds and Kranhold as far as Pier 40 on the West Side. There, he waited along with other displaced residents to see whether crews of volunteers and veterinarians who ventured into Lower Manhattan to search for pets would return with Stoli and his two cats.

Bounds and Kranhold walked on, prepared to effect a rescue of their own.

There was no guile to explain how they were dressed. When they had retreated to Beatty's apartment the afternoon before, they brought along only the ash-and-smoke-saturated clothes on their backs. So they procured clean oversized white shirts from the wardrobe of Beatty's husband and sported the masks they bought that morning dangling from their necks.

A sizable area in the neighborhood of the World Trade Center site had been cordoned off to civilian vehicles and pedestrians, preventing even people who lived within the perimeter from returning home.

Bounds and Kranhold did what they could to circumnavigate the police lines and National Guard troops patrolling the area. Then, as they recounted in their September 14 *Journal* article, when they were about a mile-and-a-half from their Gateway Plaza complex, several reporters, assuming — based on their dress — that they were medics, tried to interview the two.

We decided disguise might be our way in.

Bounds and Kranhold proceeded to march past the barricades unquestioned and soon found themselves in the midst of what they described as a village of survivors, consisting of residents of area apartments not in direct proximity to the World Trade Center complex who had been permitted to stay.

We pushed east, going downtown, nodding to other masked civilians toting suitcases and pets as they made their way along the street uptown. When officers asked, we showed them Kathryn's driver's license, which showed we live in the area. After an hour or so of walking, ... we were almost home.

Near the entrance to their building, Bounds spotted a chunk of a human finger in the rubble and quit looking down. Posted on the entrance doors was a sign that read, "Building Closed."

Kranhold lit a candle in the darkened lobby, but the two journalists had to feel their way along the walls leading to the stairwell because the glow wasn't sufficient to penetrate the intense blackness.

As we climb the stairs, we can look straight into neighbors' ash-cloaked apartments. Our bare hands are covered in the soot, and our skin begins to burn. We call out, "Hello!" on several floors, but the only answer we hear is the rumble of excavation outside the building. Within 20 minutes, another piece of the World Trade Center will collapse nearby. Again, we will be lucky and escape. For now, we keep climbing in the dark.

When Bounds and Kranhold reached their floor, they observed that multiple doors had been busted open, either by the concussion that followed the Trade Towers' collapse or by firefighters looking for survivors. Their hearts sank when they arrived at their door, and it, too, was ajar. Would their day's daring and risky escapade be for naught?

We step inside. And there, in the middle of the living room floor sits Stoli, a black-and-white cat now covered in soot. She looks up at us as if to say, "Where have you been?" And she meows.

———————————

The Gateway Plaza tower where Bounds and Kranhold lived had sustained extensive damage, more so than other towers in the vast residential complex. Their unit, which faced north directly towards the ruins of the World Trade Center, was blanketed with ash and soot.

Neither journalist would ever again reside in that apartment.

Before ascending the stairs to their own apartment, Bounds and Kranhold, like two cat burglars, had climbed through an open window into their friend Erle Norton's unit — accessible from the sidewalk — to rescue his cats. They deposited his pets in carriers they found in his apartment. The women temporarily left Norton's cats with a cooperative National Guardsman who they spotted making the rounds, while they proceeded up the darkened stairwell to search for Stoli.

Along with Stoli, the two women collected a few items — family photos, passports, a change of clothes, and their laptop computers — then got out.

No one who eyed Bounds and Kranhold in the wake of their successful rescue mission could have mistaken them for veteran *Wall Street Journal* reporters.

Back on the street, Bounds and Kranhold nabbed an abandoned grocery cart and placed the pet carriers in it. The two journalists proceeded to push Stoli and Norton's cats through Chinatown, headed toward the posh environs of the Upper East Side.

On an ordinary day, we would have been a ludicrous sight — two bedraggled blondes, reeking of smoke, trash and sweat, pushing three cats in a grocery cart through the streets of Manhattan.

But on this day, we are unremarkable.

———————————

Bernard "Barney" Kilgore became managing editor of *The Wall Street Journal* in 1941
(Photo courtesy of Dow Jones & Company)

• Chapter Eleven •

September 11 Didn't Happen in a Day

The 9/11 Commission Report found that Khalid Sheikh Mohammed (KSM), the principal architect of the September 11 attacks, first proposed the concept of weaponizing passenger planes to target landmark American structures during a meeting with Osama bin Laden in Tora Bora, Afghanistan, in mid-1996.

KSM knew that the successful staging of such an attack would require personnel, money, and logistical support that only an extensive and well-funded organization like al Qaeda could provide.

It took until late 1998 or early 1999 for bin Laden to approve the 9/11 operation and its planning to begin in earnest.

The preparation followed the nearly simultaneous truck bombings of the American embassies in Nairobi, Kenya, and Dar es Salaam, Tanzania. On Friday, August 7, 1998, those attacks killed 224 people, including 12 Americans, and wounded more than 4,000 others.

Osama bin Laden's name first surfaced in *The Wall Street Journal* on the Monday following the embassy bombings. At the time, no one at the paper could have foreseen just how entwined their future, his, and KSM's would become.

The *Journal* was late to call attention to bin Laden, the Saudi Arabia-born scion of a construction magnate. *The New York Times* first made mention of him, spelling his first name "Ussama," in April 1994.

On June 25, 1996, at about 9:30 p.m., the Khobar Towers housing complex in Saudi Arabia was truck-bombed. The explosion killed 19 members of the U.S. Air Force's

4404th Wing (Provisional) and wounded almost 500 U.S. and international military members and civilians.

At the time, no direct link to bin Laden and the Khobar Towers strike had been established. Nevertheless, Youssef M. Ibrahim, himself a former *Journal* reporter, wrote about bin Laden in a July 11, 1996, *Times* article headlined, "Saudi Exile Warns More Attacks Are Planned."

The skeleton of the Khobar Towers housing complex following the June 1996 truck bombing
(Photo courtesy of the U.S. Air Force)

Ibrahim cited an interview with bin Laden, published in *The Independent*, a British daily, in which bin Laden repeatedly hinted that such attacks would recur.

The *Journal* followed its initial news coverage of the 1998 embassy bombing two weeks later with a front-page story detailing retaliatory missile strikes ordered by President Bill Clinton. The President tied the attacks to bin Laden and said there was "compelling evidence" that bin Laden's network was planning further attacks against American facilities overseas, perhaps involving chemical weapons.

The *Journal*'s August 2, 1998, feature was written by Carla Anne Robbins and Thomas E. Ricks, with additional reporting by Robert S. Greenberger and Jeanne Cummings — all in Washington — and Daniel Pearl in London.

Robbins and Ricks would win the 2000 Pulitzer Prize for National Reporting as part of a *Journal* team that reported on defense spending and military deployment in the post-Cold War era. On September 11, 2001, and in the days that followed, Robbins was a pivotal contributor to the *Journal's* coverage from its D.C. bureau.

Likewise, Cummings, who watched politics and the White House, and Greenberger, a veteran State Department reporter, wrote extensively on topics related to the 9/11 terror attacks.

Beginning in mid-September 2001, Pearl, the paper's South Asia bureau chief, spent a great deal of time in Pakistan examining the role of bin Laden, the Taliban, and other critical players in the region.

Pearl was in Karachi walking to what he thought would be an interview at a local restaurant on January 23, 2002, when Pakistani militants kidnapped him. Eight days later, he was beheaded.

The blow hit many of Pearl's *Wall Street Journal* colleagues as hard, if not harder than the 9/11 attacks themselves. "Danny" was a victim they all knew, admired, and cherished.

Whether or not Khalid Sheikh Mohammed actually wielded the butchering knife that decapitated Pearl — and there is substantial evidence that he did — KSM later claimed "credit" during a March 2007 military hearing at Guantánamo.

I decapitated with my blessed right hand the head of the American Jew, Daniel Pearl, in the city of Karachi, Pakistan.

If there is a newspaper in heaven, Barney Kilgore is likely its managing editor.

In February 1941, sixteen years before Osama bin Laden was born, Bernard "Barney" Kilgore, a 32-year-old Indiana native, was appointed managing editor of *The Wall Street Journal*. At the time, he took charge of a failing, 33,000-circulation trade newspaper that had blown much of its credibility by being a pro-markets cheerleader during the Great Depression. The *Journal's* annual profits were a meager $200,000.

Kilgore died in November 1967, at age 59. But before he passed, he reinvented the paper. Kilgore broadened the *Journal's* definition of business news, established proprietary technology and a satellite network that allowed the *Journal* to reach next-morning readers nationwide, and — most importantly — instilled a work ethic and set of professional tenets that earned the paper a respected seat alongside *The New York Times*, *The Washington Post*, and the nation's other highly regarded news organizations.

One anecdote about Kilgore's exacting standards that lives on to this day surrounds a memo he posted on the bulletin board of the newsroom one floor below his office.

The next time I see "upcoming" in the paper, I will be downcoming and someone will be outgoing.

Peter Kann, who would become CEO of Dow Jones decades after Kilgore's death, attended high school in the late 1950s in Princeton, New Jersey. During his summers, he worked for the local weekly newspaper, the *Princeton Packet*, mostly, he has said, writing about bowling scores and picking up newsstand returns.

One day, on his own initiative, Kann borrowed a camera from the Packet and photographed the squalid living conditions of the seasonal migrant workers who tended the fields surrounding prosperous Princeton. His accompanying story caused a stir among outraged farmers, who bitterly complained and threatened to sue the paper for libel.

In his memoir, *A Journalists' Journey*, written primarily for family and friends, Kann recounted the paper's response.

The newspaper was proud of a story that had rattled the conscience of a smug community. And the owner of the Packet, a man named Barney Kilgore, even complimented me on it.

Mr. Kilgore, I belatedly discovered, was also the publisher of The Wall Street Journal. The Packet was a hometown hobby for him and he would show up on occasion in his black limousine, roll up his sleeves and help to set type.

Other than Kann, it's almost certain that none of the core group of journalists and executives working for Dow Jones on September 11 had ever met Kilgore. Yet Kilgore's presence and that of his chosen lieutenants and their successors were keenly felt.

Kilgore & Company were editorial ghosts, urging calm, coaxing reporters and editors to keep their focus on readers — not themselves, reassuring the staff that they *would* manage to go to press that evening, and reminding everyone that getting the facts correct was of paramount importance.

As Paul Steiger wrote in his January 2002 letter nominating the *Journal*'s 9/11 coverage for the Pulitzer Prize for Breaking News Reporting, more than 100 of the paper's editors and reporters strictly adhered to Kilgore's canons:

From the perspective of several months later, breaking-news stories in the September 12 Wall Street Journal are notable for the strength of their details, the clarity of their deadline writing and the discipline with which they confront uncertainty—by publishing no facts of which the reporters and editors aren't sure and reaching no conclusions that the known facts don't justify.

What appeared to the rest of the world as an overnight miracle — the frazzled, disorganized, and dispossessed journalists of *The Wall Street Journal* — rising above all impediments to produce the next morning's paper — was, in fact, a phenomenon six decades or more in the making.

While there were a few misfires along the way, the line of newsroom leadership from Kilgore to Steiger consisted of editors steeped in the Kilgore ethos, each of whom built upon the foundations laid by their predecessors.

Wendy Brandes and Paul Steiger on their wedding day
(Photo courtesy of wendybrandes.com)

• Chapter Twelve •

Magical Thinking

Had Paul Steiger been killed by smoke or crashing debris on 9/11, it would have been a body blow to *The Wall Street Journal* and a profound loss to the journalism profession. Steiger was and remains greatly admired, even beloved. More than a few editors and reporters at the *Journal*, then and now, attribute their career success to him.

However, it is fair to say that in the wake of Steiger's hypothetical demise, readers of the September 12 edition of the *Journal* would hardly have noticed a difference.

That is to Steiger's credit.

Steiger was the architect of the newsroom culture as it existed on September 11. It was a culture that encouraged individual initiative and rewarded risk-taking, even when the gambles sometimes ended poorly.

Moreover, during his tenure in the managing editor's office, which ultimately lasted 16 years until mid-2007, Steiger was the one who made the decisive personnel choices that built what has come to be regarded by many observers as the greatest iteration of *The Wall Street Journal* — before or since.

It was Steiger who anointed Alan Murray to succeed the inimitable Albert R. "Al" Hunt Jr., as D.C. bureau chief.

Steiger selected Marcus Brauchli, who was little known outside of Asian journalism circles, to become national news editor in New York, bringing a more international perspective and an overdue comfort with digital journalism to the job.

Steiger placed his confidence in Jim Pensiero to handle the most important administrative duties of the managing editor's office, including understanding the technology that was necessary to produce the paper daily and which proved to be essential knowledge on September 11.

Directly or indirectly, Steiger hired, promoted, and inspired almost every journalist who played a pivotal role on September 11. Even many of the non-journalists who made the September 12 edition possible, from computer engineers to printing plant operators and circulation managers, at one time or another had reason to work with Steiger and came to respect him.

Steiger's management style was to put qualified people in place, share his broad vision for excellence, and then leave it to them to make the moment-by-moment, day-by-day choices that were required.

He would praise often and publicly while rebuking in private as infrequently as possible. Reporters and editors wanted to win Steiger's approbation. Their reverence for their boss was not cultish, but it was common for those faced with pressing strategic decisions to wonder, "What would Paul do?"

One of the most noteworthy aspects of *The Wall Street Journal*'s response on September 11 was that reporters and editors — cut off from their newsroom and frequently unable to contact their supervisors — set about reporting and editing for a next-day edition of the paper that they weren't at all certain would ever be published.

That was the invisible hand of Steiger at work.

His observable roles on September 11 were less prominent.

Before the Twin Towers collapsed and then again after he resurfaced as Barney Calame's Upper West Side apartment, Steiger collaborated with Calame, Pensiero, Murray, Lipman, and others in making deployment and last-minute editorial decisions.

Steiger closely monitored the *Journal*'s composition and production efforts on the night of 9/11. And, of course, it was he who ordered up the six-column headline that ran at the top of the next day's newspaper. That headline remains one of this century's most iconic newspaper front-page banners.

Steiger's efforts on 9/11 were recognized in 2002 by the American Society of News Editors, which presented him with the organization's first-ever leadership award.

In a tribute video posted to YouTube by the National Press Foundation, Steiger's colleagues offered a chorus of praise.

———————————

Steve Adler, deputy managing editor: You can't become a great leader in a day. You can't say, "Okay, on September 11, Paul led us through this." Yes, he did. But as everybody else has said, the pieces have to be in place. And over time, he's really just created a truly outstanding staff.

Barney Calame, deputy managing editor: He set a tone with just being very calm, very deliberate.

Mike Miller, Page One editor: ...when the rubber meets the road and the copy starts flowing, and we start doing our job, his leadership has, you know, set the stage so beautifully that we can be extremely effective and collaborative.

Peter Kann, chairman and CEO of Dow Jones: [His leadership on 9/11] doesn't surprise me because he's done it for years and years.

Kann's point was especially valid. Steiger was a veteran of plenty of newsroom dogfights, facing innumerable tight deadlines in the battle to produce consequential stories. Moreover, unmentioned by his colleagues was the fact that some of Steiger's toughest skirmishes coincided, quite inconveniently, with personal health or family crises.

Still, no prior career challenge approached the level of adversity that September 11 presented.

The attacks on the World Trade Center and the Pentagon were by far the biggest story of Steiger's career, and he was responsible for ensuring that the paper's first draft of history was one that would stand the test of time.

Forget the fact that he narrowly escaped death. Forget that to his abiding regret, he couldn't avoid witnessing the Twin Towers' jumpers.

The most harrowing aspect of Steiger's day was that for a large chunk of it, he lost contact with his colleagues and acquaintances. He didn't know who or how many of them had made it out alive. Among those he could not account for was his bride, Wendy Brandes, 33, whom he married less than two months earlier.

Wendy Brandes was a vice president with Lehman Brothers Holdings, overseeing the investment bank's internal and external websites.

She began her career as a journalist after graduating from Columbia University, where she had been the Arts & Entertainment editor of the *Columbia Spectator*. She hoped to find work in that niche of the profession, but the only opening she could identify that would pay her enough to continue living in Manhattan was in financial journalism.

Brandes signed on at Dow Jones News Service, the "Ticker," and quickly distinguished herself. By the age of 24, she was given responsibility for overseeing the news desk in the afternoon. Despite an unwritten (and oft-ignored) rule stipulating that *The Wall Street Journal* would not hire staff from its newswire sibling, Brandes moved to the print edition's copy desk and, subsequently, its news desk. She became one of the youngest news editors in the paper's history.

Steiger had nothing to do with hiring Brandes and only had passing encounters with her in the newsroom, enough to notice that she was bright and attractive. He was married at the time and didn't view Brandes as anything but a colleague.

At a company Christmas party, Steiger and Brandes were casually chatting along with others when someone mentioned the poet and author, Geoffrey Chaucer, who in the late 14th century wrote *The Canterbury Tales*, a staple of high school and university English literature courses.

Drawing on his secondary education at the private Hun School in Princeton and his college classes at Yale, Steiger almost reflexively began reciting, in old English, the first line from *The Prologue to the Canterbury Tales*.

Whan that Aprille with his shoures soote the droghte
[When April with its sweet-smelling showers has pierced the drought]

To which Brandes immediately chimed in.

of Marche hath perced to the roote, and bathed every veyne in swich
[of March to the root, and bathed every vein in such (liquid)]

Steiger was duly impressed.

Brandes scored points with him again in April 1994, when Kurt Cobain, the frontman of the rock band Nirvana, was found dead from a self-inflicted shotgun wound. Members of the *Journal*'s national news desk engaged in a brief debate of whether or not to "kill" Cobain, the paper's rather distasteful jargon that referred to the short obituaries it ran at the bottom of the front page's "Worldwide" column.

The more senior news desk editors said they'd never heard of the musician and didn't think his death merited a mention. Brandes argued for inclusion and Steiger agreed.

We would not have done it if Wendy hadn't spoken up.

Steiger liked the fact that Brandes showed self-confidence and could be feisty when the occasion warranted.

Brandes left the *Journal* for CNN after her career stalled, and she later worked as the managing editor of *People.com*, from where she joined Lehman Brothers.

Steiger and his wife, Heidi, a stock brokerage firm executive, divorced. Not long after, he began to look at Brandes in a different light — perhaps, just maybe, the next Mrs. Steiger.

Their courtship evolved slowly, over years.

Brandes gave him little encouragement. She even wrote him a tasteful "Dear John" letter, pointing out, among other obstacles, that he is 25 years her senior.

But finding hope in the letter, where she intended none, Steiger felt that Brandes hadn't entirely closed the door on him.

The two exchanged holiday cards and met now and then for a friendly meal.

It was Brandes's 20-pound Pekingese rescue dog, Mr. Chubbs, who, oddly enough, rescued Steiger's romantic standing with Brandes.

On Valentine's Day 1998, Brandes had a date with a lawyer, roughly her age. It didn't go well.

Apparently not a dog lover, the lawyer mocked Mr. Chubbs, who had just been to the groomer and returned adorned with two small Scottish tartan bows on his head. Brandes's suitor, as Steiger later shared, called them "faggy ribbons."

Coincidentally, the next day Steiger dropped by to visit Brandes, and like the prospective beau the day before, was greeted by Mr. Chubbs. The canine came trotting out into the hallway.

Steiger is triumphant in recalling what happened next.

I stifled a grin. I got down on one knee and shook Mr. Chubbs's paw and said, "My, Mr. Chubbs, you look mighty debonair this evening."

Wendy and I have been together ever since.

Like Dow Jones & Company, Lehman Brothers maintained its global headquarters in the World Financial Center; only Lehman Brothers' tower — known as Three World Financial Center — was located at 200 Vesey Street, one long block north of the building that housed the newspaper publisher. Both offices were situated directly across the street from the World Trade Center.

On a typical workday, Brandes and Steiger — who she affectionately refers to on her blog as "MrB" — could walk via a long, marbled corridor to each other's lobbies, each passing the complex's distinctive Grand Staircase and glass-domed Winter Garden Pavilion roughly midway.

With radiant brown eyes, youthful bangs, and an infectious smile seldom unadorned with bright red lipstick, Brandes was always fashionable. On 9/11, she wore gray Katayone Adeli pants, a black-ribbed, sleeveless turtleneck top, and black Stuart Weitzman shoes, which she described as banker-boring.

Brandes was already at work in her interior 10th-floor office when the first plane hit.

I heard these tremendous, tremendous metallic sounds. I couldn't imagine what it was.

Steiger, whose office was about as distant from the World Trade Center as anyone in the Dow Jones building could be — was glued to his computer, oblivious to the deafening impact of the first plane hitting the North Tower.

It was Brandes who called to alert him.

Brandes: *What was that explosion?*

Steiger: *What explosion?*

Brandes: *The one that shook this whole building! I think you better go look out the window and get back to me.*

Steiger rushed across the entire length of the 9th-floor newsroom to the eastside windows facing the World Trade Center and, witnessing the upper floors of the North Tower aflame, immediately began making plans and issuing instructions to the few coworkers who were also gawking at the inferno.

On their next call, before most phones in the area stopped working, Steiger and Brandes agreed to meet outdoors at the yacht basin along the Hudson River, just west of the Winter Garden. But by the time the two had evacuated their respective offices, the situation on the ground didn't permit any such rendezvous. Security personnel forced Brandes to head north while falling debris and the encroaching cloud of smoke compelled Steiger to flee to the south.

Although unable to reach her husband by phone, Brandes wouldn't allow herself to consider the possibility that he hadn't made it to safety.

I just had this kind of magical thinking going on. I'm like, "I'm fine. So probably Paul is fine, too." I was telling myself calming things as long as I could. I refused to believe that anything could happen to Paul.

Steiger was in Battery Park, already caked in dust and debris, his cell phone inoperable, when the North Tower collapsed. His mind was racing, as he recounted in the 2002 book, *running toward DANGER.*

I'm now kind of desperate. I want to find out about Wendy... want to connect with our people to make sure nobody's been seriously hurt. I want to be sure we can put out a paper.

His wife was having a less traumatic experience.

Brandes was in email contact with a colleague of hers in London, who cautioned that more hijacked planes could be headed for Manhattan. He strongly encouraged her to get away from the area.

On his advice, even before the Lehman Brothers building was officially evacuated, Brandes corralled two of her coworkers and began the trek north.

Her prompt exit from 200 Vesey allowed her to escape the tornadoes of dust and smoke that enshrouded her husband.

While Brandes was making her way up the West Side Highway, her London colleague texted her on her BlackBerry to say the Pentagon had also been attacked. She replied, wondering why he would make light about such a thing.

Don't joke with me right now. I'm having a bad fucking day.

Ultimately, she and her companions found their way to Kevin Roche's apartment, near Gramercy Park, about a two-and-a-half-mile walk. They sheltered there. Roche was a *Journal* desk editor and a friend.

I kept saying out loud to anyone who was around me, "I'm sure Paul is fine. I'm fine. I'm sure Paul is fine."

Throughout it all, Brandes maintained her poise. But her magical thinking didn't extend to one of her employees, Randi Serin, a website editor, who she had tried, unsuccessfully, to locate before leaving the Lehman Brothers' offices.

I had darted back and forth between my office and ... Randi's desk several times, but I didn't see her. I called her extension and got no answer. I thought she might have left ahead of me, so I went to the lobby to meet my other people, but I kept worrying.

Brandes and her companions reached Roche's apartment shortly after the South Tower fell. They arrived equipped with a six-pack of beer, an overstuffed sandwich for one of Brandes's colleagues — who always seemed ready to eat — and a Cadbury Dairy Milk chocolate bar for the svelte Brandes.

Brandes left a trail of voice messages for Steiger so he'd know how and where to reach her when he was able to access a working phone. It took until he returned to their Upper East Side apartment, just before 1:00 p.m., for the two to connect. She was the first person he reached out to.

I was wildly relieved to hear from Paul. And he asked me how I was. And I tried to say I'm fine.

Instead, she burst into tears.

I don't know where Randi is.

Steiger had not yet showered or changed clothes. The city evacuation bus that he and Rich Regis, the senior news desk editor, rode from Battery Park dropped Steiger off about a block from his apartment on 86th Street.

When he stepped off the bus, it was a different world. The pedestrians in the East 80s seemed oblivious to the bedlam taking place only six miles to the south.

I am covered with this white powder, and nobody's making eye contact because, you know, the way New Yorkers are: "You want to have white powder on. Fine, you have white powder on. But don't ask me to make eye contact with you."

Brandes told her husband that she wanted to try contacting Randi Serin at her home, but her colleague's phone number was unlisted.

Steiger didn't realize that so many of his *Journal* colleagues feared he was dead. If he had, he would have called one or more of them before helping Brandes find Serin.

Instead, Steiger dialed a Bell Atlantic operator and asked, then demanded, that she put him through to Serin's unlisted number.

This is an emergency. I'm the editor of The Wall Street Journal. And, you know, you've got to put me through.

The operator complied. It was an exceptional day, after all.

Steiger didn't speak to Serin, but she had left an updated answering machine message for concerned callers, letting them know that she was safe.

With that crisis resolved, Steiger called Calame and reassured his long-time friend that he was still breathing and would soon arrive at Calame's Upper West Side apartment to resume command of the *Journal's* news operations.

———————

The next morning, short of sleep but freshly showered and in a clean business suit, Steiger prepared to head out from his apartment for South Brunswick. Brandes asked how she might be helpful.

On the floor, near the entrance, sat Steiger's black leather briefcase, which he had clung to throughout the day before like many escaping parents had clutched their infants. As best as she can recall, Brandes had bought it for him at Barney's, the iconic New York luxury department store. The attaché case was covered in dust and ash.

Maybe you can clean that for me?

The valise reeked, a sorrowful souvenir of the World Trade Center. Even Mr. Chubbs, ever curious, seemed to be avoiding the bag.

The briefcase was surprisingly heavy. Brandes carried it over to a trash can and shook it upside down. Chunks of rubble poured out while dust and ash flew up in her face. It was shocking. A day after her husband, she was now the one coughing out remnants of the World Trade Center.

Brandes and Steiger wouldn't see much of each other in the weeks that followed. He spent most days, and many nights, in South Brunswick, overseeing the scattered *Wall Street Journal* news operations from there and camping overnight in a nearby hotel.

Putting out the September 12 edition of the *Journal* was an incredible achievement, one history will likely remember him for ahead of his many other illustrious career accomplishments.

But as a time-worn journalism trope teasingly asks self-satisfied staffers: "What have you done for me lately?"

There was another edition of *The Wall Street Journal* for Steiger to shepherd on Thursday, September 13. And on Friday, the 14th, and Monday, the 17th, and so on, and so on.

———————

Section Three:
September Twelfth

• Chapter One •

Messenger of Sympathy and Love

Across America, metropolitan newspaper subscribers took it more or less for granted that early each morning, they could step outside the door of their home or apartment and find their local morning paper at their doorsteps, in their lobbies, or tossed nearby on their lawns or driveways.

By 2001, paperboys and papergirls were relegated mainly to the realm of nostalgia, their routes now usurped by professional services or adults using their personal vehicles to moonlight by the shimmer of dawn.

New York City, on the other hand, was an entirely different beast. Whether you subscribed to *The New York Times*, the *Daily News*, the *New York Post,* or *The Wall Street Journal,* your newspaper owed its presence at your home, office, and even your favorite newsstand to the 1,600-member Newspaper and Mail Deliverers Union (NMDU).

The NMDU had a lock on all bulk newspaper deliveries to the five boroughs of New York City. Its role was to bring bundles of newspapers from the printing plants to wholesale distributors in the city. The distributors, in turn, circulated the bundles to large clients, such as hotels and newsstands, and to so-called "last-mile" delivery services, which deposited the papers in the lobbies of apartments and condominiums, on the door landings of brownstones, and, where they still existed, to single-family residences.

NMDU was organized on October 29, 1901, in the days when newspapers were carted by horse and buggy to their destinations, many of which were soapboxes set up on busy street corners. Over the decades, NMDU leaders came to be known — and frequently disdained — by newspaper publishers for their tough but effective negotiating stances.

Journalist Robert D. McFadden profiled the NMDU in *The New York Times* in a November 1990 feature.

Along the way, the drivers' union ... has mounted strikes and slowdowns and tolerated violence and intimidation to prod and sometimes cripple employers in its fight for wages, benefits and job security for members who bundle and truck most of the region's newspapers and magazines.

The union's history is tainted with corruption that sent some of its leaders to jail, with father-son nepotism that kept black and Hispanic drivers out of its ranks for decades, and with unswerving self-interest that has sometimes engendered mistrust by fellow unions and, critics say, may even have speeded the death of some ailing newspapers.

One notable father-son duo was Douglas and Glenn LaChance. Douglas, the father, served as president of NMDU from 1976 to 1980, until he resigned to begin a prison term after being convicted on more than 100 counts of extortion and racketeering. He served 55 months. Douglas was again elected president in 1991 and stayed in that position until 1993. He died in September 2011, at age 69.

Glenn LaChance, born in 1963, followed in his father's footsteps, driving for NMDU, delivering *The Wall Street Journal,* rising to become a union heavyweight, and having multiple scraps with law enforcement.

According to a 2001 article by Tom Robbins in the *Village Voice,* in 1988, Glenn and another man used the butt end of a broken pool cue to beat a 61-year-old *New York Times* delivery driver senseless after the victim made the mistake of arguing loudly with Douglas LaChance on the plant floor.

Glenn LaChance did nine months in jail for that attack. He served a separate three-month sentence for his 1993 attack on Peter Trombina, a 60-year-old driver who had openly opposed his father. Witnesses said that after exchanging words with Trombina, Glenn LaChance sucker punched the older man, breaking his glasses.

"If Glenn's guilty of anything, it's of loving his father too much," says [Douglas] LaChance, who insists his son took the rap for someone else in the pool cue incident.

The father and son added to their reputation by getting arrested together in 1997 for beating a man they had argued with in a bar near Doug LaChance's home in East Rockaway. The charges were dismissed after the victim dropped his complaint.

Being a tough guy was virtually a prerequisite for NMDU drivers, as Robbins wrote.

Newspaper deliverymen were always a tough crowd. Publishers wanted them that way. To get the edge on competitors in the rough-and-tumble circulation wars of the early 20th century, newspaper tycoons recruited the nastiest thugs they could find to steal rivals' papers and generally disrupt distribution.

Robbins quoted Douglas LaChance concerning a two-century-old ocean-side hotel in East Hampton, New York, that the union boss owned. In February 1978, the hotel burned under suspicious circumstances.

The police asked if I had enemies. I said, "Try the Manhattan phone book."

The newspaper that New York City subscribers to the *Journal* ordinarily received each weekday morning was printed the night before at the plant located at Dow Jones's South Brunswick campus.

While the presses there began rolling more than an hour later than usual on the night of September 11, the process pretty much followed the standard script. Darrell Foster, who worked for Dow Jones since 1982, had only recently arrived in South Brunswick, having been based previously in the company's Orlando plant. He was responsible for overseeing the entire printing plant production and packaging, as well as relations with various related unions, including NMDU.

Newspapers destined for the five boroughs of New York and limited locations in New Jersey and Pennsylvania, were tied in 42-pound, union-sanctioned bundles. Near the end of the production assembly lines, adhesive white address labels were affixed to those copies of the paper that would eventually wind up in the homes and offices of individual subscribers.

Dow Jones owned 14 delivery trucks, but union rules prevented the publisher from actually delivering the papers to subscribers and resellers. Instead, the printed bundles were loaded onto the company's trucks, which were driven by non-union contractors to a depot located on Staten Island. From there, Dow Jones employees, who were members of NMDU, took the drivers' seats and drove the trucks to their wholesale drop-off locations.

Jack Newman, a third-generation newspaper deliveryman, reported to Foster in South Brunswick. He was a member of NMDU and Dow Jones's New York delivery foreman, like his father, Jack Sr., had been before him.

Jack Jr. joined Dow Jones in the late 1970s after dropping out of college. On 9/11, he was stationed at the Staten Island drop point. His job, along with two assistants, was to make sure his 14 drivers showed up on time, were ready to work, and complied with their NMDU obligations.

Two men who Newman knew well perished on 9/11; a cousin, who was a firefighter, and Kevin Conroy, a friend since grammar school and the best man at Jack Jr.'s 1981 marriage to his wife of 20 years, Valerie.

For all the gumption that reporters, editors, compositors, printers, and others demonstrated on September 11 to produce the next day's paper, like it or not, the *Journal* needed LaChance, Newman, and the NMDU to distribute the September 12 edition.

Delivering papers to New York's five boroughs was never an easy task. It required long and often chilly overnight shifts beginning between 9:00 p.m. and midnight, loading and unloading stacks of heavy bundles, maneuvering through pot-holed streets clogged with parked and double-parked cars and trucks, and coping with flat tires, mechanical breakdowns, and other inevitable impediments.

On 9/11, the hardships were multiplied exponentially.

The major bridges and tunnels into Manhattan were initially shut off to incoming traffic. One or more Dow Jones executives tried to reach Mayor Giuliani seeking an exemption for newspaper deliveries, but no such exception was forthcoming.

When traffic was again allowed to flow, primarily to the outer boroughs, drivers — especially of trucks — faced tightened scrutiny and often were required to navigate circuitous routes to their drop-off points.

Neither LaChance nor NMDU responded to requests to discuss the union's actions on the night of September 11 and the morning of September 12.

What is known, however, is that NMDU was able to make some, if not most, deliveries of the *Journal* to parts of Brooklyn, Staten Island, Queens, and the Bronx. Subscribers and newsstands in Manhattan were mostly left without their morning *Journal*.

Even if NMDU had been able to get a truck or trucks past the security gauntlet imposed on Manhattan, tragically, many of the *Journal*'s subscribers who lived or worked in Lower Manhattan were dead, the apartments of others wiped out, and the newsstands that served commuters no longer existed.

The men of NMDU — and union members were almost entirely male — looked out for their own. "Standing up for our members has been our #1 priority for over a century," NMDU proudly proclaims on its website, noting that it provides pension benefits for its retirees and their beneficiaries, as well as health insurance, life insurance, and death benefits.

In his 1990 *Times* article, McFadden described the paper haulers as "a hard-working, blue-collar brotherhood fiercely dedicated to tradition, strict seniority and long-established work rules."

It doesn't take a great leap of faith to deduce that Glenn LaChance and his union brothers — some of whom like Jack Newman undoubtedly lost family and friends to the terrorist assault — were as determined as Paul Steiger, Jim Pensiero, Alan Murray, Marcus Brauchli, Paul Gigot, Cathy Panagoulias, Jon Hilsenrath, John Bussey, and the dozens of other individuals responsible for the content of the paper to get a physical copy of *The Wall Street Journal* into the hands of readers on September 12.

Before September 11, daily disagreements were de rigueur at Dow Jones and *The Wall Street Journal*. Reporters haggled with their bureau chiefs and editors over wording and cuts; editors argued among themselves over news priorities and story placement; senior editors and ad sales administrators jockeyed for space in the paper; compositors and press operators fought deadlines, and publishers and their unions — especially NMDU — wrangled over the terms of and adherence to labor contracts.

On September 11 and early September 12, all of those quarrels were set aside for a fleeting moment. America had come under attack, and, as never before, the extended network of *Wall Street Journal* employees and contractors, union and non-union alike, were of one mind.

The essence of their mission was similar to that of postal carriers, as etched more than 80 years earlier in white granite on the outer wall of the then-new Beaux-Arts Washington, D.C., Post Office building, located at Massachusetts Avenue and North Capitol Street, N.E.

Messenger of Sympathy and Love
Servant of Parted Friends
Consoler of the Lonely
Bond of the Scattered Family
Enlarger of the Common Life

Carrier of News and Knowledge
Instrument of Trade and Industry
Promoter of Mutual Acquaintance
Of Peace and of Goodwill Among Men and Nations.

[According to the U.S. Postal Service, the original draft of the inscription, called "The Letter," was written by Dr. Charles W. Eliot, a former president of Harvard University. President Woodrow Wilson tweaked the text before it was inscribed on the wall of the D.C. post office.]

———————————————

Roy J. Harris Jr. with his two sons, "R.J." at left, and Dave at right, in 2000

(Photo courtesy of Eileen McIntyre)

• Chapter Two •

The Morning After

After a dark day and an interminably long night, on September 12, 2001 — to the relief of many — the sun did rise.

The World Trade Center towers were now only a bittersweet memory. The World Financial Center, home to *The Wall Street Journal*, was in shambles, as were the lives of so many people in communities throughout New York City and the surrounding suburbs. They had seen loved ones off only the day before and now would never see them again.

Pain, like oxygen, was inhaled autonomically by the tens of millions of Americans who grieved for their losses: family, friends, loved ones, and other innocent souls. Also gone was their misbegotten sense of safety and innocence.

Dozens of employees of Dow Jones and the *Journal* couldn't return to work and their daily routines. A few never would.

Yet the core of *Journal* reporters, editors, news assistants, designers, and production staff did pick themselves out of bed — many after only a few hours of fitful sleep — and set about putting out the September 13 edition of the paper.

It was their job. It helped them feel purposeful. And it was a blessed distraction from reliving the horrors of the previous 24 hours.

——————————

Despite a restless night, Marcus Brauchli, *The Wall Street Journal*'s national news editor, began his day at 5:30 a.m. on September 12.

His expectant wife and daughter still asleep, he made his way downstairs and to the stoop of his Brooklyn Heights brownstone. A single morning newspaper awaited him: *The New York Times*.

Brauchli knew the *Journal* had published a September 12 edition — he was instrumental to making it happen — but delivery to his and other Brooklyn homes was obviously disrupted.

Reading the *Times*, which would go on to win Pulitzer Prizes for Explanatory Reporting and Public Service for its coverage on and after September 11, he began to cry, as he wrote in an email to his extended family soon thereafter.

As I stared, my eyes filled with tears, undoubtedly for the people who were lost, and maybe because of my own traumas, possibly because I was happy my family was asleep, intact, upstairs.

Brauchli, 40, left for an early morning run along the Brooklyn Promenade. It was another picture-perfect day; only the sun cast a strange orange glow on the plumes of smoke rising from the World Trade Center site. Flashing lights from emergency vehicles in Lower Manhattan and on the Brooklyn Bridge were ubiquitous.

A block from Brauchli's apartment was the Long Island City College Hospital. He ran there, intending to donate blood. They had no need for donations. "Too few casualties," they told him.

Outside another Brooklyn blood repository, where he next sprinted, it was 6:45 a.m., and a line of those wishing to give blood had already formed. It would be two hours and 15 minutes before that blood bank opened.

On September 11, the nearby Marriott Hotel in Brooklyn had served as an emergency blood donation center. So Brauchli jogged there. No luck. The hotel's donation center was gone. In its place was a safe harbor room for survivors who had been staying in Lower Manhattan at the Marriott World Trade Center before its destruction. Most of the refugees were wearing New York Fire Department t-shirts, provided to them, as Brauchli explained to his family, by the firefighters who had helped evacuate them.

Brauchli walked back toward his apartment. He passed a newsstand near the entrance to a now-desolate subway station.

On display were copies of the September 12 editions of the *Daily News* and *The New York Post*. "IT'S WAR," blared the *News*. "ACT OF WAR," echoed the *Post*.

And then Brauchli spotted it, a single unsold copy of the September 12 edition of *The Wall Street Journal*, with its six-column headline running across the front page.

For a second time that morning, my vision clouded with tears, to see the paper come out, knowing that the staff had been scattered by the disaster, knowing that everything had changed in its world. That beautiful, tragic Wednesday morning, at 9:00 a.m., twenty-four hours after the first plane hit the World Trade Center, I left my house for my first week working in [South Brunswick,] New Jersey.

In Hingham, Massachusetts, nestled along Boston Harbor, Roy J. Harris Jr. slid open the glass patio door in his living room and ambled onto his home's large deck facing Martins Lane.

As he did every weekday morning before breakfast, Harris retrieved his copies of *The New York Times*, *The Boston Globe*, and *The Wall Street Journal*.

U.S. ATTACKED
HIJACKED JETS DESTROY TWIN TOWERS AND HIT PENTAGON IN DAY OF TERROR

— The New York Times

New day of infamy
Thousands feared dead after planes hit towers, Pentagon

— The Boston Globe

TERRORISTS DESTROY WORLD TRADE CENTER, HIT PENTAGON IN RAID WITH HIJACKED JETS

— The Wall Street Journal

Less than a month shy of his 55th birthday, Harris was the senior editor of Boston-based *CFO Magazine*, to which he commuted daily by ferry. On September 11, Harris and his colleagues who had already arrived at the office watched together on live television, in horror, as the Twin Towers disintegrated into piles of smoking rubble.

A second-generation newsman, Harris took special note of the *Journal* that morning, having spent 24 years reporting for the paper from its Pittsburgh and Los Angeles bureaus. His former chief in both cities, Barney Calame, was still with the paper, one of the four New York-based deputy managing editors. Harris was keenly aware that the *Journal*'s main newsroom was situated directly in harm's way.

A widower, Harris remarried in 2000. He and his wife, Eileen McIntyre, had made plans back in August to rendezvous in Manhattan on September 11. McIntyre had kept an apartment on 36th Street in the Murray Hill neighborhood, and on September 11 was in the Big Apple, visiting with her son, Jesse, who still lived there.

Jesse was about to start his junior year at the University of Chicago. He had attended

Stuyvesant High School not far from the World Trade Center and had a clear view of the remains of the Twin Towers from his 18th-floor unit.

The original plan had been for Harris to rent a car, drive to Manhattan to pick up Jesse on the afternoon of September 11, and then drop him off several days later at school. Along the way, the two aimed to catch some Major League Baseball games in Pittsburgh and Cincinnati.

The best-laid schemes o' Mice an' Men...

Robert Burns's 1785 poem, "To a Mouse," fittingly describes how events overtook Harris, Jesse, and millions of other Americans on September 11.

Gang aft agley (Often go askew)

When Harris arrived by taxi at the Avis counter at Boston Logan International Airport after work on September 11, the counter clerk was stunned to see him. The airport itself was closed.

Two of the planes involved in the World Trade Center attacks — American Airlines Flight #11 and United Airlines Flight #175 — had departed the Boston airfield early that morning.

There were no other customers in the Avis rental office.

Take any vehicle on the lot.

Harris picked out a white Chevrolet SUV. He reasoned that Jesse would be carting clothing and other belongings back to the University of Chicago, so the spacious vehicle would be convenient.

Instead of leaving as planned, Harris chose to spend the night of September 11 in Hingham with his sons Dave and Roy J. Harris III ("R.J."), aged 15 and 14, respectively. Only a year before, the three of them had taken the ear-popping elevator to the observation deck at the top of the Twin Towers.

I felt I needed to explain to my boys what had happened and to try to answer their questions about why people on the other side of the world hated Americans so much.

After his sons headed off for school on the morning of the 12th, Harris navigated his rented SUV along the interstate through Connecticut. It took roughly five hours to drive from his home to the parking garage, located on 40th Street, between Second and Third Avenues in Manhattan.

Harris arrived on the city's outskirts around noon, just as the first waves of cars were allowed to cross the reopened Triborough Bridge. On the front passenger seat was his home-delivered copy of that morning's early edition of *The Wall Street Journal*. He brought the paper with him to show his wife.

Harris, six-two and a slender 195 pounds, was dressed casually, wearing an outfit suitable for attending baseball games. As it turned out, of course, he and Jesse would not be able to partake of America's pastime. In the aftermath of the attacks, MLB Commissioner Bud Selig halted all play for six days.

As Harris walked the four blocks from the parking garage to Jesse's apartment, carrying his *Journal* under one arm, an unexpected thing happened. Complete strangers, no fewer than a half-dozen of them in all, stopped Harris to ask the same two questions.

Where did you get your Wall Street Journal? May I have a look?

Harris warmly complied. He surmised that the curious inquirers were regular *Journal* readers, who, like most Manhattan subscribers, hadn't received that day's edition of the paper.

After they finished browsing the front page, several of the strangers uttered a third rhetorical question.

How did they ever manage to get a paper out?

Rebecca Distler, her younger brother Andrew, and their dad Thomas were left alone on the morning of September 12 to celebrate Rebecca's birthday, open her presents — including the refrigerator magnets that mom Joanne Lipman had purchased in the World Trade Center concourse the morning before — and enjoy the birthday cake that Lipman had lovingly baked.

Lipman couldn't wait around to wish her sleeping daughter a happy birthday. Like Marcus Brauchli, Paul Steiger, Jim Pensiero, and so many other members of *The Wall Street Journal* crew that was responsible for pulling together that morning's paper, Lipman felt the call to get right back to work, producing the September 13 edition.

That night, when Lipman finally arrived back at her apartment, she showed her 11-year-old the September 12 edition of *The Wall Street Journal* and explained the extraordinary story of how — despite overwhelming odds against it — it came to be. Lipman recounted the special mother-daughter memory in the book, *running toward DANGER*.

I explained how proud I was of all the people I work with. How proud I was of the paper. And how brave all the people I work with are. I will carry that forever.

Section Four:
Five Lives

Five Lives: When Terror Struck Twin Towers—'I'm Not Coming Out'

Continued From Page A1

hit our building," he said. "I have to go."

IN THE OTHER TOWER, Diane Murray was still admiring the picture of the little boy when she heard a whooshing sound and saw a claw of flame reach around the windows to her left.

"Fire!" she screamed, and pushed two of her colleagues, Peter Webster and Paul Sanchez, toward the stairway. Her heels clicked on the steps as she descended, and she began to pray, telling God she couldn't die yet, for the sake of her eight-year-old daughter. "It's not my time," she prayed.

FIVE FLOORS ABOVE, Shimmy Biegeleisen phoned his wife from his office at money-management firm Fiduciary Trust International Inc. "There's been an explosion next door," the 42-year-old vice president said. "Don't worry. I'm OK."

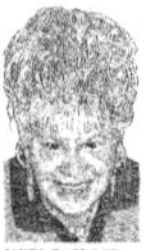

ANITA DeBLASE was nearby working at a polling place; two of her sons, Anthony and James, were in the twin towers.

After a few minutes, Mr. Biegeleisen grabbed his black canvas bag, walked past a cluster of cubicles and headed toward the stairwell. But when he reached the doorway—a step behind a project manager who worked for him—he stopped, leaned his big body against the open metal door and rummaged through his bag. "Whatever you're looking for, it's not important," the manager told her boss. "Please come." She started down the stairs.

IN THE NORTH TOWER, now engulfed in fire, Moises Rivas called home from Windows on the World. His wife's daughter-in-law answered the phone.

"Where's your mommy?" he asked. "In the laundry," the girl replied. "What's happening?"

"Tell her I'm OK," he said. "Tell her I love her no matter what."

DIANE MURRAY and her two Aon co-workers followed a crowd into the lobby of the 55th floor of the south tower. A voice on the loudspeaker said that there was a fire in the north tower, but that the south tower was secure.

Two elevators were jammed with people—going up. In another elevator, a tall, well-dressed man reassured the throng in the lobby. "Everything's all right," he said. "Stay calm." But his elevator was going down.

"If everything's all right, how come you're not going up to your office?" Ms. Murray shouted at him as the doors slid shut.

One of her colleagues said he wanted the egg-and-tomato sandwich that he had left on his desk. "No way," she told him, and elbowed them onto the next elevator down. It stopped for no apparent reason after a few floors, and they stepped into a lobby where people were gawking at a television showing smoke spewing from a gash in the north tower. With her orange jacket tied around her waist, Ms. Murray led her co-workers down the stairs.

As they reached the 42nd floor, they heard a dull thud above them and felt the building shift, tossing them back and forth between the stair railing and the wall.

WHEN ANITA DeBLASE heard that the towers were burning, she thought of her middle son, 41-year-old Anthony, a bond broker on the 84th floor of the south tower. She called his office, and the person who answered the phone told her he had left. She thanked God that her youngest son, Richard, 37, had left his job at Cantor Fitzgerald in the north tower a few years earlier.

She raced outside Public School 126 on the Lower East Side, where she was working at voting booths for the New York City mayoral primary, and saw the billowing smoke about a mile away. She crossed herself and said, "God help those people." Then she set about comforting other election volunteers who had relatives working in the towers.

THE WORD "FIDUCIARY" filled the caller-ID panel on the kitchen phone in the Biegeleisen home in the Flatbush section of Brooklyn. Miriam Biegeleisen knew it was her husband calling again from his office. "I love you," he told her.

He hadn't made it to the stairs when the wings of the second jet ripped diagonally through the south tower just four floors below Mr. Biegeleisen's cubicle. Fire engulfed the tower's stairwells. Mr. Biegeleisen was trapped.

Mrs. Biegeleisen handed the phone to Dovid Langer, a friend who volunteered for an ambulance service and had run over when he heard that ambulances had been dispatched to the towers.

"Dovid," Mr. Biegeleisen told him, "take care of Miriam and take care of my children." Mr. Langer heard a recording in the background saying over and over that the building was secure and that people should stay put. (A Port Authority spokesman said, "We are not aware of any recorded announcement made by building management.") Mr. Biegeleisen continued: "Dovid, I'm not coming out of this."

Mr. Langer connected Mr. Biegeleisen to Gary Gelbfish, a vascular surgeon and friend who was watching the towers burn on TV. "I'm having difficulty breathing," Mr. Biegeleisen told him. Black smoke was filling the room.

"You've got to do two things," the doctor said. "Stay low to the ground. And do you have a towel or a rag? Put water on it and put it over your mouth."

Mr. Biegeleisen walked past three cubicles to the water cooler. He wet a towel and raised it to his mouth. Then he walked back to his desk and lay down on the slate blue carpet in his black suede shoes, black pants, oxford shirt and black felt yarmulke. Mr. Biegeleisen was a Chassid, a devoted follower of the Belzer Rebbe, the leader of a rabbinic dynasty that dates to 1815.

"Is there a sprinkler?" Dr. Gelbfish asked. Mr. Biegeleisen looked up but couldn't see through the smoke. He and the five colleagues trapped alongside him decided to try to get to the roof. Mr. Biegeleisen hung up the phone.

ANITA DeBLASE WAS still consoling her fellow poll workers when her husband, James, swept into the school, a Pall Mall in his hand and a worried look on his face. "Jimmy Boy is in there," he told his wife. In the morning's confusion, she had somehow forgotten that her eldest, Jimmy, 45, had joined Cantor Fitzgerald as a bond broker after her youngest, Richard, had left.

Mrs. DeBlase snatched up her purse and left the polling place, making her way to the East River, where she turned toward the burning buildings.

COFFEE CUPS AND SWEATERS littered the south tower stairwells, now packed with a stop-and-go exodus. Diane Murray and her Aon colleagues emerged onto the glass-enclosed mezzanine overlooking the plaza between the towers.

Nearby, Jimmy Barbella was helping direct the evacuation of the south tower, waving the crowd toward the mall beneath the towers. "We gotta make sure everybody gets out of the building," he told a co-worker. Debris pelted the plaza through a cloud of ash. People scurried to shelter, holding chairs over themselves for cover. A falling man pawed at the air before smashing into the ground.

The eldest of seven children in a devout Catholic family, Mr. Barbella had soured on the church and lately had been meditating near a statue of the Buddha he had put in his backyard in Oceanside, N.Y. Now, gazing at the plaza, he made a hasty sign of the cross.

He moved to the operations center beneath the south tower. "Jim, did you call your family yet?" a co-worker asked. At 9:20, he called his wife, Monica, at home. "Oh, thank God you're OK," she said, standing in the TV room. He asked what she had learned from TV. A plane had hit each building, she told him. "OK, I gotta go," he said.

Mrs. Barbella, 50, assured her children—JoAnn, 25, James, 23, and Sarah, 20—that Daddy would be fine. On the wall nearby were two commendations he had received, one from the Marines for fighting a brush fire near a fuel tank in Okinawa in 1969, the other for work during and after the 1993 World Trade Center bombing, which he barely escaped.

There's no way he's leaving that building, Mrs. Barbella thought.

Mr. Barbella next ran into some Port Authority police officers who said people were stranded in Windows on the World in the north tower. He went to show them the way and ended up in the north tower's lobby, standing ankle-deep in fire-sprinkler water and pointing the way out with his radio antenna. On the channel he was using, somebody said, "The building's in danger of collapsing."

Three fire-alarm technicians descending the tower showed up on the scene. "Jimmy, what are you doing?" one asked, incredulous that Mr. Barbella hadn't fled. "Go," Mr. Barbella told him. "Keep going." Another technician veered away from the exit toward a command post, but Mr. Barbella shooed him out, too: "Get out of the building."

Just after evacuating, the third technician heard Mr. Barbella on the radio talking about Windows on the World: "All those people, we've got to help them."

THE PHONE RANG in the Biegeleisen home. Again, "FIDUCIARY" flashed on the display. The intense heat had kept Shimmy Biegeleisen from reaching the roof. "We couldn't even go into the hallway," he said into the phone.

The Biegeleisen home was filling with worried friends and neighbors. Women clustered in the living room, trying to calm Mrs. Biegeleisen. Men paced in the kitchen, taking turns speaking to her husband. One phoned 911. They waited while Mr. Biegeleisen tried again to reach the roof.

He didn't make it. At 9:45, he phoned home again. "Promise me you'll look after Miriam," he told one of his friends. "Tell Miriam I love her." Lying on the floor beneath photographs of his five children that sat atop his filing cabinet, he now spoke of them and gave instructions for handling his finances.

Mr. Biegeleisen and his 19-year-old son Mordechai were supposed to travel in five days to Jerusalem to spend the Jewish new year with the Belzer Chassidim and meet with the Belzer Rebbe. Mr. Biegeleisen made the trip every few years at Rosh Hashanah. Most inspiring to him was the second night of the holiday, when the Rebbe read aloud the 24th Psalm.

Now, in a voice hoarse with smoke, Mr. Biegeleisen began to recite that psalm in Hebrew over the phone: "Of David a Psalm. The Lord's is the earth and its fullness ..."

The friend on the phone began to shake. He handed the phone to another friend, who urged Mr. Biegeleisen to break a window. "You can get some air and go to the roof," the friend said. Mr. Biegeleisen called out to a colleague. "Let's go! Let's break the window!" At 9:59, the two men hauled a filing cabinet to the window. "I'm looking out the window now," Mr. Biegeleisen said into the phone. Then he screamed: "Oh God!"

The line went dead.

ON THE TELEVISION in his Bronx apartment, John Haynes saw the south tower disappear into rolling clouds of soot. The north tower still stood.

Mr. Haynes began dialing phone numbers at Windows on the World. Nothing but busy signals. "Get out," he thought. "Get out by any means necessary." He began reciting names aloud: Heather. Karim. Blanca. Moises.

Mr. Haynes knew them by heart because he was a cook on the morning shift at Windows, the same as his friend Moises Rivas. They backed each other up: if Mr. Rivas had not been at work that morning, Mr. Haynes would have.

Mr. Haynes's phone rang. A union organizer was calling Windows workers, hoping to find them at home. "How many people do you think were in there?" the man asked.

"There was a big party," Mr. Haynes said. About 200 guests were expected.

"Oh, s—," the union organizer said. "Oh, s—."

Mr. Haynes was looking at the TV when the north tower disintegrated.

LOUIS BARBELLA, the 36-year-old brother of property manager Jimmy Barbella, stood on a sidewalk six miles

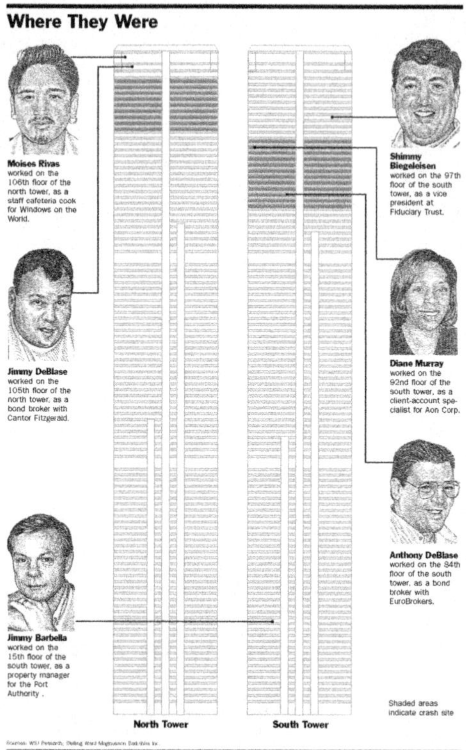

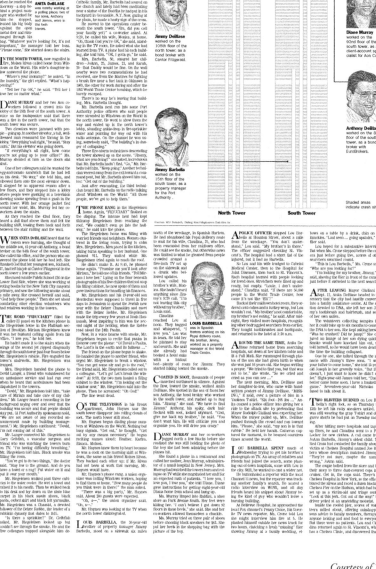

Where They Were
Moises Rivas
worked on the 106th floor of the north tower, as a staff cafeteria cook for Windows on the World.
Jimmy DeBlase
worked on the 105th floor of the north tower, as a bond broker with Cantor Fitzgerald.
Jimmy Barbella
worked on the 15th floor of the south tower, as a property manager for the Port Authority .
Shimmy Biegeleisen
worked on the 97th floor of the south tower, as a vice president at Fiduciary Trust.
Diane Murray
worked on the 92nd floor of the south tower, as a client-account specialist for Aon Corp.
Anthony DeBlase
worked on the 84th floor of the south tower, as a bond broker with EuroBrokers.
Shaded areas indicate crash site
North Tower
South Tower

Sources: WSJ Research; Skilling Ward Magnusson Barkshire Inc.

north of the wreckage, in Spanish Harlem. He had abandoned his Pepsi delivery route to wait for his wife, Claudina, 35, who had been evacuated from her midtown office. He could see the smoke, but otherwise news was limited to what he gleaned from people crowded around a five-inch TV set up on the sidewalk and a drunk who bellowed updates.

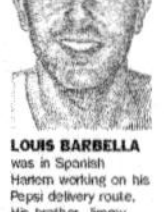

LOUIS BARBELLA was in Spanish Harlem working on his Pepsi delivery route. His brother, Jimmy, worked as a property manager at the World Trade Center.

Lou called his brother's wife, Monica. She hadn't heard anything since Jimmy's 9:20 call. "I'm not leaving this city without my brother," Louis said.

Claudina reached Lou at noon. They hugged and whispered, "I love you." Lou was in tears. He told her he planned to stay and search. She said she already had booked a hotel suite with a foldout bed—plenty of room for Jimmy. They started hiking toward the smoke.

COATED IN SOOT, thousands of people marched northward in silence. Against the flow, toward the smoke, walked Anita DeBlase. She spotted in the sea of faces her son Anthony, the bond broker who worked in the south tower, and rushed up to hug him. "Jimmy," she said. "We have to find Jimmy." Anthony, his spiky, dark hair flecked with soot, looked skyward. "God, give me back my brother," he said. "You don't want him. He will criticize you and organize you. He will drive you crazy."

DIANE MURRAY and her co-workers jogged north a few blocks before she realized she was still holding the photo of the boy she had been admiring before the planes hit.

She found a phone in a restaurant and called her mother, Jean Murray, administrator of a small hospital in New Jersey. Mrs. Murray had watched the towers burn and collapse on TV while she marshaled her staff for an expected rush of patients. "I love you, I love you, I love you," she told Diane. Diane gave instructions for getting eight-year-old Diana home from school and hung up.

Ms. Murray limped into Baldini, a shoe store on Park Avenue South. Her feet were killing her. "I can't believe I got down 92 floors in these heels," she said. She and her co-workers allowed themselves a chuckle.

Ms. Murray tried on three pair of shoes before choosing black sneakers for $43. She put her heels in the shopping bag with the picture of the boy.

A POLICE OFFICER stopped Lou Barbella at Houston Street, about a mile from the wreckage. "You don't understand," Lou said. "My brother's in there." The officer suggested checking St. Vincent's. The hospital had a short list of the injured, but it had no Barbella.

So Lou and his wife trudged to Cabrini Medical Center, then to the Hospital for Joint Diseases, then back to St. Vincent's. Each hospital teemed with people looking for loved ones. Stretchers were lined up and ready, but empty. "Louie, I don't understand," Claudina said. "If there are 50,000 people in the World Trade Center, how come it's not like 'ER'?"

Back at their midtown hotel room, they ordered crab cakes and a turkey wrap, but Lou wouldn't eat. "My brother's not comfortable, my brother's not eating," he said. After midnight, they visited more hospitals, recognizing other bedraggled searchers from earlier. They bought toothbrushes and toothpaste, and returned to the hotel at 3:30 a.m.

AROUND THE SAME TIME, Anita DeBlase returned home from searching hospitals, sat down at her kitchen table and lit a Pall Mall. She rummaged through photos of the son she had given birth to when she was just 16 years old. She began writing a prayer. "We tried to find you, but that was not to be," she wrote. "So we cried and cried as you can see ..."

The next morning, Mrs. DeBlase met her daughter-in-law, who came with handwritten posters of Jimmy DeBlase. "MISSING," it said, over a picture of him in a Yankees T-shirt. "Six foot—295 lbs ..." Anita coaxed a police officer into giving her a ride to the attack site by pretending that Mayor Rudolph Giuliani was expecting her. When the mayor pulled up, Mrs. DeBlase pushed through the crowd and ran toward him. "Please," she said, "my son is in that rubble." He held her hands. Cameras captured the moment, to be beamed countless times around the world.

LOU BARBELLA SPENT much of Wednesday trying to get his brother's photograph on TV. An army of relatives and friends had joined the search, some phoning out-of-town hospitals, some with Lou in the city. Still, he wanted to cast a wider net.

He buttonholed a reporter with the local Channel 11 news, but the reporter was tracking another family's search. He scored a radio interview on WINS, and all day friends heard his snippet about Jimmy being the kind of guy who wouldn't leave a burning building.

At Bellevue Hospital, he approached the local Fox channel's Penny Crone, his favorite TV news reporter. Ms. Crone told Lou she might interview him live at 5. He planted himself outside her news truck for two hours, clutching a fresh "missing" flier showing Jimmy at a family wedding, elbows on a table by a drink, chin on his knuckles. "Last seen ... going upstairs," the flier said.

Lou hoped for a substantive interview. But when Ms. Crone stepped before the camera just before going live, scores of other searchers swarmed round.

"This is Lou Barbella," Ms. Crone said. "Who are you looking for?"

"I'm looking for my brother, Jimmy," he said, shoving the flier in front of the camera just before it swiveled to the next searcher.

AFTER LEAVING Mayor Giuliani on Sept. 12, Anita DeBlase headed to the armory that the city had hastily converted into a family assistance center. At the section devoted to DNA, she left her son Jimmy's toothbrush and hairbrush, and some of her own saliva.

The volunteers collecting samples told her it could take up to six months to connect the DNA to her son. She kept asking herself, "Was he crushed? Did he jump?" She conjured an image of her son dying quickly. Smoke would have knocked him out, she told herself, so he would have been dead by the time the building collapsed.

One by one, she talked through the scenario with Jimmy's three sons. "I want your father to come home," she told 13-year-old Joseph in her gravelly voice. "But if he doesn't, I just want to know he didn't suffer." Eight-year-old James told her, "Daddy better come home soon. I have a basketball game." Seventeen-year-old Nicholas refused to talk about it.

TWO BLISTERS BURNED on Lou Barbella's right foot, so on Thursday the 13th he left his ratty sneakers untied. He was still wearing the gray T-shirt and dungaree shorts he had put on Tuesday morning.

After hitting more hospitals and taping up fliers, he and Claudina went to a Foot Locker for new clothes. A call came from JoAnn Barbella, Jimmy's oldest child. The Red Cross had contacted the family about a victim at Chelsea Hospital named Joe Barbera whose description matched Jimmy's. "They're not sure, maybe the name's wrong," JoAnn said.

The couple bolted from the store and told their story to three dust-covered cops in a cruiser. Get in, the cops said. There's no Chelsea Hospital in New York, so the officers blared the sirens and raced a dozen blocks to Chelsea Pier on the Hudson, which had been set up as a victim-aid and triage center. "Look at this jerk. Get out of the way!" the driver yelled at an unyielding motorist.

Inside the roofed pier, scores of volunteers milled about, offering missing-persons advice to family members, therapy to anyone looking sad and food to everyone. But there were no patients. Lou and Claudina returned again to St. Vincent's, which has a Chelsea Clinic, and discovered that a Joseph Barbera had been treated there and released. Jimmy was still missing.

The next day, Friday, the couple went to confession. "If he's gone," the priest told Lou, "he's in a place so glorious he doesn't want to come back." For penance, Lou attended the wake of a fire chaplain killed in the attacks.

AS ANITA DeBLASE WALKED in her Knickerbocker Village neighborhood that Friday, a woman stopped her and asked, "Any good news?"

"No," Mrs. DeBlase said.

"Day by day," the woman told her, shaking her head and looking down.

Later, Mrs. DeBlase said, "I want to buy a shirt that says, 'Don't bother me.' Everybody is full of advice. They're beating the s— out of me."

LATE THAT NIGHT, Diane Murray sat in her Newark home reading from Psalm 91: "Though a thousand fall at your side, ten thousand at your right side, near you it shall not come ..."

Outside, a thunderstorm cracked and boomed. She walked to her front door and stood with her Bible in one hand and a phone in the other, wondering if she should wake Diana and leave. Was that really thunder? Or the sound of bombs exploding? She felt relieved when she saw a lightning bolt tear through the sky.

LOU BARBELLA abandoned his search on Saturday, Sept. 15. He didn't want to, but the injured lists had stopped growing. He told Claudina he felt he had let down the family: "I didn't do what I said I was going to do."

They took a subway to Queens, where Lou had left his car on Tuesday. Then they went to Long Island, where they visited Jimmy's wife and attended Mass with his elderly parents. That evening, at his parents' home, Lou said something to his sister Ruth Ann at once ordinary and remarkable: "Hi, Ruth. How are you doing?"

The siblings had had a falling out two years ago. No one recalls the cause, but the two had stopped communicating. The rift had upset the family, especially their mother and Jimmy. Ruth knew the greeting ended the spat.

At breakfast on Sunday, Lou recounted his five-day odyssey for Ruth and the others, and they laughed as in old times.

DIANE MURRAY TURNED 30 that day. She attended the 11 a.m. service at Franklin St. John's United Methodist Church in Newark. The Rev. Moses Flomo asked for people to "testify" about the trade center disaster. Ms. Murray had never been much for public speaking, but today she stood up.

She faced the congregation, packed into rows of wooden pews in the red-brick church where she had been baptized. Through tears, she said she believed God had sent her Aon colleagues, Messrs. Webster and Sanchez—her "Peter and Paul"—to lead her away from the building. The congregants clapped and shouted out "Amen!" and "Praise the Lord!" Outside, they hugged her and told her how glad they were to have her alive.

SEVEN DAYS AFTER her husband's phone line went dead, Miriam Biegeleisen stood in synagogue on Rosh Hashanah murmuring a prayer about God and fate: "How many will pass from the earth and how many will be created. Who will live and who will die. ... Who by water and who by fire."

By tradition, she and her family would have begun their shiva, the weeklong mourning period for her husband, the day after his death. But no body had been found, and the Biegeleisens for days had held on to hope that Shimmy was alive. Now Shimmy's father decided that they were ready to mourn. Before they could, it had to be established that Mrs. Biegeleisen wasn't an agunah.

In Jewish law, an agunah is a woman who is separated from her husband and cannot remarry, either because he won't grant her a divorce or because it isn't known whether he is alive or dead. With no trace of a body, a rabbinic court must rule whether death can be assumed.

Minutes after Rosh Hashanah ended, Mr. Biegeleisen's father phoned Efraim Fishel Hershkowitz in Brooklyn. The 76-year-old rabbi said he would convene with two other rabbis to decide the case at once. He asked that the men who had spoken to Mr. Biegeleisen on the day he disappeared come to the rabbi's home. He also wanted a tape of the 911 call.

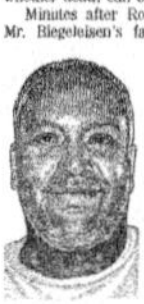

JOHN HAYNES was in the Bronx on his day off from Windows on the World while Moises Rivas worked the shift they shared.

THE THRONG on the sidewalk outside the Hotel Employees and Restaurant Employees Local 100 union hall on Tuesday, Sept. 18, hugged and cried and talked in Spanish and Mandarin, Arabic and Cantonese. This was the first meeting for Windows on the World employees and families of the missing. Seventy-nine workers had been at the restaurant. Not one made it out.

John Haynes approached, his sunglasses, as always, perched on his head. A waiter rushed over to hug him. "Oh my God, you weren't in," he said. Others came up to embrace the 43-year-old cook and shake his hand. Because Mr. Haynes worked the breakfast shift, they had figured he was gone.

Up walked Hector Lopez, another Windows employee. "I thought about you, man," Mr. Lopez said. "I'm so glad you weren't there." Mr. Haynes nodded. Then Mr. Lopez said, "But Moises was covering for you, man."

"Yeah," Mr. Haynes said.

Mr. Haynes wouldn't have had Sept. 11 off if it weren't for a fight Moises Rivas had picked a year before.

The cooks had worked together for six

Please Turn to Page A10, Column 1

• The Origin •

Who Doesn't Know That It
Was a Horrific Turn in History?

It was Friday night, October 5, 2001. Four reporters were huddled on Manhattan's Upper East Side, hoping to rescue content that had been excised from the drafts they'd submitted earlier in the week to Bryan Gruley.

Gruley was arguably the strongest writer in their group of five *Wall Street Journal* all-stars and their de facto leader. He had remained in Washington, D.C., where he was based.

Combined, the five reporters had written a 426 column-inch draft, or nearly 22,000 words. Even without headlines or illustrations, it would take up nearly three-and-a-half full pages. Gruley took upon himself the chore of winnowing the draft into a manageable, lucid feature roughly one-third its unedited size.

During a conference call, he told his colleagues that his first impression of their submissions was favorable.

This is going to be awesome.

However, when the other four read Gruley's compacted version, no one was satisfied.

The five journalists — Gruley, Helene Cooper, Ianthe Jeanne Dugan, Phil Kuntz, and Joshua Prager — had been pressed together as a team less than a month earlier. It was an emotional roller-coaster from the start. Working more or less independently, their assignment was to contribute meaningfully to a single front-page feature slated to run on the one-month anniversary of the September 11 terrorist attacks.

Their story would recount the seismic impact that the day's events had on five individuals and their families:

- James W. "Jimmy" Barbella, a property manager for the Port Authority who worked on the 15th floor of the South Tower

- Shimmy Biegeleisen, a vice president at Fiduciary Trust who worked on the 97th floor of the South Tower

- James DeBlase, a Cantor Fitzgerald bond broker who worked on the 105th floor of the North Tower

- Diane Murray, a client-account specialist at Aon Corp. who worked on the 92nd floor of the South Tower

- Moises Rivas, a Windows on the World cook who worked on the 106th floor of the North Tower

Cooper, Kuntz, and Prager crowded around Dugan's computer in her East 89th Street apartment, reading and rereading Gruley's edited draft.

There was pizza and wine, camaraderie and rivalry. At times, tears flowed, as each journalist, like a defense attorney making a closing argument, pleaded for their contribution to receive greater prominence.

Their effort contrasted with the *Journal*'s Pulitzer Prize-winning deadline reporting of September 11. The reporters and editors who contributed to the September 12 edition of the paper were chosen primarily by fate — who was available at a moment's notice, who had first-person or eyewitness accounts of that day's events, who could bypass the transportation closures and delays, and wend their way to South Brunswick.

But Cooper, Dugan, Gruley, Kuntz, and Prager were hand-picked for this story, given full leave — except Prager, who was off writing a book about baseball — from their ordinary newsroom duties.

The quintet's sweeping front-page feature would carry a stacked headline, in keeping with the paper's page-one style:

Five Lives

When Terror Struck: 'I'm Not Coming Out'; 'My Brother's in There'

From 'Have a Nice Day' To Havoc and Horror And the Bitter Aftermath

---

A Mother's Prayer for a Son

"Five Lives" is also an apt title for a retelling of the profound effect that reporting and writing their feature had on Cooper, Dugan, Gruley, Kuntz, and Prager. As Kuntz would write in an email the day after their story appeared:

Reporting it was the most amazing professional if not personal experience of my life.

"Five Lives" staggered many subscribers, for whom 9/11 remained an open, festering, emotional wound.

Reader Patricia Flashnick wrote to the *Journal*:

... it's the personal stories that have brought home the immense scope of this tragedy. The horror of it all still looms so large that it's almost unfathomable. Nonetheless, your personalized accounts of that day made the moments so vivid, so sharp, that the article actually helps, in perhaps a bizarre way, to bring that day into focus. To make the unimaginable imaginable, because we see it through the eyes of ordinary people.

Another reader, Peter Kessler, echoed the sentiments of many:

Your article is one of the most profound pieces I have ever read. I am seldom at a loss for words but, after reading it, I am without words.

Deputy Managing Editor Dan Hertzberg agreed, describing "Five Lives" as one of the finest stories to ever appear in the *Journal*. Peter Kann, Dow Jones's CEO and a 1972 Pulitzer Prize winner, emailed the authors.

Despite all I have read and seen of the Sept. 11 tragedy, your story affected me as no other has.

To achieve its emotional snap, "Five Lives" broke several *Wall Street Journal* conventions. The final, edited, 7,350-word feature began with a note on sourcing.

This article is based on interviews with more than 125 witnesses to the Sept. 11 attack on the World Trade Center and its aftermath. These witnesses include survivors and their relatives, friends and co-workers, as well as relatives, friends and co-workers of those who died or remain missing. All dialogue was witnessed by reporters or confirmed by one or more people present when the words were spoken. All thoughts attributed to people in the article come from those people.

The note highlighted a couple of crucial storytelling techniques, more commonly employed in novels. In such a lengthy narrative, it spared the authors — and readers — from constantly interrupting the intense tale with common newspaper attributions, such as "he said," "she said," "they recounted," "they explained," and the like.

The lack of attribution also helped delay the revelation of which of their five lead characters — Barbella, Biegeleisen, DeBlase, Murray, and Rivas — had survived the terrorist attacks. After all, readers would quickly have deduced that if any of the five were quoted reflecting on September 11 in its aftermath, they must have made it out alive.

Gruley elaborated on the journalists' rationale in a September 2002 Q&A with the Poynter Institute.

The key to all this was to keep the readers in suspense about who would or wouldn't die in the towers.

Despite their own stirrings over the horrors their story subjects had shared with the journalists, Gruley told Poynter that he and his colleagues resisted the temptation to dramatize their writing.

Rather than tell readers what to think, we'd just try to show them what happened, unadorned, understated, and let them interpret.

The first version of "Five Lives" began as many Page One features do, with a brief, anecdotal introduction of the principals, followed by a so-called "nut graf," *Journal* jargon for the paragraph that informs readers the significance of what they're about to read.

NEW YORK- Just before the first plane slammed into the North Tower of the World Trade Center, Diane Murray sat down on the 92nd floor of the South Tower, took off her sneakers and slipped into black sandals with heels.

Shimmy Biegeliesen [sic] called his wife to remind her a painter was coming to finish their living room in Flatbush. James W. Barbella talked about a career move with his boss. Moises Rivas chopped fish and vegetables in a restaurant. And Anita DeBlase filled out a voting card at a polling place in the shadow of the towers.

On the clear blue morning of Sept. 11, they were among the thousands of ordinary people who were about to be engulfed in a horrific tum [sic] in history. Some died and may never be found. Some lived and may never be the same. A month later, encounters with mortality have left the survivors and loved ones alike struggling with grief, anger, guilt and fear as they try to recapture their lives. By varying degrees, they're different people, and they aren't quite sure what to do about it.

Alan Murray, the D.C. bureau chief who conceived the "Five Lives" story on September 11 and the next morning began assigning staff to report and write it, quickly put the kibosh on the proposed start.

For me, the current lede just gets in the way. The nutgraf feels totally unnecessary. Who doesn't know that it was a horrific turn in history, or that things will never be the same? I'd trash it.

And so they did.

• Chapter Two •

Helene Cooper
The Worst Moment Came on Monday, October 1

NEW YORK — The alarm on Moises Rivas's nightstand went off at 5 a.m. on Sept. 11. He had been up until 2 a.m., playing slow salsa on his guitar. He shut off the alarm, snuggled up to his wife, and fell back to sleep. It wasn't until 6:30 that the 29-year-old cook raced out of the two-bedroom apartment, already late, and headed for work on the 106th floor of the north tower of the World Trade Center.

It would be a busy day. A big corporate breakfast meeting was about to begin. Mr. Rivas wore baggy black bell-bottoms that morning, but he could change into his crisp white chef's uniform when he arrived at the Windows on the World restaurant.

His instructions for the day awaited him, taped to a stainless-steel pillar in the restaurant. "Moises," said the handwritten note posted by the banquet chef the night before. "The menu for Tuesday: B.B.Q. short ribs, roast chicken legs, pasta with tomato sauce. NOTE: Please have [sic] the butcher to cut the pork chops. Cut the fish. Cut, Dice Carrot Onion Celery. Cubes of Potato for the Stew. Cook one box pasta. See you later and have a nice day."

It took Helene Cooper four days of trolling the internet and emailing friends to land on Moises Rivas as the character she'd profile. Rivas was the individual who Gruley and the others agreed should — in keeping with Alan Murray's directive — launch the published version of the "Five Lives" narrative.

Bureau Chief Murray had encouraged the group to craft a story "about all of us," not just the usual corporate types that populated so many *Wall Street Journal* features.

As Cooper wrote, 79 workers had been at the Windows on the World restaurant on the morning of September 11. None of them survived.

Cooper was based in the D.C. bureau, serving as a hybrid editor/reporter focused on international trade. She knew Gruley and Kuntz well because they were also in Washington. She was aware of the reputations of Dugan and Prager as extraordinary feature writers.

I felt under incredible pressure to produce somebody who will be good because Phil was a really, really good investigative reporter. And Gruley is a really great narrative reporter. I was terrified that my own [contribution] would be lame.

The first night before we even met up [in New York] ... I was like, 'Shit, I got to find somebody really good just to keep up with them.'

In the days immediately following September 11, all five reporters would encamp in Manhattan in order to conduct their newsgathering. Cooper had become leery of flying, so she took a train from D.C. and set up shop at the Midtown Hilton Hotel. There no longer existed a New York newsroom where she or any of her colleagues could assemble.

Cooper reasoned she might find a profile candidate at the Hotel Employees and Restaurant Employees Local 100 union hall. She made her way there on Tuesday, September 18, a week after the terrorist attacks and her fifth day with no eligible protagonist.

By coincidence, the first gathering of Windows on the World employees and families of the missing was about to begin. There were joyous reunions — *Oh my God, you weren't in* — and plenty of tearful hugs and commiserations uttered in English, Spanish, Mandarin, Arabic, and Cantonese.

As Cooper wrote, John Haynes, a 43-year-old cook who ordinarily worked the morning shift, attracted the embraces of waiters and others who had presumed that he was dead.

Up walked Hector Lopez, another Windows employee. "I thought about you, man," Mr. Lopez said. "I'm so glad you weren't there." Mr. Haynes nodded. Then Mr. Lopez said, "But Moises was covering for you, man." "Yeah," Mr. Haynes said.

Cooper recognized that Haynes would be perfect for sharing his 9/11 story, as well as the saga of Moises Rivas and his family. She told Haynes that she would need to shadow him for a couple of weeks, and he consented.

In addition, the journalist was welcomed into the Rivases' Washington Heights apartment by Moises's widow, Elizabeth. Cooper's first visit came the morning after Moises's mother arrived from Ecuador, distraught over her son's death.

There was already tension between the two women; they were arguing about where to bury Moises — the U.S. or Ecuador — if they ever found a body. It was exactly the kind of thing you would expect from a family going through grief.

In many ways, the Rivas family reminded Cooper of her own.

Born in Liberia, Cooper and her family fled to the United States when she was 13 years old. Cooper is the great-great-great-great-granddaughter of Elijah Johnson (c. 1780-1849), a freeborn Black and former U.S. soldier who was repatriated to Africa in 1820 and went on to found Liberia.

Growing up, Cooper's family was among Liberia's elite — wealthy and in control of the government. But a military coup in April 1980 unended her pampered life. The country's president, William Tolbert, was disemboweled, his body dumped into a mass grave. Cooper's father was shot and wounded. Her cousin was executed on the beach by a firing squad.

Cooper's mother, Calista, was gang-raped in the basement of their home by soldiers of the Armed Forces of Liberia. On the condition that the defilers leave Helene and her two sisters, ages 8 and 16, alone, Calista submitted to the soldiers.

Calista bribed anyone and everyone in order to obtain exit permits for her and her daughters. (Cooper's father was still hospitalized from the gunshot and would join his family later.) On May 16, 1980, the Coopers arrived safely in New York. In 1988, after living as an undocumented resident, Cooper received a green card as part of President Ronald Reagan's amnesty program. A decade later, already a reporter for *The Wall Street Journal*, she became a U.S. citizen.

Like the Coopers in the early 1980s, the Rivases were multigenerational immigrants; eight members of an extended family living in a cramped two-bedroom apartment and struggling to make ends meet.

It was hard to explain. I felt like I knew these people. I mean, I knew what all that economic uncertainty felt like.

Once Cooper met John Haynes, an African American, at the union hall, and visited with Elizabeth Rivas, her apprehensions about not finding a suitable profile subject melted away.

I wanted somebody Black to begin with or somebody who was a minority. Somebody who wasn't like a buttoned-up corporate exec because we were getting a lot of Cantor Fitzgerald type stuff [reported in the Journal.] I wanted to do somebody different.

The reporting went smoothly after that, although Cooper struggled each night to process her emotions.

She checked out of the Midtown Hilton. She was unfamiliar with that area of Manhattan, felt isolated, and came to regard the hotel more or less like a morgue.

Cooper relocated to the W Hotel in Union Square, closer to the union hall and closer to the *Journal's* vacated newsroom. She persuaded Gruley and Kuntz to lodge at the W as well.

I wanted to be around people.

It was hard. It was like I was crying all the time. I felt like — during periods — that I was having an emotional breakdown. I couldn't stop crying. I mean, AT&T commercials would make me cry.

Contributing to her emotional turbulence were the flashbacks to her youth.

I hadn't felt that unsafe in my own skin since the military coup in Liberia that my family had gone through. And, you know, being a Liberian refugee here in America, I felt safe. And, suddenly, I didn't feel safe anymore.

Like her four co-authors, Cooper found it challenging to maintain a journalistically requisite impartiality from Haynes and the Rivas family.

A couple of times, I worried that I was becoming a crutch for [Haynes]. He said, at one point: "What am I going to do when you're gone, and nobody's really interested in hearing this story anymore?"

The worst moment for Cooper came on Monday, October 1, at the Cathedral of St. John the Divine on Manhattan's Upper West Side.

More than one thousand chairs filled the sanctuary, each with a candle placed upon it, as a two-hour memorial service was held for the Windows on the World workers.

The most heartbreaking part for me was picking up the program during the Windows memorial service and seeing Moises Rivas's name.

Rivas was listed in the third row of names, sixth from the top.

I felt like I was reading a graduation program, only I wasn't.

Juan Colon, a union organizer, announced the names of each of those who perished: Stephen Adams, Sophia Buruwa Addo, Doris Eng, and so on until he called out all 79 names.

Cooper's account of the service made it into the final version of "Five Lives."

As Mr. Colon inched closer to the R's, Mrs. Rivas started shaking her head. "No, no, no," she said.

Mr. Haynes looked at Elizabeth Rivas. He felt certain that she was thinking: Why couldn't it have been him instead of Moises at the restaurant that day?

"Moises N. Rivas," Mr. Colon said.

Mr. Haynes stiffened in his chair, exhaled and said quietly, "Mo."

———————————

• Chapter Three •

Ianthe Jeanne Dugan
Are You Really with The Wall Street Journal?

Garry Cleveland Myers and Caroline Clark Myers founded *Highlights for Children* magazine in the tiny borough of Honesdale, Pennsylvania, in 1946. Their mission: to help children become their "best selves" by developing their reading, thinking, and reasoning skills.

Over the decades, the monthly *Highlights* magazine became ubiquitous in the waiting rooms of pediatric doctors and dentists. The brand expanded into games, websites, and other extensions aimed at kids from birth to age 12.

No wonder, then, that in the immediate aftermath of September 11, sources returning calls to *The Wall Street Journal*'s Ianthe Jeanne Dugan were puzzled when the voicemail system answered "Highlights for Children" rather than "The Wall Street Journal."

Previously a financial journalist for several respected news organizations, Dugan joined *The Wall Street Journal*'s *Money & Investing* team in October 2000 from *The Washington Post*, where she had covered Wall Street and proved her chops as an investigative reporter and feature writer. At the *Journal*, Dugan mostly wrote front-page stories on Wall Street and finance. She considered it a dream job.

On September 11, after dropping her daughter, Caitlin, a third-grader, at school, Dugan was driving down the FDR Drive toward Lower Manhattan when she caught a glimpse of an explosion and rippling smoke. From her vantage, it looked as if the origin of the conflagration was the 32-story New York Telephone Building, located adjacent to the World Trade Center.

At the southern tip of Manhattan, the FDR Drive flows into the Battery Park Underpass. The tunnel connects the east side of the city to West Street, which ran past *The Wall Street*

Journal's offices at 200 Liberty Street, as well as the site of the Twin Towers.

Once inside the subterranean passage, Dugan witnessed news crews and police running north toward the World Trade Center. The air reeked of smoke.

Something crazy is happening.

When she emerged once more into daylight, Dugan saw the top of Twin Towers aflame. Her gut told her the buildings were doomed.

She u-turned and headed back up the FDR Drive, collected her daughter, and then drove two-plus hours northwest on New York State Route 17 to her mother's home in Milanville, Pennsylvania. It was a getaway that Dugan had used periodically during her years at *The Washington Post* to write in seclusion. Built in 1815, her mother's home was situated on two acres of waterfront land along the Delaware River. In the backyard was a tiny house, more of an overgrown shed, where Dugan had previously generated some of her best prose.

Dugan reasoned she could contribute to the *Journal's* 9/11 coverage from the home of her mother, Sheila, speaking to her editors and colleagues, interviewing sources, and transmitting her stories, while Sheila looked after Caitlin. But the Milanville house had just one phone line and no cell service.

Dugan felt uneasy tying up her mother's phone the entire day. She walked across a nearby bridge over the Delaware and began making and receiving her business calls from a campground payphone.

I eventually went back to the house, and I was on the phone. My mother needed to make a call.

So she went over to the campground to use the payphone, and it rang. [Sheila picked it up.] It was somebody calling for me.

There had to be a better way.

Like almost everyone who lived in the vicinity, Dugan knew that *Highlights for Children*, one of the largest office-worker employers in the area, was based in nearby Honesdale. She drove to the magazine's offices, explained her predicament, and asked if she could work from there.

The *Highlights* folks were very understanding, providing Dugan a desk, phone, and voice-mail extension.

It was so strange, making these calls and calling people about this horrendous story and telling them I'm with The Wall Street Journal. People would call me back, and they'd get "Highlights for Children," and I knew they were thinking, "Who are you anyway? Are you really with the Journal?"

Dugan's search for a "Five Lives" profile subject began at *Highlights for Children*, as she combed through lists of World Trade Center victims and began, delicately, placing calls to their families.

Working alone in the magazine office on the evening of September 12, she reached a Bronx pediatrician who had last heard from her husband as he left home for a conference at the World Trade Center.

As she stoically described her college sweetheart, a baby cried in the background. I had to push the "mute" button for a moment to muffle my own sobs when she told me she believed her husband would return.

Dugan came back to Manhattan and continued her search for a suitable profile candidate. She made her way to the Plaza Hotel, located just south of Central Park off of Fifth Avenue. Several large companies had set up crisis centers at the Plaza to help families with psychological counseling, insurance services, daycare, and the like.

For a time, Dugan fixed her sights on a psychiatrist who was counseling families of Cantor Fitzgerald and Aon employees.

Located on five floors near the top of the North Tower, Cantor Fitzgerald, a financial services firm, lost 658 employees, nearly one-fourth of all the Trade Center victims. One hundred and seventy-six employees of Aon, an insurance and professional services firm with offices high in the South Tower, perished in the terrorist attacks.

Dugan found herself in a cavernous banquet room at the Plaza, where she spotted a tough-looking man — large, with big muscles and short spiked hair — in conversation with an insurance counselor. Later, she saw the same man, Richard DeBlase, 37, leaving the hotel, carrying a pile of manila envelopes. He was in tears.

I approached him and asked, "Did you lose someone?" "Yeah," he said, "My brother worked at Cantor. My other brother escaped from the other tower." He himself had left a job at the Twin Towers a few years earlier "to escape the rat race," he said, "but now it's sucking me back in."

Richard's eldest brother, James "Jimmy" DeBlase, 45, was a Cantor Fitzgerald bond broker. On the morning of September 11, Dugan later recounted in "Five Lives," Jimmy was on the phone with his wife discussing a fence they were planning to install at their Manalapan, New Jersey home.

They were talking about her plans for the day -- going to the bank, the dry cleaner, the post office -- when a sound like thunder interrupted them.

"Hold on," Mr. DeBlase said. In the background his wife, Marion, heard a voice shouting,

"What the f--- is that?" Mr. DeBlase got back on the phone. *"An airplane hit our building,"* he said. *"I have to go."*

Marion never spoke to Jimmy again.

———————————————

Two days after that phone call, Dugan spent five hours with Marion and her mother-in-law, Anita DeBlase, in Jimmy's Manalapan home.

Dugan interviewed the two women. She also spoke with Richard and Jimmy's middle brother, Anthony. The latter was at work on the 84th floor of the South Tower on 9/11 but escaped unscathed. Other family members and friends streamed through.

Dugan was fascinated by each of them. She wrestled with the question of who should be the focus of her portion of "Five Lives." Eventually, Dugan chose to tell Jimmy's story through the eyes of Anita, who gave birth to Jimmy when she was just 16 years old.

Photos of the feisty 62-year-old mother, gazing up at Mayor Giuliani on the morning of September 12, holding the city leader's hands, and imploring him to help her find her son in the rubble, to this day resurface regularly accompanying September 11 commemorations.

Anita, as Dugan recounted, was distributing "MISSING" posters featuring Jimmy — six-foot, 295 pounds, wearing a Yankees T-shirt.

A street-smart New Yorker, she concocted a story that Mayor Giuliani was expecting her. Anita convinced a police officer to give her a ride past the pedestrian barricades to await the mayor's arrival.

When the mayor pulled up, Mrs. DeBlase pushed through the crowd and ran toward him... Cameras captured the moment, to be beamed countless times around the world.

Dugan made several trips to visit the DeBlase family in New Jersey and also spent time at Anita's apartment in the Knickerbocker Village housing complex not far from City Hall. On September 25, Dugan joined Anita at P.S. 126 on the Lower East Side for a step-by-step re-enactment of Anita's day on 9/11, when she was a volunteer poll worker for the New York City mayoral primary.

At first, when Anita saw the billowing smoke from the World Trade Center, about a mile from P.S. 126, she crossed herself. She did what she could to comfort other poll workers who had family in the towers.

Only when Anita's husband, James, rushed into the school crying, "Jimmy Boy is in there," did it strike her, like a bolt of lightning, that her eldest son would have been at work at Cantor Fitzgerald when the planes hit.

Pressing against the flow of thousands of soot-covered people heading away from the burning towers, Anita made her way southward in the direction of the World Trade Center site.

She spotted in the sea of faces her [middle] son Anthony, the bond broker... and rushed up to hug him. "Jimmy," she said. "We have to find Jimmy." Anthony, his spiky, dark hair flecked with soot, looked skyward. "God, give me back my brother," he said. "You don't want him. He will criticize you and organize you. He will drive you crazy."

Pools of sorrow, waves of joy
Are drifting through my open mind
Possessing and caressing me

Nothing's gonna change my world
Nothing's gonna change my world
Nothing's gonna change my world

The chorus of The Beatles song, "Across the Universe," kept getting louder and louder as the silver BMW accelerated well past the speed limit on its way to the funeral of a family friend who had perished in the Twin Towers.

Anthony DeBlase was at the wheel, distraught over the loss of his brother and his friend. His foot, heavy on the accelerator, Anthony shouted along with The Beatles. He was in no condition to drive.

Dugan, who was alone in the car's backseat, kept glancing at the speedometer.

Oh, man, I'm going to die in here.

Anita, who was seated up front, didn't seem to notice either the music or the speed. She popped a Tylenol and told Dugan she also brought along Valium.

Ostensibly, that afternoon in Westchester, they would be burying partial remains recovered from Ground Zero. Anita confided in Dugan that she thought the authorities were just saying that in an effort to bring some closure to the victim's family. Anita believed the coffin was empty.

On Thursday, September 27, Dugan was with Anita and her husband in their Knickerbocker Village home when the two quarreled over what he should wear to Jimmy's funeral.

... he said he wanted to wear casual clothes to his son's service. He sat on their gold velour couch reading a pamphlet titled "How to make $10,000 a day for 30 days." Anita wanted him to wear his black suit to the funeral.

"This isn't a wedding," he said. "Why should I wear a suit?"

"Because it's your son," she said.

She fished out the white shirt that had sat in its original plastic wrapping in a drawer for years.

"No, no, no," he said.

She laid her black-wool pantsuit on her bed. Her husband called her into the living room.

Channel 2 news was playing "God Bless America," and there was Mrs. DeBlase on the screen, running up to Mayor Giuliani.

More than 1,000 attended Jimmy DeBlase's memorial service in Manalapan. Jimmy's father wore a suit.

The organist played "Ave Maria." Anita told Dugan, crying, that never in a million years did she imagine she'd live to hear that requiem played for her eldest child.

This can't be for my son. I don't even have a body.

• Chapter Four •

Bryan Gruley
Comfort the Afflicted, Afflict the Comfortable

Reporter Augustus J. "Gus" Carpenter grew up in a yellow clapboard house on the southern shore of Michigan's Starvation Lake, about 230 miles northwest of Detroit.

The 34-year-old unmarried journalist spent more than a decade working for the *Detroit Times*, most of it covering the auto industry.

In 1996, he came across the kind of Pulitzer Prize fodder that journalists wait their whole career to uncover. One of the Motor City's major vehicle manufacturers had designed their pickup trucks situating the fuel tanks between the chassis and the outer shell. In crashes, the tanks ruptured like an egg in a vise. Hundreds of people had been severely burned or killed as a result.

Until Carpenter exposed the design flaw, the company managed to keep its explosive problem under wraps by dolling out hush money to the injured or the families of the deceased.

Carpenter hadn't set out to be a newspaperman. He worked summers at the local marina, swabbing boat decks. In his sophomore year at the University of Michigan, he'd taken a journalism course. Carpenter, who loved hockey, thought he'd try sports reporting over the summer. One of his neighbors was the executive editor of a tiny weekly, the *Pine County Pilot*. With an assist from his mother, Carpenter landed his first journalism job.

The *Pine County Pilot, however,* did not need a sports reporter. So Carpenter resigned himself to covering general news, including town council, police procedure, zoning variances, and the like.

Almost by accident, the rookie reporter landed his first big scoop. It had the whole of

Starvation Lake wagging their tongues.

Carpenter was sold on a career in journalism.

I propped my feet up on the desk and reread my story about twenty times. I kept thinking, This is just what my professors taught: Comfort the afflicted, afflict the comfortable...

If something could make me feel this good for even one night, and it didn't hurt anyone who didn't deserve to be hurt, maybe it was something I could actually do, something I might actually be good at, something that might actually make somebody proud of me.

Years later, Carpenter was one of three finalists for a Pulitzer Prize in National Reporting.

The Wall Street Journal's Bryan Gruley crafted Gus Carpenter as the protagonist in his first mystery novel, *Starvation Lake*, published to wide acclaim in early 2009. None other than Harlan Coben, the mega-bestselling author of mystery novels and thrillers, dubbed *Starvation Lake* "a great debut from a major talent."

Whether the genre was fiction or nonfiction, no one at the *Journal* who has followed the career of Bryan Gruley ever doubted his uncommon skill as a writer and editor.

It was Gruley, who on September 11, sat zoned in at his computer terminal in the middle of the *Journal's* chaotic D.C. newsroom and curated the memos of dozens of his remote colleagues into the Page One roundup on September 12, "Nation Stands In Disbelief And Horror," recounting the riveting storylines of survivors.

They were like scenes from a catastrophe movie. Or a Tom Clancy novel. Or a CNN broadcast from a distant foreign nation.

But they were real yesterday. And they were very much in the U.S.

Gruley was also the pillar of the "Five Lives" feature. When D.C. bureau chief Alan Murray ordered up a "second track of coverage" on the morning of September 12 — aiming to distinguish the paper's reporting from *The New York Times* and other competitive news outlets — it was Gruley to whom Murray turned to refine the concept and serve as the lead writer.

Gruley developed the ultimate construct for the "Five Lives" story. Their feature would follow the chosen characters from beginning to resolution, as a few minutes on September 11 upended their lives.

We were all worried about competition. Wouldn't everybody be writing gripping stories about escapes and coping with mourning and such? What could we do that would transcend those stories?

The answer: detail and — most importantly — development of character.

Gruley contributed one of the five profiles, that of Diane Murray, who had worked for Aon in the South Tower. And, once again under severe deadline pressure, he condensed the drafts submitted by Cooper, Dugan, Kuntz, and Prager into a governable final manuscript.

Like the fictional Gus Carpenter, the central character in all three books in the *Starvation Lake* mystery series, Gruley is a hockey enthusiast, grew up in Michigan, and used to love spending time at a lake cottage his parents owned in the northern Lower Peninsula. Gruley's initiation into journalism came as a summer reporting intern at an obscure nearby newspaper.

In a Q&A at the back of *Starvation Lake*, Gruley writes that Carpenter is an amalgam of many people he's known, while acknowledging that his years working for newspapers small and large informed much of his fictional character's behavior and choices.

Storytelling has been a big part of my journalistic career, both as a reporter who loved to write nonfiction narratives and an editor who encourages others to write them.

"**Five Lives**" is only two degrees of separation from Thornton Wilder's 1927 Pulitzer Prize-winning novel *The Bridge of San Luis Rey*. Set in the early 18th century, Wilder describes the fictional backstories of five travelers who perish when an ancient Inca rope bridge that they're traversing collapses, sending them plunging into the river far below.

The tragedy is witnessed by a friar, Brother Juniper, who sees the hand of God in their deaths and spends the next six years learning and documenting everything he can about the victims in an attempt to find a justification for their violent demise.

John Hersey read *The Bridge of San Luis Rey* as he crossed the ocean to interview survivors of the atomic blast at Hiroshima, Japan, and was inspired by Wilder's narrative methods. The resulting article, "Hiroshima," was published in August 1946 in *The New Yorker*, taking up the magazine's entire issue.

Nicholas Lemann, who spent a decade as the dean of the Graduate School of Journalism at Columbia University, reflected on Hersey and "Hiroshima" in an April 2019 feature article in *The New Yorker*, "John Hersey and the Art of Fact."

[Hersey adopted Wilder's technique] of braiding the stories of an ensemble of characters. From the dozens of people he interviewed, he chose six, alternating among them so that each character appeared in every major phase of the chronology.

Hersey's writing voice is calmly recitative, bordering on affectless — "deliberately quiet," as he later put it.

Bryan Gruley channeled both Wilder and Hersey when he settled on the approach for "Five Lives."

Gruley discovered Diane Murray thanks to a friend and former *Journal* colleague, John Keller. Keller was having his hair cut on September 13. The gossipy barber told him about three people who worked in the South Tower who had survived: Murray, Paul Sanchez, and Peter Webster. Keller elicited Sanchez's phone number from the barber and passed it along to Gruley.

Sanchez was effusive in his praise for Murray. He relayed how Murray saved their lives by insisting that he and Webster descend the stairway from their 92nd-floor cubicles in the South Tower even as the public address system repeatedly assured everyone that despite the fire in the North Tower, the South Tower was secure.

As Gruley subsequently wrote, Murray was an Aon client-account specialist and commuted daily from Newark, New Jersey. The 29-year-old had an eight-year-old daughter, Diana.

Gruley didn't meet Diane until September 14. He described his first interaction with her as challenging.

Once she told me the essential story of her escape, she wasn't eager to talk further. She wanted to get on with her life.

Nevertheless, Gruley wheedled several interviews with her.

Additional anecdotes in his "Five Lives" story came from Murray's mother, Jean, the administrator of a small hospital in New Jersey, and from Sanchez and Webster.

The retelling of Murray's September 11 experience did not carry the emotional punch of Moises Rivas, Jimmy DeBlase, Jimmy Barbella, or Joshua Prager's profile subject, Shimmy Biegeleisen. After all, those four men died and left behind grieving families.

But Murray's story did allow Gruley to infuse the final "Five Lives" article with the kind of rich 'fly-on-the-wall' details that would have been nearly impossible to capture without her first-person account.

She set down her pineapple-orange muffin, glanced out at the flawless blue sky and took her seat. She slipped off her tennis shoes and put on the black sandals she had carried on her commute... The dressier shoes hurt her feet, but she liked how they looked with her black skirt and orange linen jacket.

Ninety-two flights of stairs later and blocks of jogging away from the wreckage in heels, Murray hobbled into a shoe store on Park Avenue South. She plunked down $43 for a pair of black sneakers. Her feet, Gruley wrote, were killing her.

The South Tower elevators still were running when the winded Murray, Sanchez, and Webster found themselves in the lobby of the 55th floor, weighing their chances of making an easier egress. Gruley's elevator anecdote made it into the final "Five Lives" story.

Two elevators were jammed with people — going up. In another elevator, a tall, well-dressed man reassured the throng in the lobby. "Everything's all right," he said. "Stay calm." But his elevator was going down.

"If everything's all right, how come you're not going up to your office?" Ms. Murray shouted at him as the doors slid shut.

The fact that Diane Murray lived to tell her own "Five Lives" story made Gruley's job in profiling her simpler than the tasks faced by Cooper, Dugan, Kuntz, and Prager in reconstructing their characters' day on September 11.

In retrospect, it's fortunate I chose her. As the only main character who escaped the buildings, she acted as ballast for the others, contributing a touch of humor — the shoe shopping — and some hope.

Gruley used the bonus time that his Murray profile afforded him to help his colleagues with their drafts and to write the final, truncated version that the group submitted to the Page One editors, Mike Miller and John Blanton.

Murray stood resolute when an Aon manager phoned to instruct her to report to the company's temporary quarters in Midtown Manhattan on October 1. No, she replied. She intended to go on worker's compensation and puzzled over whether she would ever return to Manhattan.

She had skipped Aon's memorial service at St. Patrick's Cathedral because she was spooked by the prospect of going back to New York. She wanted to work from Aon's Parsippany, New Jersey office, or her place in Newark.

When Murray finally made her way home on September 11, her daughter was asleep. She read from Psalm 91.

"Though a thousand fall at your side, ten thousand at your right side, near you it shall not come…"

Outside, a thunderstorm cracked and boomed. [Murray] walked to her front door and stood with her Bible in one hand and a phone in the other, wondering if she should wake [her daughter] and leave. Was that really thunder? Or the sound of bombs exploding? She felt relieved when she saw a lightning bolt tear through the sky.

• Chapter Five •

Phil Kuntz
Did You Hear About Jimmy Barbella?

Sarah Barbella, 20, the youngest child of James W. "Jimmy" Barbella, was practicing her typing skills at a business school near her family's home in Oceanside, Long Island.

It was just after 9:20 a.m. on September 11. Her father, a property manager at the World Trade Center, had just phoned her mother, Monica, to say he was okay. Monica had watched in horror the live broadcast of the second plane hitting the South Tower, where Jimmy's office was located.

When Jimmy called, she relayed the good news to her two other adult children.

Monica: *Oh my God, it's Jimmy. Oh, thank God you're okay. Where are you?*

Jimmy: *I'm in the Operations Control Center.*

Monica: *Okay.*

Jimmy didn't have much time to talk, and in the rush of emotion, Monica hung up, cutting off her husband in mid-sentence. He dialed back immediately, inquiring about what details she had learned from the news. She briefed him.

Jimmy: *Okay, I gotta go.*

Monica: *Okay, goodbye.*

At school, Sarah overheard her typing instructor talking about the attacks on the Twin Towers. She dashed out of the classroom to find a phone, covering her mouth to stifle her sobs. When Monica answered, Sarah released a torrent of tears.

Sarah: *Where's Daddy?*

Monica: *He just called me. He's okay. He's okay.*

Not so.

Jimmy Barbella would die sometime that morning, although no one knows precisely where he was or how he died. What is known is that Barbella had multiple opportunities to safely evacuate between the time the two planes hit and the two towers collapsed. The ex-Marine, however, remained behind to help others escape and to guide first responders to those still in the building who needed rescuing.

Sarah got a ride home from her boyfriend. His white button-down shirt was smeared with the makeup streaming down her face. By the time Sarah arrived at her parents' two-story, wood-shingled home, the South Tower had collapsed. Watching the destruction on television, Monica dropped to her knees, then to all fours. Sarah barged into the house.

Sarah: *Mommy, Mommy, Mommy, Mommy.*

While Monica and her other two children each coped with the presumed death of Jimmy differently, Sarah was filled with venom over her loss.

She and her boyfriend joined family members and friends in Manhattan the next day, making the rounds to area hospitals and missing-persons centers, hoping for some word of Jimmy. At Chelsea Piers, an insensitive worker asked Sarah about her father.

Is he circumcised?

Sarah refused to give up hope. She imagined her dad stuck in the rubble, looking at family pictures in his wallet. She was convinced she'd find Jimmy limping down the street or sitting on a bench, covered in soot. He'd be thirsty, so she bought a bottle of water and carried it all day.

An hour after sunset in Manhattan, she and her boyfriend headed home.

Sarah's experience, adroitly reconstructed by the *Journal's* Phil Kuntz, was gripping.

Not a word of her tribulations, however, made it into the paper.

The entirety of what readers missed in the 14,650 words that were axed from the original versions that Cooper, Dugan, Gruley, Kuntz, and Prager submitted is unknowable.

Kuntz is the only one of the "Five Lives Five" to have kept his original submission, or at least the only one of the group who nearly two decades later could still locate their initial version.

Only 1,572 words of the 5,455-word draft — or 29% of his text — survived the rigorous editing process.

Fretting that the Barbellas would be disappointed with the paired down rendition of the story as it appeared in the paper, Kuntz, who had grown close to the family, knowingly violated journalism norms and sent Monica his original manuscript.

Among other particulars of Kuntz's "Five Lives" submission that the *Journal's* redactors chopped, were:

- Jimmy was working on the B-2 level of the World Trade Center in February 1993 when he and his chair were knocked over by the shock wave from the blast of the first Twin Towers bombing. Among the six people killed that day were coworkers with whom Jimmy had been invited to lunch later that day.

- Frank Barbella Sr., Jimmy's father, survived the Battle of the Bulge in World War II. Jimmy was named after his father's brother, James, a tail-gunner shot down over Germany in 1943.

- Jimmy's eldest daughter, JoAnn, was born on September 11 and turned 25 years old the day her father died.

One poignant detail in Kuntz's "Five Lives" story survived the final cut and left many readers wondering how Kuntz knew about Jimmy's behavior the morning he died.

The eldest of seven children in a devout Catholic family, Mr. Barbella had soured on the church and lately had been meditating near a statue of the Buddha he had put in his back-yard in Oceanside, N.Y. Now, gazing at the [World Trade Center] plaza, he made a hasty sign of the cross.

Kuntz never met Jimmy Barbella. By coincidence, the reporter was on a bus one day in the aftermath of the attacks, riding along with displaced Port Authority employees. Seated next to him was a Trade Center technician who introduced himself as David Bobbitt. Amazingly, Kuntz's random seatmate knew Barbella and had spent time with him on September 11.

Bobbitt, whose name appears only in a footnote to the "Five Lives" story, shared his tear-ful recollections at a nearby pizza parlor.

Mr. Barbella walked onto the plaza and looked up at the north tower. "Jim, let's get off the plaza. We're going to get hit," Mr. Bobbitt called out from the revolving doors. "This is unbe-lievable," Mr. Barbella said after returning. For a while, Mr. Barbella directed would-be gawkers away from the shattered windows, waving them toward the escalators. From 20 paces away, Mr. Bobbitt turned and saw [Barbella] again looking out at the plaza and motioning very quickly with his right hand, touching his forehead, then his belly, then his left and right shoulders - the sign of the cross.

———————————

In the wake of the September 11 attacks and his nightmarish experience witnessing and fleeing the raining debris and horrific scenes in Lower Manhattan, Phil Kuntz was floundering.

I was so fucking devastated.... I didn't know what to do with myself, either personally or professionally.

Kuntz called Alan Murray and told his bureau chief that he wasn't doing well emotionally.

Murray, who was assembling the "Five Lives" team, asked Kuntz to see if he could find a suitable profile subject.

Murray may have assigned Kuntz because he knew the reporter needed something to snap him out of his malaise or because he knew Kuntz was a talented reporter and writer. It was likely both.

But as Kuntz would later reflect, "Five Lives" and the time he spent with the Barbellas proved a life-changing experience for him.

I would have been lost without them. I needed something to focus my attention on, I needed it, and it had to be related to what happened. And I found this family that was so loving and took me in.

———————————

Phil Kuntz was surveying his friends in New Jersey, hoping to find a suitable candidate to profile for the "Five Lives" story.

Did you hear about Jimmy Barbella?

One acquaintance, who lived next door to a Port Authority employee, asked Kuntz if he had heard about the World Trade Center manager who died trying to save people trapped in the choked-off Windows on the World restaurant.

Kuntz knew he had found his lead character.

The 41-year-old journalist had been with *The Wall Street Journal* since 1994, first as a reporter, then as an assistant D.C. bureau chief and news editor. In 2000, Kuntz oversaw a series on defense spending and military deployment in the post-Cold War era that earned the *Journal* a Pulitzer Prize for National Reporting. A talented investigative journalist, Kuntz conceived, edited, or reported on a variety of topics, including terrorism, homeland defense, law enforcement, lobbying, and campaign finance.

Kuntz reached out to a reluctant Monica Barbella.

I initially told [her] just that I was thinking of doing a story about her husband and wanted to chat with her.

Monica had gotten calls from other reporters and rejected them. She didn't want to cooperate with Kuntz, either.

The journalist persuaded Monica to at least meet face-to-face to discuss the prospect of featuring Jimmy. On Kuntz's initial visit to her home, Monica was joined by a group of immediate and extended family members.

Kuntz offered those who were gathered a bargain, and not one that journalists generally feel is appropriate when trying to maintain their objectivity.

My skill is as an investigative reporter…. I promise you if you cooperate with me, and I throw myself into the story of Jimmy, I'm going to find out what happened to him.

For the Barbellas, and so many other 9/11 families, the not-knowing was excruciating. They said, "yes."

Kuntz sat in the middle of the family room and hardly had to ask questions. Like a group therapy session, each of those present shared their memories of Jimmy and the agony of September 11.

Kuntz scribbled notes gingerly on a pad but soon switched to his laptop as the family members talked rapidly and across each other.

True to his word, Kuntz went above and beyond what was needed for the "Five Lives" feature, searching for clues about what happened to Jimmy Barbella. It consumed a great deal of his time.

I traced every single person I could find who in any way had come across Jimmy that day, from the guy he was with on the train ride to his boss who talked to him when he got there that day. I tracked down everybody who I could possibly find.

Before 9/11, Kuntz had maintained scrupulous journalistic integrity when he was uncovering rules violations that led the U.S. House's Ethics Committee to reprimand then-Speaker Newt Gingrich, and when Kuntz exposed laundered donations at a fundraiser Vice President Al Gore held at a Buddhist temple.

But Kuntz wasn't investigating the Barbellas, and he permitted himself to eschew any pretense that he was keeping an unbiased detachment from the family.

I hung out with them for hours, even while not doing interviews or even taking any notes. I did my laundry at their house. I ate dinner over at Jimmy's parent's house; we had eggplant from Jimmy's garden .... I spent maybe five minutes clearing up a few questions. The rest of the time, I just enjoyed their company.

Two decades later, distant from the context of the times and the gut-wrenching experiences that Kuntz and his *Wall Street Journal* colleagues endured, critics can argue that Kuntz crossed the line in bonding with the Barbellas. He acknowledges as much.

In many ways, I became way too close to them. I think I became closer to my characters than anybody else did. And I just said to myself, "Well, fuck it. I got to do what I got to do."

To this day, Kuntz believes that Jimmy Barbella never received the public acknowledgment he deserves for giving his life trying to save others.

Barbella loved the World Trade Center, where he'd spent most of his career. He was hired by the Port Authority in 1973, not long after the construction of the Twin Towers was completed. He worked his way up from being a polyester-jacketed janitorial supervisor to a property manager responsible for floors nine to 40 in the South Tower.

In his original "Five Lives" draft, Kuntz wrote that over the 28 years that Barbella worked for the Port Authority, he and the towers became one.

In the end, Kuntz never did discover what Barbella's final movements were. In his unpublished draft, Kuntz quoted fire-alarm subcontractors who encountered Barbella at the base of the escalator in the lobby of the North Tower at about 9:50 a.m., less than ten minutes before the South Tower collapsed.

He was wearing a dark emergency flak jacket and waving people toward the mall. Emergency lights cast a dim pall and the fire sprinklers were going, making the indoor scene seem like an early evening torrential downpour. Mr. Barbella was up to his ankles in water.

"Hey Jimmy, what's up?" asked John DePaulis, one of the fire-alarm techs.

"How're you doing, Johnny?" Mr. Barbella responded, shaking his hand.

"What are you doing?" Mr. DePaulis asked, incredulous that his colleague hadn't fled yet.

At home in Oceanside, unlike her youngest daughter who hoped that somehow her father had survived and would still be located, Kuntz recounted that Monica told him she knew her husband was dead as soon as she saw the towers fall.

I said, "How?"

And she said, "Because there was no fucking way he was ever leaving that building."

Ten days before "Five Lives" was published, Monica emailed Kuntz.

I want to take this opportunity to say thank you for all you have done for my family. In those early days of this disaster you gave us a focus and even helped those who might be too destroyed by this by giving them a place to talk and laugh about Jimmy …

Sometimes you can make a friend in the strangest places, and I do consider you a friend to us. I have many things to say to you but I just can't seem to be able to string them together but know that you are in my heart.

Kuntz attended Jimmy's funeral, which disquieted him.

This is trite to say, but after the funeral was over, I sat on a bench outside the church — out of view of everybody, thankfully — and sobbed uncontrollably for a long time.

In the days and weeks that followed, the Barbellas resigned themselves to never knowing for sure what happened to Jimmy. The final words Kuntz wrote in his original draft of "Five Lives" never made it into print.

The family's search now over, some of the Barbellas began returning to work, but much of the coming weeks was spent gathered at different homes with friends and family.

Monica's house sported a yellow ribbon and a sign on the door: "It is possible to move a mountain by carrying away small stones."

She took up smoking again but is otherwise the family's pillar of strength. Lou [Jimmy's brother] missed a day of work, but otherwise functioned. Jimmy's parents had a whole crowd over for dinner one night and served mostly goods from their son's garden, including eggplant parmesan.

• Chapter Six •

Joshua Prager
And He Thanked Me for Calling

The most famous play in sports history, as it's frequently been called, occurred on October 3, 1951.

It was the bottom of the 9th inning. The home-team New York Giants were trailing the Brooklyn Dodgers 4-2. The winners of that afternoon's contest at the Polo Grounds would go on to face the New York Yankees in the World Series. For the losing team, well, there was always next year.

On the mound for the Dodgers was Ralph Branca, a 25-year-old reliever who entered the game with one out and Giants players already on second and third base. At bat was the Giant's 28-year-old right-handed third baseman, Bobby Thomson.

Thomson took the first pitch, a fastball, for strike one. Then, at 3:58 p.m., as Russ Hodges, the Giants radio broadcaster called it, Thomson unleashed the shot heard 'round the world.

Branca throws. There's a long drive. It's going to be — I believe! The Giants win the pennant! The Giants win the pennant! The Giants win the pennant! The Giants win the pennant! Bobby Thomson hits into the lower deck of the left-field stands. The Giants win the pennant! And they're going crazy! They're going crazy! Oohhh-oohhh!

It took just shy of fifty years to expose the truth.

Joshua Prager had established his credentials as a gifted feature writer for *The Wall Street Journal* well before joining the "Five Lives" team.

His first breakout story, "Runaway Money," was published on the paper's front page almost a year to the day before the September 11 attacks. Prager's feature profiled Albert Edwards Clarke III, a 57-year-old scoundrelly vagabond and ex-con who, as a child, was bequeathed the royalties from 79 of author Margaret Wise Brown's catalog of children's books, most notable among them, the classic *Goodnight Moon*.

Only 130-words long, *Goodnight Moon* yielded Mr. Clarke nearly $5 million over the years and, with its quasi-hypnotic ability to lull toddlers to sleep, became one of the best-selling picture books of all time. For readers of the *Journal* who needed a refresher on the contents of Brown's "great green room" — two little kittens, a pair of mittens, a little toy house, and a young mouse, among them — and their literary relevance, Prager offered a review.

... the story moves from page to page like an incantation. Security and possession are its themes. Its cadence and increasingly shaded illustrations are as soporific as warm milk.

The contrast between Brown's innocent story and Clarke's hardscrabble life captured the public's attention. Prager's unmasking of the historical paradox continues to ripple to this day.

But Prager's *Goodnight Moon* revelations, and for that matter, none of his other absorbing articles up until then, excited readers quite like his January 31, 2001, front-page story: "Inside Baseball: Giants' 1951 Comeback, The Sport's Greatest, Wasn't All It Seemed."

Prager's story, which relied on exemplary journalistic sleuthing, proved beyond any doubt that Bobby Thomson's game-winning home run against the Dodgers was aided by an elaborate scheme involving a confederate in the outfield and a spyglass. The ploy allowed Thomson and his Giants teammates to learn in advance what type of pitch — fastball, curveball, other — the opponent's pitchers were about to throw.

Many people abhorred Prager's story, although they couldn't stop talking about it. At the 2001 national baseball writers dinner, the emcee dismissed Prager's reporting as "scandalous."

Millions of baseball fans, many of whom, like Prager, weren't born for decades after 1951, revered the mythical version of the Thomson-Branca duel. To his critics, Prager responded that what he reported was the truth, regardless of how unpalatable.

The Washington Post columnist George F. Will, a baseball aficionado, weighed in on Prager's article.

[Prager] demonstrated that baseball's most storied comeback, which culminated in baseball's most famous moment, was assisted by cheating.

... The importance of protecting the integrity of competition from the threat of advantages obtained illicitly is underscored by the sense of melancholy, of loss, that baseball fans now feel

about the no longer quite so luminous season of 1951.

Prager pitched "Inside Baseball" as a book, and it was quickly picked up. He took a leave of absence from the *Journal* to write what would eventually become *The Echoing Green: The Untold Story of Bobby Thomson, Ralph Branca And The Shot Heard Round The World.* *The Washington Post* named it a "Best Book of the Year."

On September 11, Prager was on leave researching *The Echoing Green.* In the immediate wake of the destruction and human misery caused by the terrorist attacks, Prager felt he should put his talents to a greater purpose than writing about a baseball game five decades earlier.

Prager was unaware of the "Five Lives" project but phoned the *Journal* to volunteer his help covering the 9/11 aftermath. Given his credentials as a feature writer, there was no question of where he could contribute the most.

Thus, the story that might otherwise have run as "Four Lives" now had a fifth contributor and would soon include a fifth World Trade Center family.

———————————

In the course of producing their Page One feature, the "Five Lives Five" became good friends, or in the case of Cooper, Gruley, and Kuntz, who already knew one another, better friends. But they also locked horns, especially when it came to ensuring that each of their profile candidates received a comparable amount of space in the final version of the story.

All five of the journalists agreed, however, that the closing scene of their "Five Lives" feature should be the one submitted by Prager.

Prager knew from personal experience how people, such as the survivors and families of 9/11 victims, could, in the blink of an eye, have their lives divided into two parts - "before" and "after."

"Before," of course, represented every life experience from birth until the morning of September 11. "After," nothing would ever be the same.

For Prager, the divide occurred on May 16, 1990, at age 19. He was a healthy, athletic teen one minute and a hemiplegic with a broken neck, on a respirator, not long after.

Prager grew up in a Modern Orthodox Jewish home. He attended an elite Jewish high school in Manhattan and intended to spend a gap year in Israel before enrolling at Columbia College.

It was in Israel, riding in the back seat of a minibus on its way to Jerusalem, that a truck driver named Abed lost control of his vehicle and plowed into the corner of the coach where Prager was seated.

A week after the accident, Prager, still on a respirator, was airlifted by a medical jet to New York for treatment in the ICU and eventual rehab. He could not speak, move, or feel anything below his neck.

As Prager relearned the basics — of speaking, dressing, and standing — he spent four years in a wheelchair. In time, he was able to walk with a cane and an ankle brace.

Prager joined the *Journal* in New York as a reporting assistant in August 1996, followed by a tour of duty as a full-fledged reporter in the Atlanta bureau. At the time, he used the byline, "Joshua Harris Prager."

He was never particularly impressive as a straight-on business and financial journalist, but he excelled at feature writing. By 1998, the powers-that-be allowed Prager to focus primarily on generating in-depth, well-written articles. A stickler for details, it was common for him to spend four months or more on a single story.

The *Journal* nominated the "Goodnight Moon" and "Shot Heard 'Round the World" stories for the Pulitzer Prize.

Prager, who came to prominence revealing the unknown history of noteworthy people and events, had his own undiscovered backstory. He had composed all of his prize-worthy articles by typing them with one index finger, his only healthy digit.

The two-day holiday of Rosh Hashanah, marking the start of a new year (5761) on the Jewish calendar, began the evening of September 17 in 2001.

Prager was spending the holiday in Englewood, New Jersey, where he and his three siblings were raised.

Having been assigned to the "Five Lives" team, he was on the hunt for a profile candidate. Walking home from services, Prager overheard a conversation between two congregants of another synagogue.

As the story went, an observant Jewish man trapped on the upper floors of the World Trade Center managed to reach his rabbi by phone. In Judaism, suicide is a grave sin. But knowing his fate was sealed one way or another, the man asked his rabbi if Jewish law would permit him to jump to his death rather than perish agonizingly in the fast-approaching smoke and flames.

I set out to find the man.

What Prager found, however, was that the anecdote was apocryphal.

Nevertheless, the false start set his mind racing over the question of how the special circumstances faced by some religious Jews might serve as a metaphor for the plight of many 9/11 families in the search for closure.

The journalist soon caught onto the tale of another observant Jewish man and his family. This time, the story was verifiable.

Shimmy Biegeleisen, 42, worked on the 97th floor of the South Tower, five stories above Diane Murray. He was a vice president for Fiduciary Trust International Inc., a money-management firm.

Like Murray, he could have gotten out safely before the second plane hit. However, when Biegeleisen reached the stairwell doorway, he rummaged through the black canvas bag he was carrying and, according to a colleague who was a couple of steps ahead of him, realized he'd forgotten something.

Whatever you're looking for, it's not important. Please come.

Biegeleisen didn't, returning instead to his desk and his imminent demise.

United Flight #175 hit the South Tower at 9:02 a.m., engulfing the stairwells in flames and quickly sending thick black smoke throughout Fiduciary Trust's offices.

Biegeleisen called his wife and told her he loved her. Shaken, Miriam Biegeleisen handed the phone to Dovid Langer, a family friend who had rushed over when he learned a plane had struck one of the towers.

Dovid, take care of Miriam and take care of my children. I'm not coming out of this.

Soon, as Prager chronicled, others arrived at the Biegeleisen home to offer Shimmy advice and to console his family.

The Biegeleisen home was filling with worried friends and neighbors. Women clustered in the living room, trying to calm Mrs. Biegeleisen. Men paced in the kitchen, taking turns speaking to her husband.

A surgeon friend advised Biegeleisen to stay low to the ground and cover his mouth with a wet towel. Another friend urged Biegeleisen, who was lying on the floor beneath photos of his five children, to break a window to let in some fresh air.

Prager, who after Rosh Hashanah spent days on end with the Biegeleisens in their Brooklyn home — making the hours-long round-trip commute from his apartment on the Upper West Side — captured Shimmy's last words.

Mr. Biegeleisen called out to a colleague. "Let's go! Let's break the window!" At 9:59, the two men hauled a filing cabinet to the window. "I'm looking out the window now," Mr. Biege-

leisen said into the phone. Then he screamed: "Oh God!" The line went dead.

It took only ten seconds for the South Tower to crumple, taking with it 800 people, including Shimmy Biegeleisen.

That might have been a powerful way to end the "Five Lives" story, but Prager's heartbreaking narrative continued.

To get on with her life, Miriam Biegeleisen would now have to prove to a committee of rabbis — without her husband's body as evidence — that her husband was dead. To non-Jews and less-observant Jews, the law of *agunah* no doubt seems arcane at best, and to most modern sensibilities, cruel and absurd.

Prager and his *Journal* editors realized as much. Yet, as Prager subsequently recounted in an internal email, the issue facing the Biegeleisens had common elements with everyone who was impacted by 9/11, regardless of their religion.

The law of agunah seemed to me a poignant and apt symbol of the unique horror facing all of America in the wake of the attack: the quest for closure even as thousands of bodies remained missing.

On October 12, the same day that "Five Lives" ran on the paper's front page, Prager wrote a second article, "For Some Jews, 'Missing' Is Not 'Presumed Dead,'" explaining *agunah* in greater detail. The story ran on the front page of the paper's second section.

Of the estimated 4,815 people who remained missing one month after September 11, among those for whom any religion could be determined, roughly 170 were Jewish. Prager spelled out their predicament.

According to the Talmud, the encyclopedic 1,500-year-old body of Jewish law, if a married man disappears, his spouse is deemed an agunah -- unfit to remarry unless a beit din, a rabbinic court, is able to satisfactorily assume the death of the husband.

Undoubtedly, the last thing on Miriam Biegeleisen's mind on September 11 and the days that immediately followed was remarrying. But the law of *agunah* also meant that she and her family could not begin the traditional week of mourning, or *shiva*, which begins the day after a loved one's passing. Unlike *agunah*, which only a fraction of Jewish people observe, most self-identifying Jews follow the *shiva* mourning ritual after the death of an immediate family member.

In "Five Lives," Prager wrote that Shimmy Biegeleisen, who wore a black-felt yarmulke at work, was a devoted follower of the Belzer Rebbe, the leader of a Hasidic rabbinic dynasty dating back to 1815. In fact, Biegeleisen and his 19-year-old son Mordechai were supposed to travel to Israel on September 16 to spend the Jewish New Year with the Belzer Rebbe and other members of his global flock.

Three rabbis, wearing long earlocks, black overcoats, and traditional wide-brim velvet hats, gathered at the Brooklyn home of 76-year-old Rabbi Efraim Fishel Hershkowitz to adjudicate the status of Miriam Biegeleisen. Was she an *agunah* or not?

The rabbis called witnesses — friends who had spoken to Shimmy on 9/11 — and they studied photographs of the wreckage of the Twin Towers.

They referenced a case, from a 16th-century book of Jewish law, of a furnace fire from which there was no escape. Mr. Biegeleisen's situation was just such a case, they said. His death could be assumed. Mrs. Biegeleisen was not an *agunah*. The mourning could begin.

———————

Prager was shocked when the Biegeleisen family asked him to speak at Shimmy's memorial service. In keeping with the traditions of Hasidic Jewry, the men sat on one side of the funeral hall, and the women sat on the other side. Thousands of mourners attended.

Prager began his remarks with a confession. Although he'd never met or spoken to Shimmy, the husband, father, and man of God was ever-present in Prager's thoughts throughout his weeks of reporting.

I was trying to do right by him.

Prager told the crowd that he had Shimmy's cell phone number.

When I finished the article, I called his number. I just wanted to call his number. So I called, and the phone rings and no one picks up, of course. But there's his voice. And he thanked me for calling.

———————

The final scene in the "Five Lives" story occurred weeks earlier.

The Biegeleisens' mourning period was at its end, and Prager was with the family in their Brooklyn home.

The phone rang.

Shimmy's wife, children, parents, brother, and sister all rushed upstairs.

Despite his limited mobility, Prager chased after them. The family had encircled a phone in a closed room and placed the caller on speaker.

From Jerusalem, they were hearing the voice of the Belzer Rebbe, Issachar Dov Rokeach. The 53-year-old Rebbe spoke in Yiddish, which Prager didn't understand. Thanks to a college course at Columbia, however, he could make out a few words.

Prager's written enumeration of the Rabbi's call brought the "Five Lives" story to a close.

[The Rebbe] asked for the men and boys, one by one, and recited to each the Hebrew verse traditionally spoken to mourners: "May the Omnipresent console you among the other mourners of Zion and Jerusalem."

Finished, the Rebbe said, "There are no words." A dial tone reverberated in the room as the family echoed him, over and over: "There are no words. There are no words. There are no words."

• Chapter Seven •

The Book of Habakkuk

At their working session in Dugan's apartment on Friday night, October 5, she, Cooper, Kuntz, and Prager agreed, more or less, on which parts of their story drafts they hoped that Bryan Gruley, who was not present, would restore.

Dugan's inquisitive eight-year-old daughter, Caitlin Cooper, who carried her birth father's surname, hovered around the group. Helene took to calling Caitlin "Mini Coop," which made everyone laugh.

At the conclusion of the night, adult Cooper took it upon herself to rework the draft to incorporate their proposed changes. She crashed that night on a blue-and-white striped Jennifer Convertibles sofa in Dugan's living room.

Over the following weekend, the "Five Lives Five" frequently phoned one another with additional suggestions.

On Sunday, October 7, Gruley began his morning by attending church. One of the readings at Mass was from the *Book of Habakkuk*, in which the eponymous Biblical prophet, who lived circa 600 B.C., laments that there is no justice in the land and no punishment for wickedness.

O LORD, how long shall I cry, and thou wilt not hear! Even cry out unto thee of violence, and thou wilt not save! Why dost thou shew me iniquity, and cause me to behold grievance? For spoiling and violence are before me: and there are that raise up strife and contention. Therefore the law is slacked, and judgment doth never go forth: for the wicked doth compass about the righteous; therefore wrong judgment proceedeth.

After Mass, in the *Journal's* D.C newsroom, Gruley began working through the "Five

Lives" scenes yet again, seeking to appease his colleagues when possible and to retain the story's cinematic flair. The five agreed they'd convene by phone for one final read-through that night at 9:00 p.m.

Gruley began by reciting a passage from that week's *Book of Habakkuk* missalette. Certainly, their "Five Lives" story, if it had a subtext, would echo the prophet's cry that evil flourishes at the expense of the innocent.

At 9:00 p.m., Kuntz called in from the balcony of his hotel room in Long Island, where he was attending the funeral of Jimmy Barbella. Ianthe was in Florida with Mini Coop. Prager dialed in from his apartment in Manhattan. Helene and Gruley were working alone in the deserted D.C. newsroom.

The call lasted four hours, until 1:00 a.m.

The tone of the conversation was captured in a group email the five subsequently sent at the request of Mike Miller, Page One editor, providing details of how they pulled off their collaboration.

It was like a NATO meeting: all allies, with a common goal, but all of us extremely protective of our own characters, and the wording we wanted used, and the scenes we wanted. Early efforts at diplomacy were tossed out the window; by the end, everyone was unabashedly saying which scenes should be cut, and suggesting changes in words and phrases.

• Chapter Eight •

Awaiting John Blanton's Verdict

In four days, Cooper, Dugan, Gruley, Kuntz, and Prager would learn whether they had pulled it off. Had they done their story subjects justice, and did they produce a final anthology that warranted the trust bestowed upon them by their editors?

Alan Murray had risked his stature within the organization to shield the five reporters from some colleagues and higher-ups who argued to the D.C. bureau chief that Cooper, Dugan, Gruley, Kuntz, and Prager would have been of greater value to the *Journal* covering breaking news and writing standard features in the aftermath of September 11, rather than taken offline to reconstruct the stories of five "ordinary" families.

Nor was there universal agreement that the narrative style Gruley and his team members chose to use was journalistically sound, relying on a note to readers about attribution at the top of the story and an explanation of sourcing appended to the bottom.

Before sending his final "Five Lives" draft to the Page One desk in New York on Monday, October 8, 2001, Gruley let Murray have a last look. The bureau chief made only minor changes.

Now, there was nothing for the five to do but wait.

The final verdict on "Five Lives" fell to two men: Mike Miller, the Page One editor who was the ultimate arbiter of what did and did not qualify as front-page-worthy, and John Blanton, one of Miller's best feature editors.

Blanton was tapped to review "Five Lives" and make any necessary changes.

Blanton liked to read the drafts of Page One stories when they first arrived and then sleep on them before he began making edits. It wasn't uncommon for him to ruminate for days, even weeks, before knuckling down to refine the copy in front of him.

If the "Five Lives Five" had had to wait an extended period to learn Blanton's take, no doubt they would have been seriously annoyed, if not unhinged.

But Blanton didn't need days to reflect. The tears that flowed from the editor's eyes after he read the story spoke for themselves.

Blanton found next-to-nothing to edit, and, at 6:01 that evening, he transmitted his enthusiastic approval. Miller would subsequently describe "Five Lives" as one of the very best narratives he had ever encountered.

Helene Cooper, Ianthe Jeanne Dugan, Bryan Gruley, Phil Kuntz, and Joshua Prager were ecstatic.

When the story appeared, Gruley emailed a copy of "Five Lives" to his friend, Brian Doyle, editor of *Portland,* the University of Portland's alumni magazine. Doyle, one of eight children from an Irish-Catholic family, was a gifted essayist, storyteller, and eventual novelist. He was deeply committed to his faith.

Doyle wrote back.

This story is a prayer. It lifts us all up.

———————————————

• Author's Note •

September 11 was the type of momentous event that those who lived through it will never forget.

Only many have — at least the finer details.

Nearly 20 years on, memories fade, details blur, and some people vividly recall specific thoughts and events that my in-depth research proves never actually took place.

Even journalists — observers by profession — who were in the exact location at the same time may remember the particulars differently, sometimes contradictorily.

In curating my research, I gave extra credence to those narratives that were composed on September 11 or in its immediate aftermath. Even those accounts, at times, were inconsistent.

Rather than always offering alternate depictions, which I sometimes do, I've crafted a chronicle that I believe represents the most faithful retelling of what occurred, albeit one that is filtered through the prism of human imperfection.

Note that in the text of the book, where I use *italics* to indicate what those who I profile were thinking, the wording reflects what the individuals told me were the thoughts running through their minds or what I uncovered in their written accounts. Direct quotes come either from interviews that I conducted or from credible source materials, including books, news articles, and transcripts of live broadcast reports.

Where I've reprinted emails or portions of emails generated on September 11 and September 12, I've done so without editing them for clarity, spelling, or grammar. Under the extraordinary circumstances they faced, the reporters and editors had no time to worry about such refinements.

After reading early drafts of this book, friends, extended family, and some of my journalism peers asked me: "Where were *you* on 9/11?"

The short answer is at home in Denver, Colorado.

The longer response is that I had just returned from a week-long trip that took me to the World Trade Center and the World Financial Center.

At the time, I was running my own small news organization whose flagship was a twice-monthly ink-and-paper newsletter, the *TJFR Business News Reporter*. My company produced multiple publications, conferences, and services that peeled back the curtains on the ways influential news organizations operated and provided in-depth biographical information on prominent journalists.

I spent most of the week immediately prior to 9/11 traveling to various Manhattan locations, interviewing journalists for a video series — *The Newsmakers* — that my company was preparing.

I had spent years in the mid-1980s working from *The Wall Street Journal*'s headquarters and innumerable days crossing over the pedestrian bridges to the World Trade Center to meet with sources in one of the complex's many restaurants, especially the scenic Windows on the World.

After leaving the paper and relocating to Denver, I also enjoyed the Twin Towers, like so many out-of-towners, as a tourist. In March 2000, my wife, Talya, and I introduced our two kids to the observatory atop the South Tower of the World Trade Center. The blustery outdoor deck offered 360-degree, unobstructed views of all of New York and everything else up to 50 miles away.

The week of September 3, 2001, I visited multiple news outlets and sites in Lower Manhattan, along with a film crew that I had contracted. Before returning to Denver on September 8, I dropped by the Krispy Kreme Doughnuts store, located on the east side of the World Trade Center plaza, to bring home a dozen donuts.

Like Joanne Lipman, who kept her receipt from the Lechters Housewares store for the magnets she purchased on the morning of 9/11, I kept mine from the donut store. We didn't have a Krispy Kreme outlet in Colorado back then, as the chain was still primarily serving donut-lovers in the South. I hung onto that receipt for many years, much like those who attend a major concert or sports event hold on to their ticket stubs.

Later that day, sitting at the LaGuardia gate awaiting my return flight to Denver, I had

My son, Maxwell, and daughter, Avital, pose atop the World Trade Center's South Tower in March 2000. In the background, facing north is the Empire State Building.

two strange premonitions, neither of which came to pass.

First, I watched as airport workers — equipped with protective headphones and wearing overalls and yellow vests — entered the passenger area up stairwells directly from the tarmac and returned to the runway seemingly freely. They must have punched in a code to access the terminal. Nevertheless, I envisioned terrorists taking advantage of the relative ease of access to and from the passenger area and made a mental note of it.

My second foreboding was related to the airport's proximity to Flushing Bay, situated to the immediate east. Arriving flights to New York City had a view not only of the embayment but also the iconic "Welcome to New York" sign.

As my flight taxied for takeoff, it struck me that the airport's adjacency to the bay presented a security vulnerability. "Why," I asked myself, "mightn't hijackers reach the airport grounds relatively easily if they boated into Flushing Bay and came ashore from there?"

Among the sites that my crew (pictured) and I visited the
week before 9/11 was the New York Stock Exchange

Of course, that's not how the 9/11 hijackers did it. They simply bought tickets and boarded the four planes just like every other passenger.

On the morning of September 11, I was back home. In Denver, it was approaching 7:00 a.m. when American Airlines Flight #11 struck the North Tower. My brother, a pediatric infectious disease physician, phoned to alert us.

We sent our kids, ages nine and four, off to school and piano lessons, respectively, as if nothing had happened, reasoning there was no need to alarm them. (They quickly found out anyway.)

I worried for my former *Wall Street Journal* colleagues and almost immediately began preparing a special issue of the *TJFR Business News Reporter*. My wife and I prayed for everyone impacted by the events that day.

Multiple locations in the vicinity of the World Trade Center and World Financial Center, where we filmed only days before, were heavily damaged in the attack. Located at 74 Trinity Place, adjacent to the American Stock Exchange and one block from Trinity Church, had been the New York bureau of public television's *The Nightly Business Report*.

On September 6, 2001, Susie Gharib, a veteran broadcast journalist who co-anchored the program from its Trinity Place studios, was gracious enough to give my video crew and

I shot this photo of the LaGuardia control tower on September 8, 2001

me a tour of the *NBR* facilities. To get to her office and the television studio, we walked along a corridor that featured framed photos of Gharib, and her New York colleague Scott Gurvey, posing with various dignitaries and guests.

For background video, so-called B-roll, my videographer filmed the corridor, the studio set, and Gharib's and Gurvey's offices. I snapped some still photos on my digital Sony Mavica.

It took us more than a year to produce all of the interviews that I conducted in New York the week before 9/11. Like so many others, our focus was elsewhere in the aftermath of the attacks and our plans in disarray.

I don't remember exactly how, but I came to learn that all of Gharib's and Gurvey's memorabilia had been destroyed by fallout from the World Trade Center. Only much later, when we were finally producing *The Newsmakers* video, did we find *The Nightly Business Report* B-roll, along with B-roll of the World Trade Center and the Marriott World Trade Center — which were no more, as well as *The Wall Street Journal*'s headquarters, which had been severely damaged, but not destroyed.

To this day, I can still recall precisely how to navigate my way from the Cortlandt Street subway station to the concourse of the World Trade Center, the lobby and restaurants at the Marriott World Trade Center, the hallways and grand staircase of the World Financial Center, *The Wall Street Journal*'s newsroom and offices, and even the corridor lined with photos at *The Nightly Business Report*.

They are memories I will carry with me for the remainder of my life, both cherished and melancholy.

At left, a photo of Susie Gharib and Bill Gates, extracted from B-roll video, that hung on the wall of *The Nightly Business Report*'s New York bureau. At right, a photo I took of Gharib and Scott Gurvey conferring in his office.

(Photographed on September 6, 2001)

Where Were You on 9/11?

Most people, even those who were only children on the morning of September 11, 2001, have vivid memories of their whereabouts that day and how they responded.

We invite you to participate in a special remembrance project that TJFR Press is conducting in conjunction with the publication of *September Twelfth: An American Comeback Story*.

To participate, at no cost, visit: https://tinyurl.com/WhereWereYouOnNineEleven

Among the questions we ask: Were you in the vicinity of the World Trade Center or the Pentagon? How did you learn about the strikes? Who was with you? What were you doing? What is your most searing memory of that day?

Your reflections will be included on the website, September-Twelfth.com (subject to approval and possible editing for length and clarity) and may be included in future editorial projects from author Dean Rotbart.

September 11 is a tragic day in the history of the United States. But it is also the source of a legion of inspiring comeback stories.

Captain James Lawrence

(By J. Herring (1794-1867). Courtesy of the United States Navy.)

• Afterword •

Much Like Members of the U.S. Armed Forces Throughout Our Nation's History, the Men and Women of The Wall Street Journal Acted Independently and Collectively Problem Solved When Faced With a Dynamic Challenge

By Dr. David F. Winkler

DGUTS: "Don't Give Up The Ship."

As a naval historian, I've emphasized those words on many occasions in my writings or in classrooms where I quiz students on who uttered that rallying cry and under what circumstances.

The correct answer is Captain James Lawrence, who, mortally wounded, gave his final order to marshall the crew of USS *Chesapeake* in that frigate's fight against the Royal Navy's 38-gun HMS *Shannon* off Boston's coast on the afternoon of June 1, 1813.

Earlier in the War of 1812, USS *Constitution* had soundly defeated HMS *Guerriere* and then trounced HMS *Java,* while the USS *United States* captured HMS *Macedonian.* Victory, however, would not be had by the U.S. Navy on this day as superior British gunnery savaged the *Chesapeake* during the first minutes of the battle, killing or wounding many of Lawrence's subordinate officers.

Having crippled the American warship, the British frigate hove alongside and called "Away Boarders."

The defending American bluejackets fought valiantly, exacting a heavy toll on the intruders, but within fifteen minutes, the American flag was struck. It would be used to wrap the body of Captain Lawrence, who passed on June 5, having lingered on for four days.

Given the inglorious defeat of *Chesapeake*, we have Oliver Hazard Perry to thank for perpetuating "Don't Give Up The Ship" as the permanent watchword of the U.S. Navy.

Inspired by Lawrence's five words, Perry had them woven onto a flag which he flew from the main mast of his aptly named flagship USS *Lawrence* that led his small flotilla in a battle against a comparable British force on September 10, 1813, for control of Lake Erie.

With his flagship rendered near useless by enemy gunnery, Perry hauled down his inspirational flag and then brought it with him when he transferred to the brig *Niagara* to carry on the fight. Out of that battle came another oft-repeated phrase — "We have met the enemy and they are ours" — expressed by Perry after his forces finally prevailed.

The "Don't Give Up The Ship" flag remains on display at the United States Naval Academy Museum.

———————————

Such is the history I focus on daily at the Naval Historical Foundation – a non-profit organization located at the Washington Navy Yard in the nation's capital. On the morning of September 11, 2001, I looked out the window of my first-floor office at Leutze Park, a parade ground that fronted Tingey House – home of the Chief of Naval Operations – on the opposite side. Hardly a day goes by during the warm weather months where some retirement or change of command does not occur with band music and accompanying gun salutes.

On the previous day there was added pomp, as the president of the United States, George W. Bush, in a gesture of friendship, presented the prime minister of Australia, John Howard, with a bell from the decommissioned cruiser USS *Canberra*. The warship had been named for Australia's capital city in recognition of the strong U.S.-Australian alliance during World War II.

With that ceremonial event now in the wake, I sat at my desk, making preparations for an 11:00 a.m. executive committee meeting of the foundation's board, when my phone rang. A retired captain, Jim Bryant, who I once worked for as a naval reservist in Navy's Command Center in the Pentagon, called to tell me I ought to get to a television, that we were under attack in New York.

I turned on the ceiling-mounted set we had in the office, stunned to see heavy black smoke pouring from the Twin Towers. It seemed only moments later when my phone rang again.

Picking up, I heard from one of our board members who had decided to come in early for the foundation's board meeting. He was now stuck in traffic on Interstate 395, alternatively called the Shirley Highway, south of the Pentagon. Ahead, he could see ominous black smoke. I glanced up at the television monitor and saw a "Breaking News" alert. The Pentagon had been hit by another hijacked passenger jet.

With the terrorist attacks in New York, in DC, and news of a plane crash near Somerset, Pennsylvania, the gates of the Washington Navy Yard were closed as military and civilian leaders tried to come to grips with the situation. Up in New York, first the South Tower and then the North Tower would fail structurally and collapse. Having watched those two buildings rise upwards from my homeroom class at New Jersey's Hackensack High School in the mid-1970s, I paused to think about classmates who may have been at work that morning in Lower Manhattan as well as others, including the hundreds of first responders who had rushed to the scene of the attacks.

Then, across the Potomac River, the Pentagon was aflame. Though many of the military personnel I had once worked with there had moved on to new jobs or retired, I remained friends with many of the civil-service workers who were as dedicated to serving the nation as their uniformed peers.

It turns out my initial fear of the total destruction of my former workspace was premature. At the time of the attack, the Pentagon had just refurbished its first wedge — the one that faced Arlington Cemetery — completing the initial phase of a massive multi-year renovation to bring the World War II vintage structure into the 21st century.

The modernization involved upgrading the wiring to accommodate increasingly complex computer networks and replacing the heating and cooling systems to make the building more energy-efficient. Additionally, the walls were structurally reinforced in the wake of the bombings of the Oklahoma City Federal Building and the Khobar Towers in Saudi Arabia.

Had the hijackers of American Airlines Flight #77 crashed the plane into any of the other four sides of the Pentagon, the loss of life certainly would have been greater. As it were, 184 people perished, 125 in the Pentagon and 64 on the plane.

The Pentagon's reinforced first wedge contained the new Navy Command Center, where the watch section was closely monitoring the situation on the southern tip of Manhattan Island, anticipating the movement of naval forces to address further threats.

Navy Command Center watchstanders often are navy reservists, who, rather than conduct a monthly drill, rotate into the center to assist with the command and control of the Navy's ships and aircraft deployed around the globe.

Seeing the situation in New York unfold, the commanding officer of the reserve unit that supported the Navy Command Center, Captain Edward S. "Sonny" Masso, called his operations officer to assemble members of the reserve unit to form a Crisis Action Team to augment the watch team in the Navy Command Center.

"I was near the top of the fourth corridor escalator when what felt like an earthquake and sounds of explosion wracked the building," Masso subsequently recalled.

As announcements were made to evacuate and hundreds of Pentagon employees filled the corridors to depart for the exits, Masso, along with first responders, pushed forward against the exiting flow to the area of impact.

Upon reaching the entrance to the Navy Command Center, Masso heard screams and smelled the stench of smoke in a darkened and destroyed corridor. With busted water pipes and sprinklers showering the captain, Masso pinpointed the cry of a woman from within a restroom.

Venturing into the darkened space, he affected her rescue and then turned back to the entrance of the Navy Command Center that no longer was accessible as a collapsed wall now blocked the front door.

Knowing a back way in, Masso made his way to the outdoor corridor between the C- and D- Rings of the Pentagon. In front of him, Masso saw the back wall of the D-Ring had collapsed, leaving a potential escape route for those trapped inside the Navy Command Center. Blocking the way, however, was a locked chain-link fence. Looking up at the floor over the gaping hole, Masso noted desperate Army personnel trying to smash the shatter-proof windows that had been installed during the renovation. With flames and smoke visible behind them, time was critical.

A fleeting sense of helplessness quickly passed when Masso turned to see Rear Admiral Phillip Balisle, who ran the Navy offices responsible for surface ship development and oversight, appear with a number of surface warfare officers. Alternatively called SWOs or ship-drivers, these naval officers who worked within his branch had undergone extensive damage control training throughout their many tours at sea to remain true to the watchwords, "Don't Give Up The Ship."

Acting like an experienced Chief Petty Officer in charge of a Ship's Damage Control Repair Locker, Balisle took charge. Using his keys to unlock the chain link fence, the SWOs, armed with fire extinguishers, charged forward and into the debris of what was the Navy Command Center, helping people to safety while beating back the flames that were feeding off an assortment of combustible materials.

Meanwhile, with the Army personnel on the upper floor successfully busting out their windows, volunteers below locked their arms together to form human safety nets. "Of the scores of jumpers I witnessed, not one touched the ground," Masso recalled.

It is said the military has contingency plans for contingency plans, and such was the case for the Navy on September 11.

Besides the Naval Historical Foundation, a better-known occupant within the walls of the Washington Navy Yard was the Naval Criminal Investigative Service, or NCIS. (It has since moved its headquarters to Quantico, Virginia.)

One of the capabilities that NCIS had incorporated into their Navy Yard facility was the Multi-Threat Analysis Center, commonly referred to as M-TAC. It would serve as an ideal command post to allow the Chief of Naval Operations (CNO), Admiral Vern Clark, and other naval leaders to regain their situational awareness and respond to the needs of the nation.

One of those leaders was Vice Admiral John Totushek, the Chief of Naval Reserve. Totushek's office had been in the E-Ring just to the right of the point of impact.

Rushing out the corridor, the vice admiral yelled: "Come this way! Come this way!" directing people towards a safe egress. Upon clearing the building, Totushek discovered that cell-phone communications were dead. Rendered helpless in being able to mobilize naval reservists to respond to the terrorist attacks, Totushek and members of his staff hopped in a car and drove over to the Washington Navy Yard.

Stopping at his residence in the Yard to gain access to a landline, Totushek answered his ringing house phone to hear the surprised and then suddenly delighted voice of Admiral Clark. The CNO had phoned to console Totushek's wife, given his belief that Totushek had perished when Flight #77 hit the Pentagon.

Although the vice admiral had been taken out of the command chain loop and even presumed dead, thousands of citizen-sailors across the nation, such as Masso and his Navy Command Center reserve unit, were preparing to help in any way they would be needed.

True to the watchwords "Don't Give Up The Ship," naval reservists who were members of Captain Masso's unit and others assembled the next day at the old Navy Annex that stood on a nearby hill astride Arlington Cemetery to help staff a makeshift Navy Command Center.

If the objective of the al Qaeda terrorists was to destroy the American military's ability to command and control its forces, then they failed miserably.

Totushek later observed: "The response of the reserve was incredible – as you would expect." And why not? For nearly 250 years, the men and women of America's armed forces have demonstrated a consistent ability to assess situations and take leadership prerogatives without awaiting instructions from superiors.

Faced with dynamic challenges, our servicemen and servicewomen are known to collectively problem-solve and implement solutions much to the detriment of our nation's enemies.

These admirable characteristics are not unique to those serving in the American military.

In *September Twelfth*, Dean Rotbart makes a compelling case that the ability for Americans to act independently and collectively problem-solve is not restricted to the armed forces. Just as with the Navy, the "Command Center" of *The Wall Street Journal* was rendered non-operational with the collapse of the World Trade Center towers. A key cog in the leadership chain was presumed dead. And yet, as Rotbart details, in the newspaper business there is always the looming deadline that must be met.

That the staff of *The Wall Street Journal* overcame tremendous obstacles to publish the next day's edition on time speaks volumes of a corporate culture and professional ethos and the vital contribution the fourth estate brings to the viability of the grand American experiment.

For those who played a role in getting the *Journal*'s September 12 edition out, they can take pride for the rest of their lives that when they were tested, they did not give up the ship.

Dr. David F. Winkler, a retired Navy Reserve commander, is a historian with the non-profit Naval Historical Foundation in Washington, D.C. He is the author of *Amirs, Admirals, and Desert Sailors: The U.S. Navy, Bahrain, and the Gulf* (Naval Institute Press — 2007) and *Ready Then, Ready Now, Ready Always*, a history of the U.S. Navy Reserve published by the Navy Reserve Centennial Book Committee.

Dr. Winkler earned his Ph.D. from American University.

• Source Notes/Bibliography •

In order to meet tight print deadline requirements, this book went to press without the inclusion of detailed "Source Notes" or "Bibliography" sections.

I plan to include both references in future print and digital editions. Meanwhile, I've posted a listing of credits at www.September-Twelfth.com.

The factual foundation of this book is based on dozens of original interviews, and scores of newspaper and magazine articles, books, television and radio transcripts, and government reports. My examination included hundreds of never-published contemporaneous internal *Wall Street Journal* and Dow Jones emails, as well as personal diaries.

• Acknowledgements •

This book is an outgrowth of a biography of Paul E. Steiger that I began researching and writing in July 2020.

Paul is a peerless journalist. He not only served 16 years as the managing editor of *The Wall Street Journal* — the longest anyone has held that influential job — he also went on to found and lead ProPublica, a global leader in investigative, nonprofit journalism.

Paul and I were speaking weekly so that I could record his oral history. When we got to the topic of 9/11, I was floored, not only by his experience that day but also by the events that impacted all of Dow Jones & Company and the *Journal*, and the responses of Paul's colleagues.

It was a story that had been told in parts but never in-depth.

Knowing that the 20th anniversary of the 9/11 attacks was approaching, Paul most graciously accommodated my request to set aside work on his biography to allow me to turn out a dedicated volume that would tell the epic tale of the *Journal's* amazingly dedicated staff and their great American comeback story.

That was in mid-December 2020. I had so much good material from Paul and others that I couldn't resist the challenge of turning out a book in the nine months that remained before September 2021.

I approached publishing houses to handle the manuscript and quickly learned that there was simply no longer enough time to get this book into their Fall 2021 catalogs.

If I wanted *September Twelfth* published ahead of the 20th anniversary, I would have to do it myself.

Only, I didn't have to.

September Twelfth owes its existence to an ad-hoc team of sources, researchers, fact-checkers, proofreaders, publishing experts, and others who believed in the project and unflinchingly lent me their support.

I will attempt to acknowledge these teammates herein, with my apologies to anyone who I leave out.

Every individual quoted in the book merits my deepest appreciation, especially those who patiently indulged my inquiries on multiple occasions, enabling me to be as accurate as possible.

"As accurate as possible" is the correct description. Any errors you spot — factual, grammatical, spelling, and stylistic — are 100 percent my responsibility. Please point them out — corrections@september-twelfth.com — and I'll address them on the book's website, September-Twelfth.com, or in subsequent editions of the book.

Let me also highlight two omissions that I'm well aware of.

One: There are many other great September 11 stories of courage and fortitude from those working for *The Wall Street Journal* and its siblings — including *The Wall Street Journal Online, Dow Jones News Retrieval,* and *Barron's* — that are absent from this book.

Two: I interviewed dozens of helpful sources who I was unable to mention by name in the text.

In proceeding to publication, despite those regrettable omissions, I am guided by the advice that Marshall Loeb, the legendary Time Inc. editor, once offered me: "It's better to go to press on time with a story that is 80 percent what you hoped it will be, than to miss the window-of-opportunity striving for 100 percent."

Most aspects of the comeback stories that are embodied in this book are timeless — and will be just as relevant in a year, a decade, or even decades from now.

The experiences of those showcased in this book are, and deserve to be, part of the conversation whenever the world reflects on the events and lessons of September 11.

Philip Revzin spent 31 years, from 1974 to 2005, working for *The Wall Street Journal* and Dow Jones & Company. He began as a reporter, was promoted to bureau chief, and subsequently served as editor and publisher of *The Wall Street Journal Europe,* the *Far Eastern Economic Review,* and publisher of *The Asian Wall Street Journal.*

After leaving Dow Jones, Phil spent almost six years as a senior editor at St. Martin's Press. Among the bestsellers he acquired there were *Our Iceberg is Melting* by John Kotter, and *Soprano State*, a chronicle of 30 years of New Jersey politics.

A native of Chicago and a life-long fan of the Chicago Cubs, Phil wrote his first book, *Just One Before I Die*, chronicling the team's 2016 World Series-winning season.

When I turned to Phil to ask him to serve as the editor of *September Twelfth*, he was gracious and immediately agreed.

Throughout the editing and proofreading process, Phil was encouraging and displayed his enormous sense of wordcraft.

I have to confess that I didn't always follow Phil's recommendations, especially when it came to axing what Phil considered superfluous content. If you've read this far and have concluded that my book needed a good editor, please know that it had one. I just didn't always follow Phil's advice.

Ray Bard is a publishing legend, endowed with a gift for turning good authors into great authors, and small-press books into global bestsellers.

In 1996, Ray launched the Bard Press imprint, a boutique house that has been satisfied with turning out only one or two books a year. Since its founding, the independent publisher has laid claim to 18 national bestsellers, including two books — *The One Thing* by Gary Keller with Jay Papasan, and the *Little Red Book of Selling* by Jeffrey Gitomer — each of which has sold more than two million copies.

Bard Press published *The Wizard of Ads Trilogy*, a troika of bestselling books by Roy H. Williams, a marketing and advertising wizard (hence his book titles) who teaches creative thinking, writing, and persuasion to journalists, educators, ministers, and business people around the world.

Roy, a good friend and role model, along with his wife Pennie, founded the nonprofit Wizard Academy, a mecca for business owners, entrepreneurs, and creatives that offers two- and three-day communication arts courses from a magical 21-acre campus located in the Texas Hill Country.

Officially, Ray Bard is retired, having relocated from his base in Austin, Texas, to the quiet village of Ranchos de Taos in New Mexico.

But Ray taught me — or at least tried very hard to teach me — what I needed to know to put on the hat of a publisher and navigate the many shoals of book-selling. I cannot possibly thank him enough or ever repay his kindness.

Debbie Luczak Hoffman merits an award.

After all, for more than 22 years at *The Wall Street Journal*, Deb managed the process of nominating its reporters for all major journalism honors. During her tenure, the paper won 22 Pulitzer Prizes, more than a score of Gerald Loeb Awards, 14 Overseas Press Club Awards, and a dozen George Polk Awards, in addition to hundreds of other prizes from organizations including the Society of Professional Journalists, the Scripps Howard Foundation, the National Press Club and the Associated Press Media Editors Association.

Deb, now on her own, continues to help news organizations prepare their awards entries. I hired her to help me research my biography of Paul Steiger, and she readily segued into my research assistant on *September Twelfth*.

Deb has an encyclopedic institutional memory, especially of current and past Dow Jones and *Wall Street Journal* staffers. She spent a great deal of time archiving documents, photos, and the like for the "Dow Jones Museum" in South Brunswick. If an important memo, email, or in-house publication was produced during her time with Dow Jones, the chances are excellent that she cataloged it.

In the days before cell phones and the internet, when I needed contact information for a source, I'd dial 411. When researching this book, I merely dialed Deb.

Who else do I want to thank beyond absolutely everyone cited in the book?

At Dow Jones & The Wall Street Journal:

Timothy Lemmer, *Letters* editor
William Power, news editor, and archivist
Colleen Schwartz, senior vice president, communications

Additional Current or Former Dow Jones/Wall Street Journal Staff:

Danforth Austin
Michael Boone
William Casey
Mary Lu Carnevale
Ron Chen
Michael Connolly
Gene Goch
Tracie Feldman
Bill Godfrey
Laurie Hayes

Acknowledgments

Howard Hoffman
Larry Hoffman
Rich Jaroslovsky
Johnnie Katsimanis
Pat Macri
Michael Marvaso
Norman Pearlstine
Bland Smith
Richard Tofel

At National Association of Business Economists:

Melissa Golding
Bruce Kratofil

At News Corp:

James E. Kennedy, EVP and chief communications officer
Robert Thomson, chief executive

Others:

Margaret and Riyaz Adat, of Toronto
Brad Ballee, Lakeside Book Company
Celeste Berteau, Mystery Book Author
Athena Bryan, Melville House
Maeve Gaynor Scott, Newseum Collection - Freedom Forum
Peter Osnos, Founder, PublicAffairs Books
Joel Reidy, Lakeside Book Company
Robert A. Rosenthal, RAR & Associates
Todd Sattersten, Bard Press
Joel Susel, of Denver
David J. Stephenson, Rocky Mountain Thunder Law Firm

————————

In March 2021, I moderated four Zoom reunions focused on different aspects of *The Wall Street Journal*'s and Dow Jones's response on September 11. I want to thank each of the panelists for sharing their recollections.

[The videos are available for free to anyone who purchases this book. See details on pages 318-319 or at September-Twelfth.com.

Panels:

Reporters and Editors

Gwendolyn "Wendy" Bounds
John Bussey
Philip Connors
Daniel Henninger
Jon Hilsenrath

Scattered

Marcus Brauchli
Phil Kuntz
Joanne Lipman
Dave Pettit
Michael Siconolfi

South Brunswick and Washington, D.C.

Jesse Lewis
Alan Murray
Cathy Panagoulias
Jim Pensiero
Lawrence "Larry" Rout

Five Lives

John Blanton
Helene Cooper
Ianthe Jeanne Dugan
Brian Gruley
Phil Kuntz
Joshua Prager

Dean and Talya Rotbart
(Photo: Time in a Bottle Photography)

• About the Author •

Dean Rotbart is a former reporter and columnist with *The Wall Street Journal*, which nominated him for a Pulitzer Prize for Explanatory Reporting. His investigation into the methods of Wall Street short sellers, "Market Hardball," won the John Hancock Award for Excellence in Business and Financial Journalism.

Rotbart serves as the chair and editor-in-chief of the *Business News Visionary Awards* and *News Luminary Awards*, programs which recognize outstanding achievements by journalists. Previously, he published the *TJFR Business News Reporter*, a trade newsletter focused on influential business and financial news organizations.

Since June 2012, Rotbart has produced and hosted *Monday Morning Radio*, a popular weekly small business podcast.

Working with the non-profit Strider Education Foundation, Rotbart was the co-creator of the nationwide All Kids Bike® drive, a grassroots effort to teach children how to ride a bike before they reach the first grade. Rotbart continues to serve as a national ambassador for the movement.

His previous books include:

- *Improbable Lives: A Scot, a Tanzanian and Their Canadian Love Story* (2020) by Dean and Talya Rotbart
- *Perfectly Ordinary, Yet Extraordinary: Making a Meaningful Difference in the Lives of Others* (2020) by Dean and Talya Rotbart
- *The Story Behind the Smiles* (2019) by Avital Rotbart and Dean Rotbart
- *Surviving Infidelity: Making Amends, Restoring Trust, Finding Forgiveness, and Living Together Happily for the Rest of Your Lives* (2018) by Abe Kass, MA MSW RMFT and Dean Rotbart

Rotbart is a graduate of the Medill School of Journalism at Northwestern University and the Columbia University Graduate School of Journalism.

A native of Denver, Colorado, Rotbart lives there along with his wife Talya. They have two adult children, who like their parents, are published authors.

• Website and Social Media •

September-Twelfth.com is a dynamic website containing testimonials, photos, documents, and research materials that complement this book.

Members of the general public are invited to share their personal 9/11 remembrances, which are posted in a dedicated section of the internet site. For additional details, visit the webpage or fill out the form available at: tinyurl.com/WhereWereYouOnNineEleven.

On September-Twelfth.com you'll also find links to Dean Rotbart's social media accounts, including LinkedIn, Twitter, and Facebook.

Please address all comments about this book to TJFR Press • 200 Quebec Street, Building #300 • Suite 111-26 • Denver, Colorado 80230. You can also email: comments@tjfrpress.com.

• Coming in 2023 •

Steiger: A Journalist in the Public Interest

Paul E. Steiger

By the author of *September Twelfth*

• Also Available from TJFR Press •

Meet Margaret and Riyaz Adat, two perfectly ordinary individuals who have accomplished extraordinary things in the service of others. Together, they epitomize the ability of anyone to make a meaningful difference in the world.

This text aims to inspire readers to take up the challenge of homegrown charitable projects, be they in a community half-a-world away or within walking distance.

Many, many people want to do good. They want to make the world a better place. But they don't have the confidence and knowledge that they need. This book offers a roadmap to success.

Improbable Lives

A Scot, a Tanzanian, and Their Canadian Love Story

BY DEAN & TALYA ROTBART

The unlikely true love story of a young man and woman — from two distinctly separate cultures and corners of the world — who meet in a new land and together defy convention and overcome obstacles time and again.

Margaret was raised in government housing in Glasgow, Scotland — one of six daughters of a bus driver and a seamstress. For much of her early childhood, she and her family had no private bathroom or hot water in their tiny, government-subsidized rental.

Riyaz was raised in rural Tanzania at a time of significant government upheaval that ultimately robbed his family of its hard-earned livelihood and required him to smuggle himself out of the country.

The Adats found each other and a welcoming home in Canada.

As improbable as the story of Margaret and Riyaz is, it is also inspirational. The couple had the will and the fortitude to succeed, to defy the prognostications of all the naysayers, and to demonstrate that, in the end, love really is the most potent force in the universe.

• www.GutenbergsStore.com •

The Boy Who Answered the Call of Kilimanjaro

By Talya Rotbart

Children worldwide have been captivated by the tale of nine-year-old Riyaz, a Tanzanian boy who dreams big and isn't afraid to act on his yearnings.

Daily, Riyaz stares out the window of his schoolhouse in Dar es Salaam, gazing at the giant Mt. Kilimanjaro, ever-present on the horizon. In Riyaz's imagination, the peak beckons him to come for a visit.

Based on a real-life boy and his adventures, these bilingual, illustrated children's books share the account of Riyaz's trek with two schoolmates, traveling on their own almost 300 miles from Dar es Salaam to Mt. Kilimanjaro.

What Riyaz and his friends expected would be an easy one-day journey – there and back in time for dinner – turned into a six-day odyssey requiring Riyaz to use all of his survival instincts to overcome unforeseen challenges and lurking dangers.

Along the way, Riyaz acquires valuable lessons about goal-setting, integrity, family, and friends.

First in the *Adventures of Riyaz* Series

English

Spanish-English

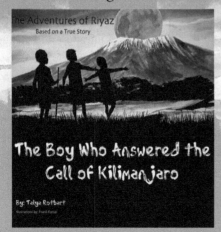

French-English

Swahili-English

Mandarin Simple-English

Mandarin Traditional-English

Korean-English

Hindi-English

Coming Soon in Japanese and Hebrew

• Meet the Journalists •

On four separate nights in March 2021, via Zoom, TJFR Press assembled panels featuring author Dean Rotbart and a total of 20 journalists who played significant roles in *The Wall Street Journal*'s coverage of the September 11 terrorist attacks and their aftermath.

Reporters and Editors

(Clockwise) Daniel Henninger, Jon Hilsenrath, Gwendolyn "Wendy" Bounds, John Bussey, Philip Connors

South Brunswick and Washington, D.C.

Jesse Lewis, Lawrence "Larry" Rout, Jim Pensiero, Alan Murray, Cathy Panagoulias

As an exclusive bonus for purchasers of *September Twelfth*, TJFR Press is making each of these hour-long reunions panels available to stream at no charge.

To view the videos, please take less than a minute to confirm your purchase by answering four quick questions at: <u>tinyurl.com/September12Videos</u>

Discover how the events of 9/11 continue to impact the lives of these reporters and editors more than two decades later.

Scattered

Michael Siconolfi, Joanne Lipman, Marcus Brauchli, Phil Kuntz, Dave Pettit

"Five Lives"

Helene Cooper, Joshua Prager, Ianthe Jeanne Dugan, Bryan Gruley, Phil Kuntz, John Blanton

• Character Index •

A

Adler, Stephen J. 117, 156, 164, 167-68, 192
Afridi, Ayub Khan 81
Ansberry, Clare 70
Apergis, George 178
Armstrong, David 101

B

Badger, Cheryl 137
Baker, Gerard 148
Barbella, Frank 245
Barbella, James W. "Jimmy" 218-20, 240,
 243-49
Barbella, JoAnn 245
Barbella, Lou 249
Barbella, Monica 243-45, 247-49
Barbella, Sarah 243-44
Barringer, Felicity 171
Barrionuevo, Alexei 101-02
Barta, Patrick 30, 32
Bartiromo, Maria 39, 41
Bartley, Robert "Bob" 49-52, 55-6, 58, 65
Bausé, Rick 94-5
Beatty, Anne 179, 181
Beatty, Sally 179-80
Belopotosky, Danielle 93
Biegeleisen, Miriam 255-57
Biegeleisen, Mordechai 256
Biegeleisen, Shimmy 218, 220, 240, 255-57
Binkley, Christina 70
bin Laden, Osama 64, 69, 185-87
Blanton, John 241, 265-66, 292
Blumenthal, Abby 98, 105
Blumenthal, Jennifer "Jen" 105
Blumenthal, Karen 63, 68, 97-105
Bobbitt, David 245
Bolton, Matthew 145-46
Bounds, Gwendolyn "Wendy" 143-45, 148,
 175-79, 181-83, 304
Brandes, Wendy 123, 145, 190, 193-99

Brandstrader, Janet 138, 140, 143, 147-49
Brauchli, Marcus 32, 71, 77-87, 100, 124,
 130, 167-68, 191, 206, 209-210, 213,
 292, 305
Brecher, John 157-58
Bridis, Ted 66
Brooks, Rick 103
Brown, Melanie 121
Bush, George W. 104, 109, 278
Bussey, John C. 20, 37-46, 54, 86, 111, 119,
 123, 131-32, 134, 139, 142, 179-80,
 206, 292, 304

C

Calame, Byron "Barney" 86, 117, 144, 156,
 162, 164-68, 170-72, 192-93, 199,
 211
Calame, Kathryn 166, 168
Callahan, Patricia 101
Capparell, Stephanie 93
Carey, Phyllis 121
Carey, Susan 101
Carlino, Deb 127
Carpenter, Augustus J. 237-39
Cender, Gary 127
Champion, Jim 127
Chubbs, Mr. (dog) 195, 199
Cloud, David S. 68-9
Cole, Jeff 140
Colon, Juan 226
Connors, Philip J. 56-9, 177, 292, 304
Cooper, Caitlin "Mini Coop" 229-30,
 261-62
Cooper, Calista 225
Cooper, Fred 121
Cooper, Helene 217-19, 223-26, 239, 241,
 244, 253, 261, 265-66, 292, 305
Coston, John 121
Courter, Sheila 129

Cummings, Jeanne 186-87

D

DeBlase, Anita 220, 232-34
DeBlase, Anthony 232-33
DeBlase, James "Jimmy" 231-34, 240
DeBlase, Richard 231
De Witt, Ken 55, 130
Distler, Rebecca 153, 167, 213
Dizney, Joe 154-55, 159-62, 169-70
Dougherty, Philip H. 157
Doyle, Brian 266
Dugan, Ianthe Jeanne 217-19, 224, 229-34,
    241, 244, 265-66, 292, 305
Dunn, Dave 127

E

Emshwiller, John 102
Ennis, Tom 121

F

Farley, Margaret "Maggie" 80-1, 83-88
Farr, Kristine 122
Flashnick, Patricia 219
Foreman, Park 85-6
Foster, Darrell 205
Fraust, Bart 130
Frazier, Claire 121
Friedland, Jonathan 46, 63, 68, 101-02

G

Gaiter, Dorothy 158
Garcia, Mario R. 159
Gharib, Susie 272-74
Gigot, Paul 44, 49-52, 54-6, 58, 130, 206
Giuliani, Rudolph 95, 103, 113, 145, 206
Godfrey, Bill 166, 290
Goyden, Gary 127
Greenberger, Robert S. 186-87
Griffeth, Bill 46
Gruley, Bryan 63, 70-2, 110-11, 217-20, 223-
    25, 237-41, 244, 253, 261-62, 265-66,
    292, 305
Gugliotta, Guy 71-2
Guilfoyle, Joe 140

Gurvey, Scott 273-74

H

Haines, Mark 39-40, 42-3, 179
Harris Jr., Roy J. 208, 211-13
Hashey, Ed 159
Haynes, John 224-27
Helliker, Kevin 99-101
Henninger, Daniel 51, 53-4, 292, 304
Hersey, John 239-40
Hertzberg, Daniel 86, 117, 156, 164, 166-68,
    219
Hilsenrath, Cristina (Tiberio) 23-5, 28-9,
    33-4
Hilsenrath, Danny 29-30, 33-4
Hilsenrath, Jon 19-23, 25-35, 93, 111, 177,
    206, 292, 304
Horvath, Adam 82-3
House, Karen Elliott 87, 117
Hunt Jr., Albert R. "Al" 65, 191

I

Ibrahim, Youssef M. 186
Ingrassia, Lawrence 130, 134
Ip, Greg 69, 72

K

Kann, Peter R. 87, 117, 188, 193, 219
Keller, John J. 140, 240
Kennedy, Karen 127
Kessler, Peter 219
Kilgore, Bernard "Barney" 171, 184, 195-97
Kilman, Scott 101
King Jr., Neil 68-9
Kranhold, Kathryn 143-45, 148, 175-79,
    181-83
Kronholz, June 70, 72
Kuntz, Phil 86, 107-13, 177, 217-19, 224-25,
    239, 241, 243-49, 253, 261-62, 265-
    66, 292, 305

L

LaChance, Douglas 204-05
LaChance, Glenn 204, 206
Landro, Laura 179

Langer, Dovid 255
Lay, Kenneth L. 102
Lemann, Nicholas 239
Lescase, Lee 80
Lewis, Brian 180
Lewis, Jesse 32, 87, 114, 127-28, 130, 134, 292, 304
Lipin, Steven 140
Lipman, Joanne 117, 153-62, 164, 167-69, 171-72, 176-77, 192, 213, 270, 292, 305
Lunsford, J. Lynn 101
Lynch, John 127

M

Martin, Richard 44
McCartney, Scott 98-101, 103-04
McFadden, Robert D. 203, 206
McGurn, William 55, 130
McIntyre, Eileen 208, 211
McKee, Steve 83
McKinnon, John D. 69
McWethy, John 147
Miller, Karen 123
Miller, Mike 52, 117, 122, 144, 164, 167-68, 193, 241, 262, 265-66
Miller, Norman C. 65
Mohammed, Khalid Sheikh 185, 187
Mollenkamp, Carrick 103
Mossberg, Walter S. 91-95, 109
Murray, Alan 63-73, 83, 86, 106, 124, 130, 167-68, 191-92, 206, 220, 223, 238, 246, 265, 292, 304
Murray, Diane 218, 220, 239-41, 255
Murray, Matt 205-06

N

Newman, Jack 205-06
Norton, Erle 143-45, 176, 178-79, 181-83

O

O'Donnell, Laurence G. 156
O'Grady, Mary Anastasia 49, 54
Opdyke, Jeff 30, 32
Oster, Chris 103

Otten, Alan L. 65

P

Panagoulias, Cathy 118-20, 122, 129-30, 132-34, 139-40, 206, 292, 304
Pearl, Daniel 80, 186-87
Pearlstine, Norman 92, 156
Peers, Martin 180-81
Pensiero, Jim 71, 86-7, 117-120, 122-26, 128, 130-32, 134, 145, 166-68, 170, 191-92, 206, 213, 292, 304
Pettit, Glen 23-4, 34
Pinkston, Will 103
Prager, Joshua 217-19, 224, 239, 241, 244, 251-57, 261-62, 265-66, 292, 305
Putka, Gary 63, 68, 101
Pybas, David 159

Q

Quimby, Art 121

R

Regis, George 141
Regis, Nora 138-39, 145-46, 149-50
Regis, Richard "Rich" 86, 137-50, 176, 198
Revzin, Philip 87, 288, 311
Ricks, Thomas E. 186-87
Riley, Jason L. 54
Rivas, Elizabeth 224-26
Rivas, Moises 218, 220, 223-24, 226, 240
Robbins, Carla Anne 63-4, 67-8, 71-3, 186-87
Robbins, Tom 204-05
Roche, Kevin 197
Rokeach, Issachar Dov (Belzer Rebbe) 256-57
Rorex, Clela 78-9
Rout, Lawrence 40-2, 122, 128-30, 132, 134, 175, 292, 304
Royster, Vermont Connecticut 56
Rupp, Lindsey 100

S

Sandberg, Jared 119
Scharff, Edward E. 140

Seib, Gerald F. "Jerry" 63-4, 69, 72-3, 106
Serin, Randi 197-98
Skilling, Jeffrey K. 102
Skinner, Peter G. 37-8, 86
Smith, Bland 127, 291
Smith, Rebecca 102
Sorenson, Erik 180
Spurgeon, Devon 101
Steiger, Paul E. 13, 20, 26, 32, 52, 58, 64-6,
        71, 86-7, 93, 100, 117-19, 123-25,
        130-32, 134, 144-45, 148, 156-59,
        164-72, 176, 188-99, 206, 213, 287,
        290, 299
Steinberg, James B. 64, 66-7
Suskind, Ron 158

T

Tanouye, Elyse 130
Templin, Neal 30, 32
Tiberio, Cristina (Hilsenrath) 23-5, 28-9,
        33-4

V

Vickery, Lisa 180

W

White, Joe 101
Wilder, Thornton 239-40
Will, George F. 252
Woeltz, Jessie 161-62
Wong, Dona 159

Z

Zannino, Richard 133-34

September Twelfth
An American Comeback Story
Dean Rotbart

Published by TJFR Press
Denver, Colorado

Copyright @2021 TJFR Press
All rights reserved.

Ordering Information
For additional copies visit Amazon or e-mail orders@september-twelfth.com. Quantity discounts are available.

ISBN 978-1-7344841-7-5

Library of Congress Control Number: 2021914618

First Edition
***
Book Editor: Philip Revzin

Copy Editing and Proofreading: Maxwell Rotbart

Research Assistant: Debbie Luczak Hoffman

Text Production: Time in a Bottle Photography

Jacket Design: Hespenheide Design

First Printing: August 2021

• Praise for September Twelfth •

The most detailed and dramatic look yet at the [Wall Street Journal's] Pulitzer-winning work following the terrorist attacks.

— The Poynter Institute

September Twelfth is an amazing story about how *The Wall Street Journal* produced Pulitzer-winning coverage while overcoming incomparable obstacles. It's a story about perseverance, diligence and a commitment to doing a job, and doing an excellent job — something that everybody can learn from.

— Christopher S. Roush
Dean and Professor, School of Communications
Quinnipiac University

There could be a movie about this. This is a truly compelling story. It is so relatable.

— Dan Gaffney
The Dan Gaffney Show
Delaware 105.9 FM / News-Talk

One fantastic story. I'm sure that it will be a global bestseller.

— Malcolm Gallagher
Anchor, BizVision Network
England

Grips you as soon as you begin reading the book. It's really the proverbial page-turner because these are real stories that you're reading.

— Rob Cornilles
Founder & CEO
Game Face, Inc.

An incredible book. Absolutely amazing.

— James Lowe
Syndicated Radio Talk Show Host
iHeart Network

I am proud that my friend has chronicled the play-by-play of that miraculous day, but I must also say that I am not surprised. This was a story that had to be told.

— Roy H. Williams
Bestselling Author, The Wizard of Ads Trilogy

Made in the USA
Las Vegas, NV
21 July 2022

51920215R10174